# Post-Theistic Thinking

# Post-Theistic Thinking

### The Marxist-Christian Dialogue in Radical Perspective

*Thomas Dean*

Temple University Press
*Philadelphia*

Temple University Press,
Philadelphia 19122
©1975 by Temple University
All rights reserved
Published 1975
Printed in the United States of
America
International Standard Book
Number: 0-87722-037-9
Library of Congress Catalog Card
Number: 74-83202

To G. P. D. and F. K. D.

# Contents

# *Preface*

What follows is a thought-experiment.

Imagine that you no longer believe in God. For some time, you continue to believe in the truth of your religious tradition, until one day even this becomes too much to affirm. Nonetheless, something within you refuses to be identified simply as an American, or a liberal, or a believer in the latest cause.

Then comes a proclamation—by theologians—that God is dead, and with it a new gospel of secular man come of age. This is followed by the development—again within theology itself—of a radically political self-consciousness. Suddenly overnight your religious heritage is transformed. The possibilities of your tradition have become live options again. You become involved in the heady dialogue between this new theology and the most radical elements in secular life and thought. For you the old world of religion and theology is shattered forever, and the voyage toward a new, as yet unknown world has begun.

What would the story of such an extraordinary journey look like? How might it begin, what might happen to you along the way, and where, insofar as one can speculate, might it lead? Even if none of us should ever choose to take such a journey, by taking one in our imagination perhaps we can gain some insight into the actual road ahead. What follows is an imaginary account, told in the first person, of one such journey.

We begin by going back ten years or so to the late 1950's and early 1960's. For that was when we were first hearing from theologians a strange new story about the death of God. If someone had taken me aside at that time and tried to tell me what was soon to follow, I should have thought him mad or hopelessly utopian. And yet, in a few short years, what happened to the voices of Barth and Bultmann, of Niebuhr and Tillich, in the land?

I remember I was a young divinity student at the time, fresh out of a large midwestern state university, and just beginning, somewhat belatedly (about a half-century too late, I was to learn), my own quest for the historical Jesus. The status of God was already somewhat uncertain for me, but never mind, for a Christian a strong enough sense of the historical Jesus would make up for a shaky sense of the reality of God. By the end of the first year of my quest I had found a wife, but the historical Jesus had (as Schweitzer had said he would) eluded my grasp.

Well, then, what next? Who, or what, was responsible for this frustrating state of affairs? (At the time this was known as "the hermeneutical question.") It turned out to be a rather forbidding Teutonic thinker by the name of Martin Heidegger. Heidegger—the father of modern-day secular existentialism, the philosopher of human finitude for whom the meaning of life was to be found only through a resolute acceptance of man's essential being-toward-death. It was Heidegger whose philosophical interpretation of man and being, when imported into biblical scholarship and contemporary theology, effectively put an end not only to my youthfully conceived attempt to get back to the historical Jesus, but to any lingering hopes I may have had of finding an intelligible metaphysical basis for a doctrine of God.

I made the pilgrimage to Germany with my wife in 1963–64. It was there, studying the works of Heidegger, that the full weight of the death of God and the end of the quest for the historical Jesus came home to me. It was the year, too, that a handsome young president was assassinated. We felt a long way from home. Not only our theological but our secular illusions had been taken from us. By the time of our return, the new president was bombing a small country on the basis of a fabricated excuse, his election opponent was threatening to do even worse, and the warnings of our German friends that Hitler could happen anywhere, including "Amerika," began to seem more true. It was good to see the harbor of New York again, but the death throes of our old world had commenced. What would emerge on the other side?

We came back to upheavals in the world of theology too. In rapid sucession there appeared Paul van Buren's *The Secular Meaning of the Gospel* (1963), a series of manifestos by William Hamilton and Thomas J. J. Altizer proclaiming the advent of *Radical Theology and the Death of God* (1963–66), and Harvey Cox's invitation to celebrate the new freedom of *The Secular City* (1965). It was an exhilarating time. What a sense of release and expansion we felt.

This first wave of the new theology had a distinctively American character. Its orientation was primarily antimetaphysical, antitheistic, but for the rest it was an affirmation of the modern secular world as an American knew it. It was, in other words, a radical theology of American bourgeois liberalism. It as yet lacked a political sense. But we were also experiencing, on a more practical level, the arrival at the divinity schools of the new generation of student radicals. They came to Union Theological Seminary in the fall of 1964. The bombing in Vietnam was to lead to a whole new series of explosions in the world of theology as well. Immediately there sprang up a student-faculty journal, *Christianity and Revolution,* consciously opposed to the dominant Christian realism of the Niebuhrian journal, *Christianity and Crisis.* By the following year another graduate assistant and I had organized an interdisciplinary seminar on "The Philosophical and Biblical Foundations of Social Ethics" as a vehicle for theological reflection upon the radical critique that was being directed against American society. We drew our resources for radical social criticism from the prophetic, eschatological, and apocalyptic literature of the Bible. For us the radicalism of the new theology had begun to acquire a specifically political dimension.

That was also the year when some of us first began to read Marx. Marx—the spiritual father of godless, atheistic communism, the ideological enemy of everything religious or American. I remember my involuntary shudder when I bought my first volume of selections from Marx. As I began to read it, I realized that I was not looking for ammunition with which to attack communism, but for ammunition with which to attack and rethink theology. My introduction to Marxism, however, was for me as for others of my generation through the so-called younger Marx. This Marx was not the older, battle-scarred veteran of the *Communist Manifesto* and later writings, not the implacable determinist portrayed by the ideologists of Stalinist Marxism, but an engaging, humanistic, proto-existentialist thinker whose works had not been known or published until the 1930's. In the light of this new Marx, and the humanized view of Marxism he made possible, standard texts such as Charles West's *Communism and the Theologians* suddenly seemed to be a reflection of the earlier cold war era of the 1940's and 1950's. There now seemed a need for a different kind of theology, a theology that was no longer the handmaiden of the American political establishment but represented instead a radical critique of that establishment based on a synthesis of Marxism and the original revolutionary message of the Bible itself.

By the time I took my first teaching post in the fall of 1966, the second wave of the new theology—a theology which was radical in a political rather than an antitheistic sense—was well under way. As the movement of the death-of-God theology subsided (1963–66), a group of politically oriented European theologians came to the fore (1966–69). Suddenly the names we had been hearing about were translated and became accessible to us in America as well: Jürgen Moltmann, whose ground-breaking *The Theology of Hope* (Germany, 1965; America, 1967) was soon followed by his *Religion, Revolution, and the Future* (1969); Johannes Metz, *Theology of the World* (Germany, 1968; America, 1969); Roger Garaudy, *From Anathema to Dialogue: A Marxist Challenge to the Christian Churches* (France, 1965; America, 1966); and among these a major essay by an American theologian, Richard Shaull, "Revolution: Heritage and Contemporary Option" (1967).

The excitement generated by these theologies of revolution was, if anything, even greater than that which greeted the death-of-God theology. But it was becoming increasingly difficult to sort things out. How was one to get some perspective on this rapid succession of movements that were so dramatically transforming our entire theological tradition? On the one hand there was the imposing philosophical presence of Heidegger, my original guide on the way toward a radically finitist, post-theistic philosophy of man and being. Then there were the voices of the first group of radical theologians—the American theologians of secularity who had first proclaimed the death of God. Now there were the voices of a second group of radical theologians—the neo-Marxist theologians of revolutionary social change. And somewhere back on the edges of my memory was the figure of the man who, for me, had started it all, the first theologian to have pointed out that the strange eschatological figure of the historical Jesus was quite different from and alien to what the liberal theologians of Schweitzer's day would have liked him to be. Had Schweitzer been wrong in at least this one respect? Had it turned out that the eschatological Jesus was not a stranger to our time after all, but instead, in a startlingly relevant way, our revolutionary contemporary?

Whatever the answer, I could not go on until I had somehow come to terms with these different movements. Being basically irenic, however, I wanted to work out a position that took account of what each of them had to say. So I tried the following hypothesis: What if that which was radical in the first type of radical theology—its antitheistic, radically finitist ontology—could be brought over into what was radical in the second type of radical theology? For this latter, while radical in its political orientation, had reverted to a metaphysically untroubled affirmation of God, so that ontologically it was still preradical. What needed to be shown was that the radicalism of the death of God demanded a corresponding radicalism in the political sphere as well, and that, conversely, radicalism in a political sense would be theoretically incomplete if it was not grounded in a radicalism on the level of metaphysics as well. If I could demonstrate that each of these theologies required the other, then my thought-experiment—the bringing together of Heidegger's finitist ontology, Marx's social critique, and a type of Christian thinking that was post-theistic (no longer theological, since it would lack a doctrine of God, but still Christian by virtue of its link to the historical tradition bearing that name)—would be a success.

But what could I hope to accomplish by means of such a proposal beyond resolving an intellectual puzzle to my own personal satisfaction? Well, given the assumptions from which I was starting, I hoped to be able to prove to my theologically inclined colleagues that it was no longer necessary or even possible to defend a theological—that is, a theistic—perspective on man and being. Talk about God, or about transcendence, would be shown to be a way of saying, in an upside-down or indirect way, what could be said more adequately and straightforwardly in a radically finitist and nontheistic way: we are finite beings living in a finite world; a clear-eyed recognition of that fact must inevitably have a further radicalizing effect upon our political consciousness of the conditions of human existence in the one and only world in which it is given us to live. If we accept the criticisms of Heidegger, the radical metaphysician, and Marx, the radical social philosopher, then, I wanted to say, theology can never again hope to make an intelligible or plausible case for a theistic perspective—however "radical"—on human reality.

To illustrate this speculative hypothesis, I proposed to describe two ways in which post-theistic thinking could be incorporated in the thought of a particular tradition—in one case, Marxism, in the other, Christianity. Whether or not either of the resulting positions—the Marxist humanist or the radical Christian—was actually held by anyone in every particular, success in rendering them imaginatively concrete and believable would go a long way toward confirming my original hypothesis. Of course it was necessary that I, as the experimenter, avoid giving the impression that I subscribed to either one of these positions. They were to be regarded as the hypothetical creations of a philosopher's workshop. At best they could be considered, as Kierkegaard might have said, "existence-possibilities," but never ones that could be discovered in pure form in the actual confusion of everyday lives. My own position was in any case a vague and shifting one, unclear even in its general features, and hence had little useful bearing on the case.

During the years that I worked on my thought-experiment,

several other trends in theology came and went. In departments
of religion, I found, the rate of change was faster than I for one
could keep up with. As it was, the rest of my work, apart from the
continuing labor of the thought-experiment itself, went off in
seemingly unrelated directions—religion and psychology (a
turning inward by thinkers grown weary of too much Marx?);
death and dying (Heidegger with a vengeance); medicine and
bioethics (our secular successes turning upon us to make moral
monsters, and victims, of us all?); philosophy and the behavioral
sciences (the inexorable reduction of men to machines despite
the efforts of humanists and theologians alike?). And so, by the
time my thought-experiment was ready to be published, it already seemed a skin that had been shed and left behind, with
little suggestion of a living relation to its former owner.

Let me here acknowledge my thanks to some of those who
made this thought-experiment possible. First, I should like to
thank my colleagues in the department of religion at Temple
University. Bernard Phillips, as chairman, supported a two-day
conference in April 1969 on "Marxism, Religion, and the Liberal
Tradition." Out of that conference came a book, *Marxism and
Radical Religion,* edited by John Raines and myself, and published by this press; its last chapter is, in slightly revised form, the
third chapter of the present work. Gerard Sloyan and Paul van
Buren, each as chairmen, also encouraged and supported this
project in all the ways that only chairmen can. Next, I should like
to thank my students, too, who helped this experiment along by
working through the materials with me. I hope that some of the
arguments or positions tried out here may prove to be of interest
to them in their own experiments. Finally, my deepest thanks go
to the various members of my family, beginning with my parents,
to whom this book is dedicated—Gladys Paust Dean and Frank
Karstens Dean, who began their life together thirty-nine years
ago on this day. They opened their house to us for the three long
summers in which this book was written. I include here my aunt,
Janet Dean Millar, who has supported us in this and other
projects ever since 1966, when we moved to Philadelphia and
adopted her as our local mother. Last, my thanks to my wife

Susan, who has been my partner throughout the many stages of this thought-experiment. She and our children, Maggie and Frank, have been constant reminders of a reality which gives to all our experiments in thought and in life such worth as they have.

And now, let the experiment proceed.

*Thomas Dean*
*Swarthmore, Pennsylvania*
*September 30, 1974*

*Introduction*

# Marxist-Christian Dialogue and the Radical Perspective

The Marxist-Christian dialogue has, on the level of theory, reached a decisive and perhaps historical turning point. In its initial stages it brought about a "return to what is basic" in each tradition.[1] More recently it has led to attempts to restate these essentials in newer and more open ways.[2] Both sides have moved from rediscovery of origins (the young Marx; biblical eschatology) to contemporary revision (Marxist humanism; the theology of hope). As a result, however, each of these world views is confronted today by another, more far-reaching prospect: the process of revision has gone so far that there now exists the possibility of rejecting the traditional assumptions that governed this dialogue (dialectic) of opposites and creating types of Marxist and Christian thinking that are philosophically new and quite compatible.

Our ability to push ahead with these newer possibilities of the Marxist-Christian dialogue has been limited until now by the relative neglect of its philosophical setting and determinants. While the renewed dialogue between Marxists and Christians has been going on for some time, surprisingly little attention has been given to its underlying metaphysical presuppositions. Priority has been given to more pressing questions of doctrinal clarification and the search for areas of practical agreement—a priority surely justified by imperatives for change in the Church's relation to socialist regimes in Eastern Europe or to revolutionary movements in the Third World, to cite just two examples. What is needed at this juncture is an analysis of the deeper arguments, the controlling assumptions, the presuppositions of a metaphysical sort, which are implicit in all of these discussions and which exercise a significant if not decisive influence upon their overall direction and prospects.

These philosophical presuppositions do not exist in an historical vacuum. They must themselves be understood in the context of the possibilities and limitations which characterize the general situation in contemporary metaphysics. And here the central fact of our time is the profound conceptual revolution that has resulted in a shift from *ontotheology,* the traditional Western metaphysics of transcendent being, to a radically temporal, finitist, this-worldly perspective on being, what I shall be calling a metaphysics of *radical secularity.* To make sense of the present philosophical situation of the Marxist-Christian dialogue, therefore, we must do two things. We must begin by identifying the basic issues and assumptions that have traditionally shaped this dialogue. But we must then see what happens when these issues and assumptions are confronted by the conceptual revolution which gave rise to the new metaphysics of radical secularity. Only then will we be in a position to determine whether the Marxist-Christian dialogue has in fact reached a decisive turning point and, if it has, to speculate on what its further prospects might be.

## Basic Issues in the
## Marxist-Christian Dialogue

The basic philosophical issues in the Marxist-Christian dialogue may be grouped, following an old set of metaphysical distinctions employed by Kant, into three general problem areas: theology (or ontology), anthropology, and cosmology (including philosophy of history).[3]

In the area of theology, the most obvious disagreement between Marxists and Christians has to do with the charges and countercharges concerning theism and atheism. While the variations in the controversy between Christian theists and Marxist atheists are many and complex, Christians are generally confronted by Marxists with the claim that the traditional doctrine of

God is an ideological reflection of man's alienated relations to his
fellow men. It is not always clear whether Marx himself considered the concept of God to be logically incoherent (as does, for
example, Sartre for whom God represents the impossible ideal
of a being-in-itself and for-itself ), or whether he was simply
interested, following Feuerbach, in seeing the predicates of divine being restored to their rightful place as potentialities of
man's species being.[4] What is clear is that for Marx the doctrine
of God, which claims to locate the source of human freedom in a
transcendent ground, in fact represents the expropriation of that
freedom. It serves ideologically to conceal the true source of
human initiative and responsibility, as well as the alienation of
these powers, in man's own productive activity and social relations. For the contemporary theologian, the first order of business is at the very least to clarify if not radically reconstruct his
understanding of God in such a way as to meet both the logical
and humanistic concerns of his Marxist critic.

The contemporary Marxist, in turn, has been asked by the
theologian to reconsider whether atheism is doctrinally necessary to his social theory.[5] If it is possible to develop a concept of
God capable of supporting a humanism as materialistic in its
concern for man's this-worldly existence as is Marx's, then could
not Marxism, even though it is a nontheistic humanism, come to
view itself as logically and morally compatible with such a
theism? After all, for Marx himself atheism appears to have been
merely a negative and historically conditioned preliminary to his
essential theoretical concern, which was the construction of a
scientific theory of social change. If the Marxist insists on retaining an atheistic interpretation of his humanism, however, the
theologian must then ask whether such a humanism is not, like
Feuerbach's, really dependent upon and conditioned by the very
theism it seeks to overcome. Is it not inevitably determined by
the "theological" character of its antitheistic animus to engender
logical and moral self-contradictions of its own which, without a
theistic corrective, it is theoretically unequipped to overcome?
The contemporary Marxist is challenged by the theologian to
clarify if not to abandon as nonessential the atheism which he
claims is basic to his radical humanism.

In the area of anthropology, the issues at stake in the Marxist-Christian dialogue are, as might be expected, closely tied to the dispute over theism and atheism. These include such traditional philosophical problems as the dualism of body and mind; optimism or pessimism regarding human nature; the relative significance of individual and society; and the dilemmas of freedom and determinism, autonomy and heteronomy. Again, the ways of formulating these issues are too numerous to fit into a few generalizations, but some recurring themes can be singled out. Christians are commonly said by Marxists to have an overly individualistic and spiritualized concept of man, one that distorts their understanding of the bodily and social dimensions of human existence. Because of their idealist anthropology and an alienating concept of God, Christians devalue man's needs for bodily and social fulfillment and his capacities for reshaping nature and history to fulfill those needs. This is reflected in Christianity's individual spiritual conception of man's ultimate destiny, and is reinforced by its pessimistic doctrines of original sin and man's need for God's grace. For the Marxist, to expect from such an anthropology any significant help in analyzing the true, economic and social causes of man's secular alienation is to place one's confidence in ideological illusions and mystifications when what is needed is a scientific, social theory of man. The Christian theologian's task is to show that he too possesses a doctrine of man that appreciates men's bodily and social needs and affirms their capacity for shaping the world to meet those needs, while keeping hold of his traditional insights into the individual, spiritual, and transhistorical dimensions of human existence.

The Marxist, of course, faces the opposite charge: in his stress upon the priority of those dimensions of man's existence traditionally overlooked or neglected by Christian anthropology, he has perpetrated in theory and in practice what from the Christian viewpoint are even graver errors. Orthodox Marxism, though it has less of a history behind it than Christianity, has already become identified with a rigidly collectivist, determinist, and materialist view of man. In the aftermath of its practical successes, it has inevitably justified the subjugation of individual

freedom to the necessities of state power and has subordinated
the higher expressions of the human spirit to the current dictates
of state propaganda. When confronted by the ultimate questions
of human life—the irreducibly spiritual dilemmas of death, guilt,
and meaninglessness—its hands are self-confessedly empty.[6]
The Christian theologian can hardly avoid the conclusion that
the Marxist theory of man is not a genuine humanism, a
humanism of the whole man.[7] The task of the Marxist participant
in this dialogue is to demonstrate that Marxism, no less than
Christianity, is capable of addressing itself to the subjective and
transcendental needs of man without compromising its insistence on the priority of the material, social, and historical determinants of his being—that Marxism too is concerned to work for
the liberation of the whole man.

Finally, in the area of cosmology, we come to questions about
man's relation to the world in which he lives. What does it mean
to say that man is, in the technical rather than popular sense, a
worldly or secular being, a being-in-the-world? Can man be fully
at home in the world, or is he only a pilgrim here, penultimately
in but not ultimately of the world? How does this worldly situation relate to his higher aspirations? Can he have a final vision of
his ultimate destiny, or must all his visions be provisional pending that final outcome? And what is his role in bringing about
that outcome? For the Marxist and the Christian, these questions involve a struggle between two competing world views
grounded in two different historical traditions and featuring two
different understandings of man's relationship to the world and
the proper way of realizing his secular visions.

The Marxist critique of the Christian world view focuses on its
metaphysical orientation to another world and its tendency to
devalue the reality of this world. The practical effect of this
inversion of ontological priorities is that the Christian view of the
world serves implicitly to sanction the secular status quo. The
Constantinian conversion of Christianity into the establishment
or house religion only made official in the world's eyes what was
true from the outset about Christianity's self- and world-
understanding: that here was a system of individual salvation
from the wordly powers and principalities which served to ren-

der unto God what was God's and unto Caesar what was Caesar's, that served to keep the spiritual and the worldly apart, the Kingdom of God distinct from the kingdoms of men. Christian realism (i.e., conservatism) in social ethics was merely the other side of Christian idealism where individual salvation was concerned. By refusing to commit itself without qualification to the emancipation of man in this world (Christians being in but not of the world), by regarding its involvement in the concerns of this world as never more than penultimate, then no matter what it understood itself to be doing, Christianity was in fact, according to Marx, only further alienating man from his authentic worldly life and enslaving him to the secular powers and principalities. To be sure, Christianity was the expression of real, this-worldly suffering and a protest against that suffering. But by grounding its solutions in an unreal, other-worldly appeal, it could offer Christians nothing more than "opium"—an illusory relief which amounted, as the forces of the status quo soon discerned, to a de facto reinforcement of secular alienation.[8] The task of the theologian is to demonstrate to his Marxist critic that, whatever the traditional interpretation or historical function of the Christian world view may have been, its essential ingredients allow for a radical affirmation of man's this-worldly being along with the possibility of unqualified commitment to revolutionary struggle against the forces of alienation in the name of the future of man.

The Christian critique of the Marxist world view, in turn, focuses on its deterministic reading of the movement of history and its exaggerated utopian claims for man's secular future. In Marxism's improbable combination of historical materialism and secular eschatology, the Christian critic finds the theoretical origins of that peculiar blend of nihilism and utopianism which justifies the sacrifice of existing individuals and groups to the indefinite and uncertain prospect of some future era of human emancipation. Marxism's pseudoscientific confidence in the historical inevitability of the world communist movement has from the beginning, however it has officially understood itself, in fact functioned as an ideological prop for the cynical exercise of political terror and party dictatorship. A world view which, according to the vision of its founder, held out the promise of genuine human emancipation has historically produced just the opposite. In the face of this contradiction, even the most subtle and sophisticated apologetic is rendered impossible. Marxist idealism concerning the future liberation of man has proved to be the ideological sanction for Marxist realism concerning state power. The task of the contemporary Marxist accordingly is to show that Marxism, despite overwhelming historical evidence to the contrary, is capable of the same humanization, the same demythologization and "secularization," that it demands of its Christian opposite. It must furnish more open and humanistic concepts of history, revolutionary struggle, and the secular future, and be willing to use them as critical weapons in the fight to overcome the alienation of present-day socialist societies. It must not defer the process of genuine human emancipation to some far distant future, but must prove its ability to seize the humanist initiative now, while admitting that there is still a very great distance to go.

## The Need for a Radical Perspective

If this is an accurate summary of the philosophical issues that currently confront Marxists and Christians, then it should be evident what distinguishes the needs and opportunities of this stage of the dialogue from its earlier stages. What immediately stands out of course is that, unlike their earlier counterparts, contemporary Marxists and Christians are trying to respond positively and constructively to their opponent's criticisms. They are concerned to show that their respective traditions are open to learning from one another without having to abandon their own traditional insights. What is not so often remarked, however, is that to the extent that this is true, there arises a whole new set of problems, one that implicates Marxists and Christians alike but one that might find each of them less than fully prepared. For what we have seen in our brief review of the issues above is that when Christians and Marxists move beyond superficial doctrinal or practical differences to the underlying philosophical principles that separate them, any attempt to respond constructively to their opponent's criticisms will most likely involve them in the radical reconstruction if not outright abandonment of some of the fundamental concepts and assumptions that characterize their respective traditions. The Marxist philosopher is challenging his theological counterpart to become radical in his metaphysics and not just in his social theory or practical commitments. The Christian theologian is challenging the Marxist philosopher to become radical in his philosophy of man and not just in his efforts to transform society. The problem is that neither the metaphysical tradition of Christianity nor the philosophical tradition of Marxism offers the conceptual resources for this radicalizing (secularizing and humanizing) which contemporary Marxist and Christian thinkers require of one another and themselves. This demand for the radicalization of both Marxist and Christian thought ought therefore to be interpreted as an acknowledgment on both sides of the need and the opportunity for introducing new philosophical resources into the Marxist-Christian dialogue, resources that lie beyond those provided by the philosophical traditions of either Marxism or Christianity but which can be shown to be compatible with, and in fact provide the necessary basis for, the rethinking of the basic concepts of both traditions.

The demand for introducing a more radical philosophical perspective into the Marxist-Christian dialogue arises, I am suggesting, from the internal conceptual necessities of the dialogue itself. But why has the internal logic of this dialogue given rise to this need only now and not already at some earlier stage? The answer lies in the different way in which the philosophical issues at stake are now perceived and formulated. At an earlier stage, as the rhetoric of reaffirming the essentials of each tradition clearly showed, the way the philosophical issues at stake were perceived was determined, implicitly or otherwise, by a refusal or inability to consider the possibility of a radical rethinking of the basic concepts and assumptions of the respective philosophical traditions involved. In the present situation, the need and opportunity for explicitly introducing a new metaphysics of radical secularity into the Marxist-Christian dialogue are direct results of the fact that already implicitly the participants in this dialogue have begun to perceive and express the issues in radically new, "re-visionary" ways. Christians and Marxists are beginning to grasp the radical implications of the insight that even the essentials of their respective traditions may be subject to historical and logical transformations that give birth to concepts and assumptions that are qualitatively new. The fact is that a new metaphysics of radical secularity is already present in the way Christians and Marxists today see the philosophical issues that confront them. It remains to make that metaphysics explicit and to explore its implications for the radical rethinking of Marxism and Christianity and the prospects of their further work together.

It should not surprise us that the formulation of philosophical issues in the more recent stages of the Marxist-Christian dialogue has been shaped by an implicit metaphysics of radical secularity, for the fact is that there has been a third partner to this dialogue for some time. It has been represented by the various non-Marxist, non-Christian metaphysical systems of the post-Hegelian, post-positivist era—for example, pragmatism, naturalism, process metaphysics, and secular existentialism. It is in large part because of the conceptual pressures brought to bear by these contemporary world views of process, temporality, relativity, and change that Marxist and Christian thinkers have begun to change their understanding of their own positions and criticisms of one another. In view of the largely continental setting of the present dialogue, it is also no surprise that the most influential of these new, radically secular philosophies has been the existentialist metaphysics of such thinkers as Heidegger, Sartre, and Merleau-Ponty. It is in existentialism above all that we find those new metaphysical concepts and assumptions which constitute a revolutionary break with all earlier metaphysical systems, theistic and materialist, and which have motivated re-visionary theologians and Marxists to rethink the philosophical foundations of their own world views. It is to the radical metaphysics of secular existentialism that we may look, therefore, for help in making explicit the present philosophical situation of the Marxist-Christian dialogue.[9]

Introducing existentialism as a third partner in this dialogue not only offers philosophical resources for rethinking Marxism and Christianity in the perspective of a radical metaphysics; it also points up certain conceptual and methodological issues that a radical metaphysics poses for Marxism and Christianity alike quite apart from their criticisms of one another, issues that arise not out of a specifically Christian or Marxist context but which a radically secular perspective in metaphysics poses to post-theistic thinking in general. In keeping with our threefold scheme, these problems are roughly as follows.

In the area of theology or ontology, both Christians and Marxists confront in existentialism the systematic expression of a radically temporal, finitist, and humanistic interpretation of being which, while in debt to elements in the philosophies of both traditions, nevertheless appears in its twentieth-century formulation to explode the framework and categories within which the traditional Marxist-Christian debates over theism, atheism, and humanism have been carried out. By presenting entirely new analyses and evaluations of such phenomena as contingency, temporality, and possibility, it appears to rewrite the rules by which any future controversies over God and man can proceed.

In the area of philosophical anthropology, existentialism requires that Marxism and Christianity come to terms with a new concept of man as a *being-in-the-world,* a radically secular interpretation of man's being which takes its start from the basic category of action or praxis.[10] Existentialism represents an attempt to rethink the traditional dichotomies of human existence (subject and object, body and mind, the self and others, freedom and determinism) by recasting them in terms of a more complex concept of man's being as an activity of finite self-transcendence.

Finally, in the area of cosmology, Marxism and Christianity are both challenged by existentialism to rethink their concepts of the world and history in terms of an analysis of being-in-the-world that justifies both total commitment to the world and total openness to shaping it anew.

Because it poses an independent philosophical challenge to Marxism and Christianity and offers them conceptual resources for a radical rethinking of their traditions, existentialism gives us

the methodological leverage we need for exploring the possible
ways in which Marxism and Christianity might move once the
official rules of dialogue have been suspended. By operating
from a radical perspective in metaphysics, we break open the
traditional categories and assumptions which these two world
views bring to their dialogue with one another, and thereby
create an open space for the possible emergence of something
new.[11] If, for example, both parties should come to accept a
metaphysics of radical secularity as the common basis for philosophical discussion in a post-theistic age, we could very well discover large and hitherto unexpected areas of agreement between
them concerning their basic concepts of being, man, and the
world. The question which would then confront radical Christians and Marxist humanists might be, "What *are* the differences,
once theology has been deontologized and Marxism has ceased
to be an antimetaphysical metaphysics?"[12] This, in turn, might
lead Marxists and Christians to worry more about how each
might fill out with concrete examples and paradigms the general
features of a metaphysics of radical secularity and less about how
essential or irreducible their remaining differences are. The old
dialogue, in short, might never look the same again. It might
even be that they would no longer wish to call what they were
doing a dialogue or think that it was of primary importance that
their positions be labeled either Marxist or Christian.

Whatever the outcome, it should be obvious by now that, in
the present situation of the Marxist-Christian dialogue, it is no
longer sufficient to compare established or rapidly changing
positions with an eye to arriving at nicely balanced judgments or
carefully qualified predictions. Something more is required. We
must ourselves join the ongoing process of thinking and rethinking, trying at first to think along with the participants in the
dialogue and then, where possible and necessary, to begin the
harder task of thinking over against or beyond them by following
the lead of the problems themselves rather than what thinkers
have felt obliged to say about them. In matters philosophical at
least, this, rather than the doctrinal interests of either party to a
dialogue, should be our dominant concern.

Because the arguments of this book are motivated primarily

by conceptual and methodological concerns rather than by any of the usual assumptions about what a dialogue requires, a word of explanation may be in order about the direction we shall be taking. My general concern is to explore the possibility and impact of introducing a radically secular perspective into Christian and Marxist thinking about some of the fundamental concepts and assumptions in their respective traditions. We shall begin in Part I ("Theology and Radical Secularity") with a description (Chapter 2) and critique (Chapter 3) of what to many seems the most adequate and promising of the attempts of contemporary Christian theology to respond to these issues—namely, the various political or secular theologies of hope and revolution represented by such thinkers as Johannes Metz, Jürgen Moltmann, and Richard Shaull. I shall be using the umbrella terms *radical theology* or *theology of radical secularity* to refer to this family of theological options.

Because, as I shall argue, there are a number of important places at which the radical theologians fail to respond convincingly to the criticisms of either Marxism or a radically secular metaphysics, it will be necessary in Part II ("Toward a Radical Metaphysics") to pause and reconsider just what is being referred to by the terms *radical secularity* and *metaphysics of radical secularity*. To do this we must first go back to the historical origins of radical metaphysics in the philosophical writings of the young Marx (Chapter 4) and then come forward to its contemporary formulation in the works of the secular existentialists (Chapter 5).

Having cleared the way with a critique of radical theology in Part I and with a sketch of the main features of a radical metaphysics in Part II, we shall then be in a position to return in Part III ("Post-Theistic Thinking") to a consideration of the ways in which a radical metaphysics can serve as the philosophical basis for rethinking Marxism (Chapters 6 and 7) and Christianity (Chapters 8 and 9) in a post-theistic setting. Because what emerges on the Christian side of this dialogue can, in the context of post-theistic metaphysics, no longer rightly be called theology in a strict sense of that term, I have chosen to call it *radical Christian thinking*. It is not to be confused with the related but

quite different type of position considered in Part I under the
rubric of *radical theology*. For one of the major theses of the
present work is that a species of radical *Christian* thinking is still
possible in the post-theistic aftermath of the revolution in contemporary metaphysics, but that, if it is to be consistent with the
radical character of that revolution, it can no longer be in any
sense whatsoever a species of *theological* thinking.

# I

## Theology and Radical Secularity

# 2

# The Theology
of Radical Secularity

In this chapter, we shall present the arguments of certain contemporary theologians who have tried to meet the objections of Marxist thinkers by reinterpreting traditional Christian concepts from a radically secular perspective. In the political theologies of Jürgen Moltmann and Johannes Metz, the theology of revolution of Richard Shaull, and the temporal or process theologies of Karl Rahner, Schubert Ogden, and Wolfhart Pannenberg, we find the basic elements of a theological perspective that is radical in both a philosophical and a political sense.[1] From their collective effort there has emerged a powerful new synthesis of the most radical elements in the biblical tradition and contemporary secular thought: the central rather than marginal role of eschatology in biblical faith; the dynamic, temporal world view of modern secular metaphysics; and the commitment of radical humanism to the revolutionary struggle for social and political emancipation. More than any other trend in recent theology, it is this theology of radical secularity which appears best qualified for a dialogue with Marxism and secular thought.[2]

A Radically Secular
Doctrine of God

Confronted by the theoretical atheism and militant humanism of his Marxist critic, the radical theologian's task, it will be recalled, is either to clarify the ambiguities or, if necessary, to reconstruct the traditional Christian understanding of God. The

theologians of radical secularity have opted for the latter course.
Theirs is a theology *post mortem Dei.* For them the clarification of
the old doctrine of God is no longer enough. Something radically
new is required.

It is one thing to proclaim the "death of God." It is quite
another to work out a fresh understanding of God. There are two
possibilities: the reworking of the original biblical concept, or
the outright creation of a new one. Here, at the point of initial
and basic disagreement with Marxism, the new theology has
shown itself to be both biblically and philosophically inspired.
Theologians like Metz, Moltmann, and Pannenberg have turned
to none other than a contemporary Marxist philosopher, Ernst
Bloch, for conceptual resources to recapture the biblical way of
thinking about God. In Bloch's work, a dialectical and historical
interpretation of man's being is extended into a view of reality in
general as a process of coming-to-be under the pressure of the
future. For Bloch, this temporal ontology represents a complete
break with the traditional concept of being as eternal presence.
And yet, paradoxically, it is this futural concept of being worked
out by an atheist metaphysician which the radical theologians see
as restoring philosophical sense to the original biblical vision of
the God of Exodus and Easter, the God of history and eschatological hope. As Pannenberg acknowledges, "Bloch has taught us
to understand anew the overwhelming significance of a future
which is still open, and of the hope which anticipates this future,
for the life and thought of mankind and moreover for the ontological peculiarity of all reality."[3]

But why should this paradoxical approach succeed so well
when, for almost two millennia, theologians seem to have struggled in vain to bring together the categories of Greek metaphysics and biblical faith? It is not to be attributed to the arbitrary
inventiveness or ingenuity of the new theology, nor does it
represent a fresh submission of theological thinking to the categories of pagan wisdom. It is, rather, that secular philosophy
itself has finally stolen a page from the biblical tradition, with
or without the latter's official blessing, and thus finds itself able
to return the favor to a newer generation of theologians. This is
clear from Bloch's own admission, as a Marxist metaphysician,

that it is biblical eschatology which stands behind the insight of contemporary secular philosophy into the open, futural logic of being: "Man is indebted to the Bible for his eschatological consciousness."[4] The radical theologians too are aware of this historical reason for the logical similarities between Bloch's Marxist ontology and the biblical concept of God. What has happened, says Pannenberg, is that Bloch has "recovered the eschatological pattern of thinking of the biblical tradition as a theme for philosophical reflection and also for Christian theology."[5]

How, on the basis of this new ontological model, does the radical theologian reinterpret the nature and activity of God? Already in Israel's exodus from captivity, the biblical God was experienced eschatologically as a God ahead of us, not a God above us. He is a God "who goes ahead of us and who is bringing a real future into being."[6] His word to Israel is the creative and liberating promise of a future that is greater than any they can presently conceive.[7] Philosophically speaking, then, God is the transcendent power of the future to bring into being new possibilities of existence that have never existed before.

This reinterpretation of the biblical doctrine of God in terms of a temporal ontology of the future enables the radical theologian to bring together elements long separated in the tradition of Western thought, namely, the concepts of transcendence and the future.[8] This reunion, in turn, has the singularly happy effect of suggesting a way to dissolve the related dichotomies of freedom and grace, time and eternity, finitude and infinity, the relative and the absolute. God's eternal being, for example, can now be reinterpreted as his preeminent temporality and futurity. God's unlimited, infinite, absolute being is his temporal openness to, and transcendence of, every present state or actuality of being. God's grace is nothing other than his being-for-us as the power of the open future.

This last point is particularly worth developing in light of Marxism's repeated contention that a doctrine of God inevitably compromises man's freedom. For the radical theologian, a reconstructed doctrine of God's grace, far from being a threat to our autonomy, in fact provides the necessary ontological basis and guarantee of human freedom. A concept of God's grace as the power of the open future "would in no way contradict the autonomy of the human race," argues Metz, "since it is this openness to the future which constitutes the very essence of man."[9] God is the power of being that comes to us out of the future. But precisely as such he is also the ground of our own ability to project ourselves and our world into the future. The traditional concept of the transcendent power of God is here reinterpreted as "the pressure exerted by the future on the present." But it is not a pressure that, as it were, compels. It is a pressure that, paradoxically, liberates. It is "the power of the future to contradict the negative moments of present existence and set free forces through which victory is achieved."[10] Michael Novak helps set these typically German and perhaps misleading theological abstractions in a more concrete frame of reference:

∴ . . . The empirical ground which allows men to conceive of the "absolute future" or of an "open future" is precisely the human ability to ask ever further questions . . . a capacity to change directions, to shift his presuppositions, to imagine new alternatives. . . . The ground of the concept of the absolute future is man's unrestricted drive to ask questions, his relentless openness.[11]

To talk about the power of God's grace as the pressure of the future on our present is not to contradict our own freedom, therefore; it is simply another way of talking about that very freedom, of reminding us that we ourselves as futural beings have an irreducible capacity to negate the force of present circumstances and project ourselves forward into alternative futures.

Despite the humanistic thrust of this futural reading of divine grace, even the radical theologian must at some point ask whether in the final analysis man's eschatological hopes are grounded in his own deeds or in the being of God. For the Christian theologian, however radical, the answer to this question is unequivocal and clear: the future is not man's to determine. There is a greater future, which is God's own being, "a future which is grounded in itself and belongs to itself—as a future which does not come into being out of the possibilities of our human freedom, but which calls our freedom to its historical possibilities."[12] For the radical theologian, "the future is not only to be thought of subjectively as the referent of man's hope to transcend the given in his present, but as ontologically grounded in God's own mode of being."[13] But this, by the very nature of things, is necessarily true, for as Metz points out, "only a future which is more than a correlative and projection of our own possibilities can free us for something truly 'new,' for new possibilities, for that which has never been."[14] Paradoxical as it sounds, only if man's future is greater than that which he can conceive can it be absolutely open and free.

The implications of Bloch's temporal ontology for the traditional Christian understanding of God are thus profound indeed. But its implications for the Marxist critique of Christian theism are, for the same reasons, no less profound. Confronted by new, temporal metaphors for divine transcendence, by an eschatological view of God as a dynamic revolutionary force in history, Marxist atheism begins to have a relative and dated look. With the development of a radically secular concept of God as the pressure of the future for human liberation, Christian theology would appear to have recaptured the ground earlier surrendered to the Marxists. It has also opened the way for a radical rethinking of traditional theological concepts of man and the world.

A Radically Secular
Theology of Man

Bloch used his futural concept of being primarily as a tool for revising the contemporary Marxist view of man. But theologians like Metz and Moltmann think his ontology may also be used to retrieve the original biblical understanding of man. Their task, we have said, is to prove to their Marxist critics that the biblical tradition also affirms the natural, social, and historical capacities of men, and that, unlike Marxism, it does so without abandoning its traditional affirmation of men's individual and transcendental needs. By drawing on Bloch's revisionary theory of man, these theologians are uniquely positioned to respond to the Marxist critique of the more traditional emphases of Christian anthropology.

For Bloch, man is not simply or even primarily the product,

individual or collective, of his past circumstances. He is one who hopes—that is, one whose existence is to be understood as purposeful action in the present guided by the expectation of future fulfillment. But as Bloch himself points out, this is nothing other than the message of Christianity itself. The fundamental motif of biblical faith is "the hope-laden dissatisfaction which spurs man on toward the future."[15] Therefore Bloch's philosophical anthropology is but a secular translation and confirmation of the biblical picture of man. Human existence is structured by the dialectical logic of promise and fulfillment: "Man's hopes burst open his present, connect him with his past, drive him toward the horizons of the not yet realized future."[16]

The radical theologians see in this new, yet biblical, anthropology the basis of a radically secular affirmation of man's freedom and responsibility for shaping his this-worldly destiny. As Bloch's ontology suggests, the eschatological Kingdom of God is not a distant goal that already exists, ready-made, somewhere ahead of us. It points to a task that is not yet finished, a reality that is still coming into being, an event still outstanding in our future. Man, as one who actively and creatively hopes, is therefore a participant in the realization of that coming Kingdom. "And as we move forward to it in hope, we build it up, as collaborators in and not simply interpreters of a future whose driving force is God himself."[17] By recovering what Metz calls a "militant, operative relationship to the future," the new theologians move away from the traditional Christian stress on contemplative knowledge or spiritual inwardness, and return to the original biblical stress on eschatological hope and practical action. Biblical man strives not to understand and transcend the world but actively to transform it in accord with the eschatological promises of the God of Exodus and Easter.

The future of man envisioned by a radically secular theology is not to be found, of course, in the conceptual abstractions of a philosophical anthropology, no matter how congenial. Nor can biblical man's hopes be reformulated in terms of an indeterminate program of human emancipation, Marxist or otherwise. For the radical theologian, as for biblical man, the outlines of that future are already contained in the liberation of the people of

Israel from their slavery in Egypt and in the cross and resurrection of Jesus the Christ. For the Christian, it is, above all, the figure of Jesus that provides the historical clue to the nature of a new universal humanity. As Shaull explains:

> . . . The peculiar dynamic of this position is the result of the association of this hope for men within a particular historical person, Jesus of Nazareth, in whom we have a concrete indication of what such a new humanity can mean. Jesus, the Messiah—a political, in fact, a revolutionary figure—is the instrument of human emancipation.[18]

Only in the light of the future of Christ is man's future to be understood. For Christ is "the new man; he represents a new form of human existence in the world."[19] Only by referring to this particular person and event is it possible to reflect on the general structures of human existence. The thinking of a radical Christian anthropology starts not with the generalizations of a philosophical system; it starts with the concrete humanity disclosed in Christ, and moves from there to a consideration of its implications, philosophical and historical, for the realization of a universal humanity.[20]

This emphasis upon the person of Christ as the locus of a new humanity should not be taken as licensing an individualistic or spiritualized approach to man. The significance of this Christocentric view of the future can be grasped only within the larger setting of the destiny of a people. Only through his solidarity with the social struggles and historical aspirations of the people of Israel does Jesus come to bear in his own person the eschatological identity and promise of a new, universal humanity. In the same way, our own individual quest for identity and self-realization, so far as it is a reflection of our hope in him, must take place in historical continuity with the struggles of that larger community.

The focus of a new humanity in the person of Christ can serve as a pointed reminder, however, that the goal of sociopolitical emancipation does not exhaust the possibilities of personal liberation. Even in the midst of the revolutionary struggles of our time, the radical Christian will endeavor to create space for the fulfillment of other, individual or higher needs.[21] For the new theologian, a radical Christian perspective on man affirms its solidarity with contemporary struggles for social and political freedom. But it also holds open the possibility of a higher, personal, and spiritual end. It is therefore up to the Marxist critic to reconsider which of these two visions of man is most capable of satisfying the needs of the whole man.

## A Radically Secular Theology of the World

When it comes to constructing a new theology of the world, the radical theologians no longer need to draw on the resources of Bloch's Marxist metaphysics. They can appeal directly to the precedents and criteria provided by the biblical tradition. The object of biblical hope is the coming of the Kingdom of God. This expectation is rooted in the promises made to a particular people, the historical community of Israel. But the content of that hope is the revolutionary creation of a new kind of world order, an era of social freedom, justice, and peace among all nations. A radical theology of the world therefore will be a theology that hopes for, and commits itself to, the struggle to overthrow the present world order and to build, in accord with the biblical vision, a new secular era of universal human emancipation.

The biblical world view is radically secular in this historical and sociopolitical sense from the very beginning. Already in the Genesis narratives, the biblical thinkers had broken with the dominant nature-oriented cosmology in which all aspects of life and reality were viewed as expressions of an unchanging cyclical world order. The stories of Creation and Exodus represent a revolutionary reorientation in man's attitude toward the world. The world becomes a realm of unprecedented and transforming change, a realm of events that liberate men. The world of the gods of nature is replaced by the world of the God of history— and of men. We are on the road toward the desacralizing and humanizing of the world—the path of secularization.

The historicizing of the world that takes place in the myth of Creation and the story of Exodus is later repeated in the

apocalyptic literature that provides the narrative setting for the
New Testament story:

The "universe" is no longer, as in pagan cosmology, a thing to be
interpreted in astro-mythical or pantheistic or mechanistic terms as the
sum total of the world and of our satisfaction with it. Instead it splits
into aeons in the apocalyptic process—into a world that is coming
and one that is passing away.[22]

In both the Old and New Testament cosmologies, the world is
mythologically reinterpreted in temporal-historical terms and
made the field of God's transforming and liberating activity.

If the world is now seen as a theater of revolutionary eschatological expectation rather than a cosmos of unbroken
natural necessity, the nature of man's relationship to that world
must similarly change. The move from a natural to an historical
cosmology is an invitation to the development of a political view
of the world—a theology that is political not only in the broader,
Aristotelian sense of the *polis* as "the inclusive horizon of the life
of mankind"[23] but also in the more immediately practical sense
that involves a revolutionary critique of a hitherto sacred social
order which had justified itself ideologically by appealing to a
natural cosmology. It is but a short step from the story of Creation and Exodus to the radical politics of the prophets. The
prophets are "the first revolutionaries," men for whom "liberation from old authorities, concern for human emancipation, and
a sense of duty led them to look critically at their own society and
to become very dissatisfied with it."[24] As the prophetic paradigm
shows, the biblical "theology of the world" is not a speculative
metaphysics of the natural universe or an expression of the
problematic of personal existence. It is an explicitly political
view of the world, a revolutionary perspective that brings the
pressure of the eschatological future to bear on those forces in
society which are the practical agents of its transformation.[25]

This sociopolitical radicalism of the prophets is, according to
the new theologians, the unmythological core of biblical religion. This "protest against real suffering" (Marx) is also "the real
inheritance" of the biblical tradition.[26] In the biblical politicizing
of theology—theology as "practical eschatology or eschatological praxis"[27]—the radical theologians see the origins of all sub-

sequent ideologies of revolutionary social change. In support of
this argument, the Marxist philosopher Bloch himself admits
that "all the utopian aspirations of the great movements of
human liberation derive from Exodus and the messianic parts of
the bible."[28] By the time Christianity had been transformed into
the official state religion under Constantine, the radically secular
hope of the biblical tradition had been all but abandoned by the
established Church and left to others—initially to the heretic and
sectarian traditions, in modern times to secular revolutionary
movements. But with the help of a renewed understanding of its
biblical origins and in response to the urgent pressures of our
own times, the new theology has attempted to recapture for the
Christian Church a sense of the radically secular (social and
political) character of its original eschatological mission to the
world.

The biblical tradition established the precedents for a radically
secular view of the world. But it also provides the criteria that
enable the radical theologian to distinguish his view of the world
from that of his Marxist partner in dialogue. The major criteria
are provided, once again, by the events of the Exodus and the
Resurrection.

The event of the Exodus tells us several things about the
particular shape and content of the biblical hope for the world.
By linking that hope to the destiny of a particular people
—Israel—it tells us, first of all, to look for the fulfillment of our
hope in the arena of history. More specifically, as the story of the
deliverance of a people from slavery and their journey to a
promised land of freedom, it tells us that that fulfillment will be
sociopolitical in nature and that its specific content will be the
revolutionary overcoming of a life of social unfreedom and the
establishment of a new era of total human emancipation. From
the perspective of the Exodus, it follows that the traditional
Christian view of individual salvation from the world is a serious
distortion of the biblical hope. For the radically secular theologian, the salvation for which the Christian hopes can never be
"simply or primarily the salvation of the individual—whether
this is understood as the salvation of one's soul or the individual

resurrection of the body—but salvation of the covenant, of the people, of the many."[29]

At first sight, the focus of the Resurrection on the individual person of Christ would seem to contradict the sociopolitical thrust of Old Testament hope. But the Easter faith was itself embedded in a larger eschatological drama. Jesus had preached the imminence of the Kingdom of God—an apocalyptic, world-shattering revolution that was to inaugurate a new, messianic era. His resurrection, accordingly, was viewed as the first fruits of a general resurrection of the dead which was to accompany an era of universal human emancipation. For the radical theologian, therefore, the Christian hope in the Resurrection enables us to see "in the existing reality of man and the world as at present experienced, and which it reveals in all their negativity, the positive side of the future for which it hopes for man and the world, for spirit and body, for Israel and the nations."[30]

When we look at the actual life of the historical Jesus, we see there too an explicitly "political figure—the Messiah" who is also "the new man . . . a new form of human existence in the world."[31] In the life of Jesus, we see a revolutionary figure who relentlessly attacked and exposed "the moral bankruptcy, the spiritual inadequacy, and the ultimately dehumanizing consequences of the legalism and piety of his time."[32] We see a man condemned and killed as a threat to the religious and political establishment of his time, a man whose life and teachings have become the powerful symbol of the struggle for human emancipation. In the historical person of Jesus, we have a concrete model and anticipation of what the new, liberated humanity can be.

The Exodus and the Resurrection are not arbitrary criteria for shaping a contemporary theology of the world. They can serve as effective guides to the possibilities of the future only because they have already actualized these possibilities as events in the past. On the other hand, they cannot simply be detached from their original historical setting and turned into generalized symbols of the future possibilities of man. They open up only very specific possibilities for the future because of the historically specific way in which they shaped men's hopes in the past. The

eschatological vision of a radically secular theology will not
proceed from a pseudoscientific doctrine of human progress or
historical inevitability; nor will it be the projection of a general,
unspecified confidence in the creative powers of the human
species. It will be a reaffirmation of the inner logic or historical
necessity of the events that gave rise to that hope in the first
place.[33]

The inner necessity that characterizes the movement of biblical hope (lest it be mistaken for the laws of necessity that apply to
the natural universe) is the dialectical logic of divine promise and
fulfillment—the power of God's future to break into the present
and open up the possibility of a world that is new. This was the
kind of logic or necessity that forged the chains of historical
continuity in the events surrounding God's original promises to
the people of Israel. The events of the Exodus and the covenant
at Sinai were, literally, history-making events, because they
opened up an historical space in which a people was freed to
pursue its destiny. Insofar as it repeats and extends the inner,
history-making logic of those events—that is, insofar as it too
opens up specific possibilities for a liberated future—the resurrection of Christ may be said to stand in historical continuity with
them. Similarly, Christ's death and resurrection stand in effective, not merely symbolic, continuity with our own times. By
joining with our contemporaries to overthrow the forces of
human alienation and open up possibilities for a more human
future, we too are drawing upon and further extending the
historical reality of those earlier events. It is the events of the
Exodus and the Resurrection, not a science of history or a
general philosophy of man, that provide the radical theologian
with the grounds and criteria of a future that will fulfill the
original promise of human emancipation.

This radically secular theology of the world, of history, and of
the future is an attempt to restate in contemporary language the
nonmythological core of the biblical-eschatological view of the
world. But in the context of a Marxist-Christian dialogue, it must
be asked whether it presents a view of the world that is superior
to its modern secular alternatives. The radical theologians present several kinds of arguments to show that it does. For pur-

poses of closer analysis in the chapter that follows, I shall call
them the argument from history, the argument from the future,
and the argument from the world.

The argument from history states that it was the biblical tradition that first articulated a radically secular view of the world. It
can hardly be denied that

> it was the Jewish and Christian biblical message that first recognized
> the world as history, that this message freed men to look upon the
> world as subject to human mastery, that this message saw the
> world not as something fixed in which man stood, but as a world in
> process, a world rising toward the future of God, a world for which
> man is held responsible.[34]

It was the biblical view of the world that proved decisive in the
subsequent shaping of the Western outlook, both the world of
Christendom and the world of modern secular man. By itself of
course, this argument from history does not suffice to prove the
theologian's case. It must be supplemented by other arguments
that more directly testify to the continuing validity or normative
superiority of the biblical world view.

The argument from the future holds that, as Metz puts it,
"perhaps we are also ahead in that we admit to knowing less
about the future than Marxism does."[35] Now epistemological
uncertainty or humility about the future seems a puzzling basis
for claiming ideological superiority. Furthermore, it appears to
contradict an earlier assertion that Christianity, unlike Marxism,
does speak to those ultimate questions that transcend the limits
of time and space—that Christianity provides answers where
Marxism does not. But the intention of this argument is fairly
clear. Whatever the positive content of the Christian's hope for
the future, the negative thrust of his position is that Marxist
ideology fails to distinguish between what man can know about
his own projected inner-worldly futures and what he can or
rather cannot know about the absolute future.[36] Biblical eschatology is superior to all secular utopias in that it refuses to turn our
inevitably partial and changing visions of the future into historical absolutes. Marxism may be reluctant or unable to speak about
the absolute future, but this does not mean it is free to dogmatize
about its own particular projection of the future. In this sense,

though the Christian claims to know less about the future, he already knows something more about it than someone who claims to know that something more. He knows that the only attitude we can take to the absolute future is one of hope beyond hope or faith in that which cannot yet be seen, a faith which perseveres in the expectation that the future will bring possibilities for liberation beyond anything we can presently foresee or project.

The argument from the world is simply the other side of the argument from the future. It points out that, just as Christian eschatology resists our every claim to absolute knowledge about the future, so it frees us for a commitment to the world that is both more critical and yet more radical than that of any secular utopian ideology. The biblical insight into the irreducibility of the future to the givens of the present or the past makes possible a radical critique of the dehumanizing forces of the existing world order. But it also serves as a transcendent safeguard against the tendency to absolutize the particular ways we try to overthrow that order. It therefore guarantees that our commitment to changing the world will be a radically open and humanizing one.

Michael Novak has observed that "there is a startling unity between language about God and language about social and political reform."[37] Central to both is man's vision of future possibilities which transcend and stand in critical judgment upon the existing order of things. What distinguishes Christian eschatology from every merely secular utopia, however, is that it insists that the future is even greater than what men can produce or conceive.[38] Because the Christian's commitment to the world is rooted in an absolute future which transcends every future projected by man, it is a more liberating and hence more radical commitment than that of his Marxist counterpart. The absolute power of the future to transcend every past or present is the source of the Christian's radical freedom to work for the secular emancipation of man. When Marxism, as an atheistic ideology, rules out the possibility of talking about an absolute future, it commits itself to the self-contradictory proposition that its own limited projection of the future can make sense of man's hope for a future that is radically open and free. For the theologian, on the other hand, radical humanism makes sense only if, paradoxically, it is rooted in something other than man's own capacities to project or envision the future—and that is the being of God as the absolute future of both man and the world. Apart from this transcendent perspective and power, there is absolutely no guarantee that the secularization or *hominization* of the world will also lead to its *humanization*.[39] Apart from the freedom of God as the absolute future, there is no hope for the liberation of men in this world's future. And that, in the final analysis, is what the Marxist-Christian dialogue is all about.

3
Radical Theology:
A Secular Critique

In the previous chapter, we looked at the arguments of those theologians who met the criticisms of Marxists by reinterpreting the traditional Christian concepts of God, man, and the world from a new, radically secular perspective. In the present chapter, I shall argue that this radical reconstruction of Christian theology has not succeeded in overcoming the objections of either Marxism or contemporary secular thought. More specifically, I shall not argue the weaker thesis that all such theologies have happened to fail; I shall defend the stronger claim that any such theology must necessarily fail.[1] To show this, it will be necessary to consider both matters of detail and inner consistency as well as the prior question whether a *radically secular* theology (because it is a radically secular *theology*) is possible at all.

That radical theology cannot meet the objections of its secular critics may be demonstrated in a number of ways, corresponding to the variety of arguments advanced on behalf of such theology. We shall examine in turn the arguments from history, the future, the world, man, and God, after which we shall revisit the argument from the future.

The Argument from History

One of the basic questions which the secular critic must ask of a distinctively Christian approach to secularity is one which Moltmann himself asks as a theologian: "Why dialogue precisely with *these texts* and with this past?"[2] As long as the theologian refuses to confront this preliminary question, he is still living uncritically off the inheritance of his tradition. However radical his posture, he is merely continuing traditionalism by other means.[3] Behind the obvious apologetic issue, "how can and should one understand the Christian tradition today," there lies the logically prior question, *"Why* is one compelled to preach precisely these texts, to understand and believe them?"[4] Why are we compelled to view our contemporary reality primarily (if not exclusively) in the light of the biblical perspective?[5]

The radical theologian's answer to this question rests, as we have noted, on the argument from history—that is, an appeal to descriptive and normative precedent: Christianity got there first.[6] The Judeo-Christian tradition, as even its Marxist critics agree, was of decisive influence in the formation of the Western perspective on man and the world. Hence, it is normative not only for our understanding of the past of that culture but for the development of its future possibilities. Since this argument rests on certain factual as well as interpretive assumptions, we must look to the evidence offered in their support.

"Theology," says Moltmann, "can teach only on the ground of the word given in tradition."[7] The very first question therefore is: What is this tradition? Simply as a request for information, this question immediately leads one into a maze of complexities. Not only does it involve the difficulty of getting clear about the exact nature of the biblical origins. It also presents the problem of assessing the tradition's subsequent growth and development in all of its continuity and discontinuity, its accretion of the foreign and the new in both ecclesiastical and secular history. When we add to this factual request a demand for the clarification of such normative terms as "decisive," "definitive," "unique," "distinctive," "essential," then the size of the theologian's task must be apparent.

To show the nature and importance of this issue at stake, let us examine two claims which are crucial to the success of this argument from history. It is claimed, first of all, that Jesus is, actually and symbolically, "a political, in fact, a revolutionary figure."[8] His cross and resurrection are the source and continuing inspiration of a political, more specifically a revolutionary historical, hermeneutic.[9] It is in the life and teaching of Jesus, or in the spirit of Christ, that the radical theologian finds the call for a revolutionary break with the old secular (social and political) order and the construction of a radically new one.

The radical theologian is also concerned to defend the independent integrity of a secular Christianity—that is, to show that the Judeo-Christian tradition, independently of its relationship to modern, secular culture, has its own biblical resources for supporting man's efforts to create a more human future. As Rahner contends: "Christianity as the religion of the absolute future . . . is not a modernist interpretation of Christianity or one which arose only from contact with Marxism."[10]

Now both of these claims can be brought into serious question in light of much else that we know about the origins of our modern, secular, and revolutionary self-consciousness. With regard to the second claim, even some of the radical theologians themselves admit, contra Rahner, that the new theology has already learned, and can still learn, a great deal from secular society and culture—and not merely in the accidentals of faith. According to Cox and Shaull, for example, Christian theology today needs secular thought and praxis in order to regain the essentials of its faith.[11]

But an even more damaging point can be made. The claim that Christianity does not need to be interpreted with the help of contemporary culture because it is the spiritual progenitor of modern secular and revolutionary consciousness is, it can be argued, simply not true. As Hannah Arendt convincingly shows, the origins of modern man's secular consciousness and his revolutionary praxis are to be found in the economic, social, and political achievements of the age of absolutism and the two great revolutions at the end of the eighteenth century.[12]

The same may be said for the related claim that the notion of history, with its linear development and element of inexpungeable novelty, is Judeo-Christian in origin. For it can be argued that even where the Christian philosophy of history succeeded in partially comprehending the novelty and unrepeatability of the Christ event, its understanding of both sacred and secular history remained for the most part bound within the cycles of antiquity.[13] It seems plausible to conclude, with Arendt, that "the best one can say in favor of this theory is that it needed modernity to liberate the revolutionary germ of the Christian faith, which obviously is begging the question."[14]

Then what about the assertion that Jesus has a political-revolutionary significance for radical Christianity? Both to those who argue, roughly, that Jesus was really the first communist, that he struggled for social justice, and that Marxism is just a secularized version of Christianity, and to those who, conceding that this was not the case, still urge his spiritual or symbolic significance for the modern revolutionary impetus, it must be pointed out that this quest for a revolutionary Jesus is misleading and misguided. It is misleading, because it assumes that facts about the historical Jesus are sufficient to prove the argument, whereas the question of the true historical significance or influence of Jesus is very much more complex. It is misguided, because it inevitably leads to a reduction of the historical element in the life of Jesus to a bare factual vehicle for the conveyance of larger, more malleable symbolic truths, whereas it is the actual, practico-historical content (or lack of content) of the Christ event that this particular debate is all about.

Whether the argument for the revolutionary significance of Christ appeals to historical fact or symbolic truth, it is in any case highly problematic and cannot be judged persuasive. At best, the radical theologian might be able to argue that Jesus, as a religious leader, offered important prerevolutionary insights. But as the Marxist would remind him, it is "opposition, political opposition," that must be rendered unto Caesar. Hence, the radical theologian would probably do better to find other revolutionary examples than Jesus.[15]

The reliance of the radical theologian upon this particular assertion provides a clear illustration of the way in which the argument from history can turn into a two-edged sword. Let us assume a secular historian to be asking what it was about Jesus that was so new, so unique, that he became for Christians the hinge of history. Historical precedents for much of what Jesus said or did can be found throughout the Jewish tradition, not to mention parallels in the other great religious and moral traditions. His decisive significance for the early Christians therefore must have consisted rather in the fact that in Jesus they saw the eschatological timetable as having advanced another step. Having been partially and proleptically realized in the person of Jesus, the Kingdom was then further extended in the subsequent history of the Christian community.

The problem with this answer to the historian's question is that it permits the secular thinker who finds contemporary meaning in the biblical events to draw a quite different and opposite conclusion. For a Marxist humanist like Ernst Bloch, the proper conclusion is that it is our task to complete in a secular setting that which was only partially and indirectly begun in the religious community of faith. The realization of what the Christians referred to mythologically as the Kingdom of God requires abolishing, not perpetuating, the religious expression of faith in order to promote a genuinely secular transformation of the world.

From a radically secular perspective, therefore, the radical theologian's attempt to establish the primacy of the Christ event and the Christian historical tradition for modern man's secular and revolutionary self-consciousness is at best a mistaken, and in any case an unnecessary enterprise. It is an effort to preserve the old story, the expectations of an ancient world view (eschatology —an amalgam of myth and history), under the same name but in a new and different setting. To the extent that it succeeds, with the help of the novel concepts and historical praxis of the modern secular world, it in effect acknowledges the primacy (if not the chronological priority) of the latter, and thus, in fact, it fails.[16]

The attempt at an historical defense of radical theology's claim to primacy in the essentials of our secular self-consciousness is complex and questionable enough. When there is added the claim that the biblical tradition represents a normative criterion for contemporary social and political struggle, the radical theologian would seem to have made the qualitative jump from improbability to impossibility. At the very least, the argument from history must be judged inconclusive.

But perhaps this is as it should be. Perhaps it is intrinsic to the logic of this particular theological position. For as a world view oriented primarily to the future, radical theology itself reminds us that the answer to the question of the uniqueness or superiority of the Christian perspective should not be sought exclusively in a consideration of its past history. It can be found only by expanding our search to take in the eschatological dimension as well, for history, including the past, can be finally understood only under the aspect of its future. Here, rather than in a catalog of past events, is where the decisive answer to the secular hope of man resides. The same holds true even more obviously for modern secular and revolutionary self-consciousness. Proof or disproof of the Christian origins of secularity tells us nothing definitive about the future possibilities of either those origins or their supposed derivatives.[17]

## The Argument from the Future

There are at least two reasons, it will be recalled, why a radical Christian eschatology might consider itself superior to any secular form of utopian ideology: it speaks of and promises more, and yet it knows and endangers us less.

The logical consequences of this paradoxical conjunction of arguments, when spelled out, appear to be contradictory. When secular hope seems to project itself too far, it is attacked by the theologian for failing to respect the limits of human understanding, for attempting to envision what can never be seen from our present vantage point. When secular hope is scaled down to a limited, human-sized projection, it is faulted for its inability or failure to speak to first and last things. Yet, when pressed for information or criteria concerning his own eschatological alternative, the theologian becomes reticent, contenting himself with negative, cautionary notes or, at most, appeals to faith in that which is unseen. Attributing to his secular opposite an inability to achieve a self-critical and self-transcendent vision of the future, he declares his own ideology off limits when the same demands are made on it. What would appear to a secular critic an obvious contradiction in the theologian's epistemic relation to the future is mysteriously converted into an impregnable

methodological asset: the Christian vision of man's absolute
future in God "cannot be confirmed within history but can only
be accepted in faith."[18]

The underlying difficulty with the theologian's argument is
that it leaves us without any criteria (except, possibly, negative
ones) for distinguishing warranted from unwarranted projections
of human hope. It rests in a peculiar ambivalence, a refusal to
concede that it is possible for secular philosophy to avoid confusing its vision of the world and of man as a whole with either
specific data about man and the world or limited projections of
specific innerworldly futures. From a contemporary secular
perspective, one that is increasingly capable of self-criticism and
self-transcendence, this traditional theological maneuver, with
its claim to another, higher form of insight and self-
authentication, simply fails to convince. Its appeal to an irreducible element of mystery and paradox looks like a retreat to
mystification and self-contradiction instead—a patent weakness,
not a hidden strength of the position.

The argument from the future thus leaves us with several
questions: Is the theologian's suspicion of secular utopias justified? If so, on what grounds does the theologian justify his own
claim to a superior vision, one which *does* apply to first and last
things, to the world and man as a whole? If not, what does this tell
us about secular visions of the future, and what does it imply for
theology's alleged eschatological guarantees?

If the radical theologian's vision of the future contains
metaphysical and epistemological ambiguities, then his commitment to the world should display similar difficulties.

## The Argument from the
World

The ambivalence of radical theology's attitude to the world
shows itself in a reluctance to identify with, or commit itself fully
to, specific programs of revolutionary change. It is capable of
doing so radically—but only up to a point. Its concern for the
world can never be more than provisional or penultimate, since
its ultimate source and hope lie elsewhere.[19]

For example, Karl Rahner tells us that, "regarding the material content of this [inner-worldly] future, Christianity has just as little to say. It does not set up an innerworldly ideal for the future; it makes no prognosis and does not bind man to any determinate goals for an innerworldly future." And yet, at the same time, the theologian can add that, because it is a religion of the absolute future, which is neutral to all of our particular futures, Christianity is "liberating in regard to man's individual and collective innerworldly aims," that, in fact, it "confers a final radical seriousness to the work of building an innerwordly future."[20] Because of its decisive objection to every secular vision of utopia, Christian eschatology makes possible "a radical humanism . . . more human than its autonomous counterpart."[21]

Now there is a serious problem here. It must be granted that this refusal to identify the absolute with any particular is the Judeo-Christian tradition's way of proscribing the fashioning of false idols from human hopes. But Christianity has always been unequivocally historical, and has not hesitated from earliest times to take stands and make commitments (for the most part, establishmentarian) to specific historical programs and goals. It can be argued therefore that in this period of history and at this particular juncture in the dialogue with Marxism, men's need is to hear the opposite sort of glad tidings. Men need to hear, rather, that their deepest dreams and highest aspirations are relevant to a world coming-of-age, that their most urgent utopias are perhaps more realistic, more capable of realization, than ever before.

A radically secular perspective no longer allows room for theologians to declare that the realization of man's hopes and dreams must be forever beyond his this-worldly reach. It refuses the priestly illogic that would have men move from saying "no" to some particular stage of this world to a refusal to say "yes" to the world as a whole. The ultimate thrust of a radical perspective on secularity runs directly counter to this final reservation of the new theologian, for its explicit concern is to find "a way of transcending the present world while remaining firmly within it."[22]

A radically secular perspective on man's commitment to the

world demands two things of contemporary thought: acknowledgment of man's hard-won capacity for self-critical self-
transcendence, and an affirmation of this finite, temporal, historical world as his true home, the legitimate field of his creative
activity on behalf of man's future. Anything less will necessarily
rely upon an appeal to man's weakness, ignorance, and fear, and
will be able only provisionally to affirm his knowledge, courage,
and strength. To speak of and to men's weakness is one thing, but
to play on it, to take advantage of it, to claim the only guarantee
for overcoming it, is another matter altogether.


## The Argument from Man

The same ambivalence which characterizes the eschatological
hopes and this-worldly commitment of radical theology is also
found in its argument from man. There is an implicit contradiction between its celebration of secular man's coming-of-age and
its underlying appeal to man's weakness (as distinct from his
finitude, although that too is a double-edged sword, as we shall
see).

Moltmann bases the superiority of Christian anthropology
over Marxist humanism on the latter's inability to provide
spiritual reassurance and an eschatological guarantee concerning
"the regions over which nothingness holds sway and where
human beings experience suffering and death." He contends that
Bloch's philosophy of man as a being who is open to the future
"comprehends nothingness only to the extent that the courage to
hope can 'do something'; it cannot apply hope to no-longer-
being."[23] Christian anthropology, unlike secular forms of
humanism, is more radical because, as we have noted, it holds out
the promise of a "greater future" (Metz) than any that secular
man can hope for on his own. It promises to liberate man not
only from this or that particular (finite) threat of nonbeing but
from the power of transitoriness itself. Rahner, an equally strong
defender of the superiority of Christian humanism, similarly
argues that "no economic change or social system can prevent
man from an experiential awareness of his limit in death,

thereby—though not only thereby—placing his whole being in question."[24]

Now while in general this may be true, it must be asked whether the only conclusion that necessarily follows is that drawn by the theologian—namely, that man on his own is unable to provide a satisfactory answer to this question. This is not to suggest, as Bonhoeffer sometimes seems to do, that the existential problems of James's "sick souls" are to be swept under the rug as a secular embarrassment. Such experiences are perhaps an inevitable part of the total condition of man. The question, however, is whether a theological remedy is required to face them.

This brings us to a second part of the radical theologian's argument from man—his radical reconstruction of the traditional understanding of man's freedom and God's grace. For Rahner, as we have seen, "grace is nothing other than God's gift of himself as the absolute future . . . as the future of the world."[25] The difficulty is that even on this revisionist or futural reading, divine grace is still considered necessary if man is to be freed to realize his essential humanity in a way he would otherwise be unable to do. He cannot by himself initiate or bring to fulfillment the process of genuine human emancipation. The inner logic of this Christian anthropology, in other words, even in its revised, radically secular version, still presupposes the traditional metaphysical cleavage between the essence and the existence of things.

The modern experience of man's autonomy and capacity for historical initiative requires a rather different metaphysical approach. Human existence is to be understood as a dialectical process of self-creation and self-transcendence. The essence and thus the necessities of man's being are self-determined, not predetermined or externally determined. They are the products and projections of his own practical activity. In such an anthropology, it becomes impossible to drive a metaphysical wedge between man's essential possibilities and his actual historical capacities. For a radically secular perspective, man's essential possibilities are not something already there *in potentia,* waiting to be liberated by God. They are imaginative projections which summon him to the ongoing task of the creation of man by man himself.

There are therefore two ways to read the lesson of human finitude, only one of which calls for a theological completion. Moltmann agrees with the perspective of radical secularity that "our knowledge . . . has a transcendent and provisional character marked by promise and expectation, in virtue of which it recognizes the open horizon of the future of reality and thus preserves the finitude of human experience."[26] Man's finitude just is this capacity for self-transcendence. But this, it turns out, does not satisfy the distinctively theological desire to provide a further, transcendent guarantee for the realization of man's highest hopes. Thus Shaull thinks he has adequately characterized the two options available to a radical humanism by accounting for them in this way:

This radical transcendence and transgression could have only one of two sources. It could come as the result of ascribing infinite value to one aspect of finite reality . . . the second alternative . . . reverses this whole process. The object of loyalty is not some element of the finite which has been absolutized, but the Creator who relativizes and at the same time sustains all created reality.[27]

But are we really offered two alternatives here? Are we not, rather, presented with just one choice wearing two different faces, a positive, theistic aspect and a negative, antitheistic one? Is it not possible to imagine another possibility, one that would constitute a genuine alternative—an ontology of human finitude which is just that? If so, we must first take explicit account of the final argument of the radical theologian, one we have been considering implicitly all along, the linchpin of this as of any other theology.

## The Argument from God

For the theologian, as for the radical secularist, the fundamental question underlying this entire discussion is, finally "Why God?"[28] For Harvey Cox, the question is:

Does man's unfaltering hope for a more human and just world have any grounding in reality itself? Is there reason to believe the developing universe itself sustains the human aspiration it seems to elicit, or is man's hope only his own wishful projection, something to which both history and the cosmos remain supremely indifferent? It is the contention of Biblical faith that there is a mystery from which man emerges, a reality that summons him to anguished freedom and joyous responsibility, a real ground for the hopes man entertains for himself and his race.[29]

Similarly, for Shaull, "Human life is seen as most human when it is lived in response to a higher loyalty than self, and expresses the trust that reality—coming-to-be—is ultimately favorable to man."[30] The secularist, for his part, might agree with the theologian that "reality—coming-to-be" in some sense carries greater ontological weight than man. But he feels compelled to ask whether that either necessitates or justifies our calling that greater something "God."

The theologian's argument seems to rest on two presuppositions: the theism-relative or ontologically dependent status of atheism, and the impossibility of radical transcendence on other than theistic terms. Let us consider each in turn.

One of the standard theological criticisms of atheistic humanism is that it is conceptually and existentially dependent upon the theism it rejects. For Moltmann, " 'atheism' is always a relative concept. . . . It opposes concepts and notions which describe God as . . ."[31] Even when proclaimed in the name of a prior and positive commitment to man, atheism is—if one looks closely enough at its concept of man—parasitic for its content and significance upon the theism it attempts to replace. Atheism is always antitheism, theism-relative humanism, and thus bound negatively but dialectically by the rules of the theist's onto-theologic.[32] The favorite contemporary illustration of this thesis among theologians is, of course, Sartre's anguished freedom, which views man's being as "useless passion," a futile striving to realize the impossible ideal of "being-in-itself for-itself"—that is, "to be God."

This rather subtle putdown of secular humanism is supported by the further claim that a radical doctrine of transcendence is, in any case, impossible to articulate in immanentist terms. In response to the Marxist humanist attempt to formulate such a notion, Moltmann argues that "the apocalyptic content of the

Bible . . . can be brought into the dialectical and historical process of the mediation of man and nature only if that which occurs without any mediation—the sudden and transcendent end as understood in the Bible—is translated into what is subject to mediation: transcendental immanence without transcendence." In this process, the divine reality emerges much diminished; in fact, it is "reduced to a nuclear immanence within matter." Thus, what the Marxist sees as the last step in an act of demythologization necessary to activate secular hope, the theologian sees as a remythologization of nature, a reintroduction of the divine mystification into the natural process from whence it had originally been removed (desacralized) by the biblical account of Creation.[33]

Here the theology of radical secularity, supported by the ontologies of Bloch, Whitehead, and others, moves onto the philosophical offensive. Insofar as the atheist's opposition to Christian theism rests on a rejection of the mythological language of the Bible or the metaphysical concepts of a theology grounded in the absolute and unchanging being of classical metaphysics, his objections are well taken. The new theologians agree that acceptance of either the language of myth or the language of classical ontotheology entails a denial of the full autonomy and significance of the secular world. But the rejection of "that peculiar combination of myth and traditional metaphysics called classical theism" does not entitle the atheist to the further conclusion that he has succeeded in rejecting all forms of theism.[34]

What entitles the radical theologian to make this assertion? The exegetical rediscovery of the dynamic God of biblical faith—yes. But more important—since the mythological language of the Bible can be a stumbling block—is a new ontology whose basic categories are those of temporality and historicity, a metaphysics which places relativity and the affirmation of change in the very heart of being itself.[35] This new ontology is what informs Shaull's and Cox's view of ultimate reality as a process of coming-to-be. It is what grounds Braaten's and Moltmann's assertion that "the future [is] a divine mode of being."[36] Accordingly, if God's eternity is understood as eminent temporality under the primary aspect of open futurity, then God's being, far from alienating man from his secular self-consciousness and his this-worldly being, in fact reaffirms that secularity in its very ontological depths.[37]

For the secular critic, however, this problem is not yet resolved. Just how do these categories of temporality and relativity apply to our concept of reality as a whole, to the totality of being and to God as the highest being? Shubert Ogden replies that for a secular metaphysician like Heidegger, and presumably for Bloch and Whitehead too, "finitude is seen . . . to consist not in temporality and relatedness as such, but in the limited mode of these perfections appropriate to our being as men." Therefore, if temporality and relativity are in their primal forms constitutive of being itself, then "God's uniqueness is to be construed not simply by denying them, but by conceiving them in their infinite mode through the negation of their limitations as we experience them in ourselves."[38]

But this answer simply raises further questions. Is the logic of this move from the finite to the infinite, even in its new form, acceptable? Does this new concept of God really overcome the alienating effect which the traditional concept has upon secular man?

The metaphysical use of this reconstructed concept of God as eminent temporality (futurity), despite its categorical novelty, is subject to the same Kantian strictures which applied to the older, classical metaphysics of God. The radical conversion of the predicates of divine being from immutability to relationality, from eternal presence to open futurity, should not obscure the fact that the theologian is still trying to retain, to prove the intelligibility of, the subject of these predicates. The difficulty lies not in the notion of God's being as temporal, but in its infinite temporality—a leap which post-Kantian metaphysics, processive or otherwise, is not licensed to take.

The question is therefore a more serious one. It is whether the underlying logic of either the theistic or the antitheistic position makes any sense at all. Does it any longer make sense to use such phrases as "the totality of being" (Moltmann), "reality itself" (Cox), "reality—coming-to-be" (Shaull), "the world and man as a whole" (Rahner), "the ultimate metaphysical reality" (Ogden), "the absolute future" (Rahner)? If these terms are to have any theistic significance, then they must have either an explanatory or a referential function in the setting of a metaphysics of transcendent being, and clearly that is how these theologians intend them to be taken. But since Hume and Kant, such terms have come to be understood as simply convenient shorthand expressions for the most general categories of a secular, descriptive metaphysics. The temptation of theologians to regard them as quasi-referential terms in the service of theistic proofs still leads, as it did in Kant's time, to those transcendental illusions which we have come to associate with speculative metaphysics.

There is a further problem. Even this new, temporal concept of God's being, contrary to the claims of its most revolutionary-minded adherents, does not fully overcome the alienating effect of the traditional notion of God. Again, the radical reconstruction of the divine predicates in line with the general features of man's secular being might lead one to think that the Marxist's suspicions on this score could be overcome. The unspoken assumption is apparently that Christians, by yielding to Marxists on the predicates of ultimate reality, might in turn succeed in encouraging Marxists to yield to them on the divinity of these predicates. The problem from a radically secular perspective, however, is that the dispute over the nature of the predicates of the divine is not the chief issue. The Marxist is in any case already persuaded of the dialectical character of ultimate reality. His concern is, rather, with the divinity of these predicates—specifically, with the theologian's assumption that, without divine backing, these predicates would lose their ultimate significance for man's being.[39]

Ogden's way of deriving the predicates of God's being from the predicates of man's being ("by conceiving them in their infinite mode through the negation of their limitations as we experience them in ourselves") nicely illustrates the sort of inverted logic that was the object of the original Feuerbachian and Marxist animus against the argument from God. Once again, the concept of God becomes the alienated and alienating expression of man's finite perfections. Put forward as their ground and guarantee, it in fact infinitely negates them. In addition, this newer concept of God is now more subtly alienating than when the predicates of divine being radically differed in character from their human counterparts. For with the affirmation of an ever-increasing similarity between the predicates of the human and the divine, the difference which remains in their extension— God as the eminent sublimation of human transience—seems even more oppressive. The closer the descriptive predicates of this theology of radical secularity come to our human secularity, the more obvious and problematic is their difference, as theological predicates, from a truly radical—that is, human—secularity.

As Marx concluded in his dialogue with the left-wing theologians of his day, it would seem that the theology of radical secularity must be stood on its head if its genuinely radical and secular truth is to be realized. For by insisting upon a doctrine of God as the highest being and a priori guarantee (even as eminent temporality) of an open future, the radical theologians are every bit as much transcendental-historical idealists as were Marx's Hegelian theological partners in dialogue. Their ability to affirm and work for the realization of man's secular hopes is grounded in the prior concept of a God whose eternity (ideality) is thought of as "the future of every past, the future of every present, as ontologically prior in his futurity to every event and epoch of the remotest distance from us."[40] If by idealism is meant a metaphysical world view, whether Platonic or processive, which sees the nature and destiny of finite being as grounded a priori in a realm or process of infinite and absolute being, then the theology of radically secular Christianity too is an idealism.[41]

From a radically secular perspective, the truth of "materialism"—that is, a metaphysics of radical finitude—can no longer be denied. The evidence for this philosophical claim is already visible in the world of contemporary secular practice. This will become clearer if we reconsider the practical implications of the argument from the future.

## The Argument from the
## Future Revisited

The argument from the future states that the question of the relative merits of the Christian and Marxist views of man and the world is to be settled, not so much by a comparison of their past performances as by an estimate of the respective futures they propose and their effectiveness in bringing these about. Hence, the events, the concepts, and the visions of Christian eschatology and Marxist utopian ideology ought not to be taken as the objects, laws, or predictions of a speculative science of history. They are, according to Moltmann, "not so much generic concepts for the subsuming of known reality as rather dynamic functional concepts whose aim is the future transformation of reality." These anthropological and cosmological visions are sketches for the future whose inner logic (the projective logic of promise and demand) drives them out of ideality into the realm of praxis. To understand and evaluate them properly, one must judge them in terms of their capacity to bring about their own abolition as merely speculative ideas by securing their realization as practical forces in the transformation of the world.[42]

If a theology of radical secularity is to preserve itself from the charge of being a new variation on idealism, it must indicate in what concrete respects Christian eschatology is not simply a speculative vision but one which holds its own with Marxism as a "practical attitude to the future."[43] Is Christian eschatology capable of demonstrating that, in this practico-historical sense, it too is a materialism rather than an idealism? As soon as the question is put in this way, its answer must be readily apparent. For the truth is that, in terms of the several criteria by which the pragmatic or future-practical validity of the Christian vision might reasonably be judged—theoretical guidance, practical programs, or historical initiative—the theology of radical secularity is the dependent rather than creative partner in the dialogue with secular humanism.

On the level of theory, one of the basic features of the new theology is its appreciation of the essentially futural nature of being, its belief that the essence of something is not what it was or is, but what it has the capacity to become, what it can or will be. So there is something ironic, if not self-contradictory, in the attempt of the radical theologians to ground both this insight and their defense of Christianity as essentially future-oriented in an appeal to the essentials already there in the biblical past. Thus

Metz, apparently without reflecting on the internal logic of his position, tells us that "contemporary man's orientation to the future [is] grounded in the biblical faith."[44] But by their own estimate, what any tradition essentially is, or even was, can be determined only (and even then, never definitively) by what it yet can be. The ground of contemporary (or even biblical) man's orientation to the future can be only that open-ended future itself. Have these theologians really considered the radical consequences of their own ideological affirmations?

The fact is that this theology of the radically open, the new, the revolutionary, seems unable to acknowledge the coming-into-being of something totally new unless it can show it that it was anticipated by and grounded in the essentials of the biblical perspective. Theology, as we recall Moltmann saying, "can only teach on the ground of the word given in the tradition." In short, it can only retell the old story; it cannot entertain, let alone conceive, a radically new one. But, a second irony, Christian eschatology itself has had to rely increasingly on the thought and practice of the secular world not only to comprehend the *novum* but to understand and gain a hearing for the retelling of its own story. And so it is that the theology of radical secularity comes to find itself "announcing to the secular world, as though by way of a discovery, what the secular world has been announcing to it for a rather long time."[45]

When it comes to matters of practical guidance, radical theology is confronted by the Hobson's choice of acknowledging the irrelevancy of its theistic perspective to the specifics of its social and political vision, or, as more frequently occurs, of confining itself to the level of symbolic or imaginative generalities about the future. Even then, in its dialogue with competing secular visions, as we have seen, it often views its role as primarily a negative one. The more neutral it can be vis-à-vis every particular this-worldly vision of the future, the better. The value of its dynamic futural concepts then reduces to that of a meta-reminder that we finite men ought not to absolutize our partial and relative visions. But this is a reminder that a secular man, radicalized in his commitment to the humanistic future of this world by his experience of its twentieth-century horrors, is able to provide for himself. There is no need to fall back onto a theological interpretation of its truth.

Finally, insofar as the Christian vision is a theological world view grounded in a religious way of life and concerned primarily with the activity, individual and collective, of Christians in their sociologically distinct roles as churchgoers, pray-ers, and the like, it must be said that the historical initiative, the specific methods, tools and institutions for the creation of man's future, have passed out of its hands into those of the secular world.[46] The earthly future of man is no longer to be found in sole or even primary reliance upon retelling and reliving the old story, but in the disciplines and techniques, the visions and deeds, of the new story of secularity. The question for the future is therefore not whether theology can once again accommodate itself to secularity but whether theology or religion in general can provide the secular world with the specific thought and practice which can create a more human future. That, for the Marxist at least, is the root of the matter.

*Some Transitional Remarks.* It is just here that theology's prospects are most dim. Since Hume and Kant, theism has not had any theoretical significance for understanding the world; nor, since Marx, Nietzsche, and Freud, has religion been on the practical frontier of creating the future. Plainly, theological thinking in the future cannot hope to be saved by an appropriation of secular thought. Nor can it expect to get past its secular hearers on the strength of such linguistic shockers as "Before God and with God we live without God" (Bonhoeffer) or "God is of no use whatever and that is why He is God" (Fontinell). The fact is that any presentation of theism which is able to gain a hearing from secular thought does so only by undergoing a transformation that empties it of its theistic content.[47]

It seems necessary to draw the logical conclusion and take the final step: the thinking of the future demands a decisive, a *radical* break with theological thinking as such. It calls for a radically different option, another kind of thinking altogether, one that is neither theistic nor antitheistic. As Marx already forewarned, this thinking must not exhaust itself in the negation and destruction of religion. Rather, it must clear the ground for a new, secular faith—a faith for a post-theistic world.[48] It must deliberately reverse the previous direction of thought: instead of trying to legitimate secular thought in terms of its Greek or Christian origins, it must, while acknowledging its debts to the classical and biblical traditions, move forward to create a new truth out of the revolutionary thought and praxis of our modern secular world.[49] It is to this other way of thinking, this new ontology of radical secularity, that we must now turn.

# II

# *Toward a Radical Metaphysics*

# 4      Marx's Sketch of a Radical Metaphysics

For the beginnings of a new ontology of radical secularity, or what I shall also call a radical metaphysics, we must reach back to the philosophical writings of the young Marx. It is here that we find the first clear, though not fully developed, attempt in modern philosophy to go beyond the atheism of an earlier type of radical metaphysics. Marx, as we shall see, viewed that earlier atheism as a negative or preliminary expression of the more positive and thoroughgoing project of transcending theism and atheism altogether. In its place he proposed to construct a "positive humanism," a post-theistic but also post-atheistic philosophy of man which started not from a critique of religion but from a scientific, historical view of man.[1] Marx's philosophical notebooks are the record of his first deliberate efforts to ground this new humanism in a metaphysics that would be radical in what we have come to recognize as the distinctively Marxist sense of that term, a sense that is at once philosophical and political.

If this reading of Marx's early works is correct, it will provide the first plank in our argument that there exists a post-theistic and radically secular alternative to traditional theistic and antitheistic metaphysics. More specifically, it will mean that Marx's notebooks contain a working outline and conceptual resources for the contemporary development of a radical metaphysics (Chapter 5). It will also suggest ways of extending certain possibilities and resolving certain difficulties in traditional Marxist thought, among them the exegetical debate about the relevance

of the young Marx's thought for the rethinking of contemporary
Marxism (Chapters 6 and 7). Finally, it will call for some hard
rethinking on the part of those who still believe it is possible to
think in a way that is both radical and Christian but who, in light
of the criticisms of the previous chapter, must now reconsider
just what this would mean (Chapters 8 and 9). Before we can go
any further with our present dialogue, therefore, we must first go
back for a closer look at what was going on in Marx's fragmentary
efforts to sketch a radical metaphysics of man.

## Marx's Critique of the
## "Critique of Religion"

When we think of the possible significance of "radical metaphysics" as a term for Marx's philosophy, we probably think first
of Marx's critique of religion. Marx himself, however, viewed
the criticism of religion as but a "premise" or preliminary step on
the way to the more serious business of criticizing bourgeois
society. Hence, though we shall begin our own remarks on
Marx's metaphysics with a look at his critique of religion, or
rather his *critique* of the "critique of religion," it is important to
be clear from the outset that, contrary to the assumption of a
number of Marx's critics, it is not to Marx's atheism that we must
look for clues to the nature or motivation behind Marx's
metaphysical radicalism. These clues are found elsewhere. In
view of Marx's own remarks on this subject, it is unwarranted for
critics, secular or theological, friendly or unfriendly, to perpetuate the myth that the key to Marx's radical humanism is to be
found in a logically prior and allegedly militant doctrine of
atheism. Atheism plays neither a decisive nor a determinative
role in Marx's philosophy, whether it be his social criticism or his
metaphysics.[2]

What is most significant about Marx's critique of religion is
that it is not really a critique of religion at all. It is rather a critique
of the entire enterprise of criticism of religion as representing a
failure to understand what *radical* criticism is all about. Feuerbach's criticism of religion is a case in point. In Feuerbach, says
Marx, the criticism of religion is essentially complete. And yet

Feuerbach's criticism remains curiously incomplete—in fact, false and ineffectual. Why? Because it leaves the true object of criticism unanalyzed and hence unchanged. It is a criticism of religion from within religion, a criticism that proceeds from what is at bottom itself a "religious" standpoint. The possibility of genuinely radical criticism arises only when, the smoke and furor of the criticism of religion having subsided, the critic suddenly realizes that "the chief thing remains to be done." But for that, something further is required, something that takes us beyond the realm of the criticism of religion altogether.

What Marx has in mind may be seen in his Fourth Thesis on Feuerbach:

> Feuerbach starts out from the fact of religious self-alienation, the duplication of the world in a religious and secular world. His work consists in resolving the religious world into its secular basis. But the fact that the secular basis becomes separate from itself and establishes an independent realm in the clouds can only be explained by the cleavage and self-contradiction of the secular basis. Thus the latter must itself be understood in its contradiction and revolutionized in practice. For instance, after the earthly family is found to be the secret of the holy family, the former must then be theoretically and practically nullified.[3]

Marx's first criticism of Feuerbach is that the latter goes only halfway in his criticism of religion. Feuerbach explains the origins of religion by reference to its human ("secular") basis, but he does not explain how this human basis actually comes to generate a religious world. What is it about this secular basis that gives rise to religion? Feuerbach's answer is to retreat to vague speculative theories about man and the frustration of his capacities as a species being. For Marx, this is not enough. What is needed is a criticism that is more radical and specific, an analysis that lays bare the roots of religion in the contradictions of human society. Marx begins at the point where Feuerbach leaves off: the criticism of "earth," of secular society, must follow or, rather, precedes and makes intelligible the critique of "heaven," of man's religious self-alienation.

For Marx religion is an "inverted consciousness of the world" which is accounted for by the "inverted world" of which it is the ideological reflection. Religion is the "theory" (reflective awareness) of an alienated world. But is is an inverted or alienated theory, in Marx's term an *ideological* consciousness of that world. It is an illusory and compensatory mode of awareness which substitutes the promise of an unalienated life in an other world for man's alienated existence in this one. Both theoretically and practically, it is an "unreal" response to a world of "real suffering."[4]

As Marx explains it, there is an inverse dialectic at work between the human alienation which characterizes the underlying social order and its ideological (i.e., alienated) expression in the form of religion. The alienation of man from himself, his work, and his fellow men in this world is ideologically transformed and sanctioned by the development of Christianity into an other-worldly religion. Christianity lends tacit support to the alienation of man from his this-worldly existence by abandoning this world to the rule of the powers and principalities. The chief religious motivation of Christianity, namely, the individual's concern for his own salvation—what Marx refers to as "the spiritual egoism of Christianity"—is the necessary ideological expression and counterpart to the "material egoism" and alienation of his social existence in this world. "Celestial need," though the reflection of and protest against real, this-worldly alienation, in fact leaves "terrestial need," the this-worldly rule of practical need and selfish interest, unchanged. Religion does not change the fact that in this world material needs and wants, hence social alienation, reign supreme.[5] As Marx concludes:

The religious and theological consciousness appears to itself all the more religious and theological in that it is apparently without any political significance or terrestrial aims, is an affair of the heart withdrawn from the world, an expression of the limitations of reason . . . a veritable life in the beyond.[6]

Given this dialectical relationship between religious consciousness and social alienation, what, asks Marx, can criticism of religion, restricted to the intramural confines of religion and theology, really hope to accomplish? At best, the struggle against the religious consciousness of the world can be viewed as an indirect and ideologically distorted form of the more fundamental struggle against the real, inverted world that gives rise to the religious world view.[7] In itself, the criticism of religion can accomplish nothing. Worse, under the guise of having accomplished something, it in fact leaves the world as it was before. It rests on the illusion that because our consciousness of the world has been changed (for example, perhaps we have become atheists or freethinkers), therefore the alienated social reality underlying that consciousness has also in principle been overcome. In this respect, Feuerbach's criticism of religion is, and can only be, profoundly uncritical, for it leaves the social causes of religion unacknowledged and therefore untouched. It is theoretically unable to get the necessary leverage for effective criticism of either religion or the society which it reflects.[8]

If, Marx argues, we appreciate the material or social roots of religion as an ideological formation, then we must view the criticism of religion dialectically as but a first and indirect step in a more extended process of criticism that is directed at the underlying contradictions of the secular (social) world. For the object of radical criticism is the alienation of human existence within this world, not the alienation of this world from some other, higher world beyond. Religion is not the primary bearer of life; it is only the manifestation of a prior and removable narrowness within secular life. If our aim is to overcome the alienation of this-worldly existence, we would do better, Marx tells us, not to attack religion at all but instead to extend or transform our criticism into a direct attack on the secular world itself. By overcoming the contradictions in its secular roots, the narrowness of religious consciousness will be transcended of its own accord. The criticism of religion is a premise for all other criticisms only if, having abolished an illusory happiness, men then go on to demand real, this-worldly happiness; only if, having abolished their illusions about man's nature and destiny (half celestial, half terrestrial), men then go on to demand the overcoming of those real, secular conditions which required those illusions.[9]

It should be clear that already in his earliest comments on religion Marx has concluded, against Feuerbach, that one cannot stop with the criticism of religion and that, in a real sense, one cannot begin with it either. It would appear that, unlike Feuerbach, Marx takes religion unseriously: it is simply not worth the trouble of attacking directly.[10] The main task of criticism lies elsewhere. Having destroyed the theory of an other world and a truth peculiar to it, the task of philosophy, or critical theory in general, is to "establish the truth" of this world. Its task is to unmask alienation in its secular (social) forms, now that it has been unmasked in its religious form. Having laid bare the contradictions in the secular basis of religion, criticism must proceed to revolutionize that basis in practice. This is the "practical-critical" truth of genuinely radical criticism, of which the criticism of religion is only an ideological and misdirected expression.[11] Going beyond Feuerbach, therefore, Marx concludes that "the criticism of heaven turns into the criticism of earth, the *criticism of religion* into the *criticism of law,* and the *criticism of theology* into the *criticism of politics.*"[12]

Before going on to Marx's second criticism of Feuerbach, we should note here that already in this first criticism Marx has gone beyond the normal or accustomed, which is to say the bourgeois-liberal connotation of such terms as "secular," "secularity," and "secularization." In the modern world—that is, in a bourgeois society and the democratic liberal state—"secularization" refers to the gradual separation of the spheres of secular society and political life from the network and authority of religious institutions and ideology. But for Marx, on the contrary, the modern secular world is itself still alienated, still characterized by internal contradictions which are fundamentally "religious" in nature. To be sure, bourgeois society was built upon the demystification and secularization of man and his world. But the secular reality which emerged was itself characterized by the selfsame phenomena of mystification and alienation. Modern secular man, defined and torn asunder by the contradictions of his social, economic, and political life, still leads an alienated or religious double life as a being part "celestial" (free, rational citizen of the political state) and part "terrestrial" (atomic, egoistic, self-interested member of civil society). A radical critique of religion, one that pretends to be something more than an ideological atheism, one that turns instead to the practical task of criticizing the modern secular world, points toward a new, post-bourgeois concept of secularity as *unalienated* secularity. This positive or radical concept of secularity is to be distinguished from the negative, religious concept of secularity defined by bourgeois ideology in terms of the separation of church and state but actualized in bourgeois society in the various forms of the alienation of the individual from his "species" or social being. Truly radical criticism is thus not only or even primarily criticism of religion. It is also, and much more, a criticism of secularity, a revolutionary social critique of the modern world and its official bourgeois ideology (an essential ingredient of the latter being the earlier "criticism of religion").

We come now to Marx's second criticism of Feuerbach's criticism of religion. Marx wants to argue that even on the level of theory, quite apart from the question of underlying social roots, Feuerbach's criticism of religion is fundamentally mistaken. It is Marx's contention that Feuerbach's critique itself operates from within the boundaries of a religious consciousness of the world. Even as a theoretical humanism or atheism, its basic categories and assumptions are theological in nature. Even as a theoretical criticism of religion, it presupposes the validity of the religious problematic and thus assumes the truth of the very ideas it purports to overcome. Marx wishes to argue, therefore, that there is still room, even on the level of the theoretical criticism of religion, for a more radical critique than the one advanced by Feuerbach—a critique that will be genuinely irreligious or radically secular in a way that Feuerbach's, despite its alleged radicality, was not and could not be.

What, specifically, does Marx have in mind? We have already noted that, in Marx's view, to criticize religion without criticizing its secular, social roots is to take a standpoint no less theological or other-worldly than that of religion itself. Because Feuerbach overlooks the social mechanisms which give rise to ideological formations, his conclusion about religion—that it is the projection of man's essential species capacities upon an alien being—is equally ideological in nature. For Marx, this leads to the crucial observation that had Feuerbach grasped the social contradictions underlying the religious phenomenon, he would have found it impossible to carry out his project of restoring the alienated predicates of divine being to their original home in man's social reality. He would have had to confront "the cleavage and self-contradictoriness of the secular basis" directly and on its own terms.

Instead, Feuerbach interprets the predicates of the divine as predicates of man's species being, the latter being conceived not as the totality of man's social relationships but as a Platonic essence in which each individual member of the species somehow participates no matter what the actual state of affairs.[13] Feuerbach's criticism of religion leaves the existing world as it is—that is, it leaves an alienated social order unchanged. But as a consequence, it also leaves the individuals who inhabit such a world with that psychological or existential need which is the heart of religion, namely, the sense of an unbridged gap between man's ideal species essence and his actual individual existence.

This, in turn, explains the humanistic and in fact religious appeal of Feuerbach's alleged critique of religion. The appeal of Feuerbach's transformation and restoration of the alienated predicates of man's species being to their proper origin in man lies precisely in the fact that whereas the subject term, "God," no longer has a reference, the predicates of the divine retain their infinite qualitative significance for men. Feuerbach's criticism of religion may be a criticism of speculative theology, a denial of God as the subject of these predicates, but it is not a criticism of religion, it is not a critique of the divine predicates as capable of being embodied in men.[14] In other words, Feuerbach does not challenge the basic idea of all religion, the idea that man has an ineradicable religious need, want, or capacity; he criticizes only its ontological location.

But for Marx, this means that Feuerbach's humanism is still basically religious. Feuerbach's "philosophy of the future" presents itself as a new, radically anthropological world view which, as the culmination of the inner tendency of modern philosophy, at last succeeds in overcoming and dissolving the earlier theological world view of Western metaphysics. Feuerbach abolishes this theological world view, however, only to reinstitute it within the framework of a philosophical anthropotheism. Man in his abstract, unchanging species essence is as divine, as potentially infinite and actually alienated from his secular existence, as he ever was in the religious world of Christendom.

Feuerbach's radical anthropology is religious at root, for by Feuerbach's own admission it is the essence of religion, above all, of Christianity as the religion of the Incarnation, to deify man and thereby to underscore the alienated character of his actual life situation. To deify man is to invert and project the secular alienation of man in the form of an ideal other-worldly being, and "Christianity is the religion *kat' eksochēn,* the *essence of religion, deified man as a particular religion.*"[15] Feuerbach's restoration of the attributes of God to man in his ideal species being is simply another, albeit secular or humanistic version of this process of the deification—that is, self-alienation—of man, and it is precisely this move on Feuerbach's part which Marx opposes in the name of an authentically radical and secular approach to man and society.

Because of his failure to recognize the social roots and hence the ideological or religious (alienated) character of his own critique of religion, Feuerbach mistakenly thinks that the way to overcome religion is by realizing it in the secular world, by trying to construct a humanistic, secular equivalent. According to some interpreters of Marx, Marx's reservations about Feuerbach at this point extend only to the point of criticizing Feuerbach's naïve or idealist assumption that the species essence of man is in some sense already divine. Marx's own more sophisticated and materialist position would then be that the divinization of man is, rather, a practical task or future goal still to be achieved.[16] In fact, Marx's criticism of Feuerbach's anthropology is much more radical than that.

Marx rejects the notion of man's possible divinity altogether, including the popularly held version just mentioned. For as he points out, "the religious spirit cannot *actually* be secularized, for what is it, in fact, but the *non-secular* form of a stage in the development of the human spirit?"[17] As he goes on to explain, the religious spirit can be said to have been realized or secularized only when that stage of development of which it is the alienated reflection comes to an awareness of itself and constitutes itself in the corresponding secular form. In the case of modern Christianity, for example, the corresponding human basis or secular form is the democratic, liberal political state. What almost all of Marx's critics overlook at this point is that Marx immediately goes on to add that this secular realization of religion is itself still religious or Christian in nature because, as a reflection of that particular stage of historical development (in this case, modern bourgeois society), it legitimizes the dualism between man's real, individual, earthly existence in civil society and his species essence, his heavenly, ideological identity as a citizen of the political state.[18]

The secularization of religion, in other words, though it is a significant phenomenon of modern life (its latest avatar being the welfare state of liberal democracy), is in no way to be construed as the overcoming of religion. It is rather simply the reembodiment of religion in the form of an equally alienated structure of secular existence. Marx's point is that, apart from a more fundamental and revolutionary criticism of the current stage of development *as a whole* (whether in its religious or demystified, secular form), the criticism and secularization of religion will simply perpetuate, in secular form, that alienation of individual men from their social reality that characterizes the religious mode of existence in general.

On both grounds, therefore, Marx concludes that Feuerbach's attempt to overcome religion is itself, to use Hegel's term, a negation of alienation within the ideological sphere of alienation. It is an unreal, merely ideological or religious overcoming of religion—that is, no criticism of religion at all.[19]

The irony, of course, is that in making this criticism Marx is simply turning Feuerbach's method of irreligious criticism back against Feuerbach himself.[20] It is by extending Feuerbach's critical concepts of alienation and the inversion of subject and predicate to the realm of social and political criticism that Marx's own philosophy is transformed from merely ideological or religious criticism into genuinely secular, sociopolitical criticism. It is because of this radicalization of Feuerbach's method that Marx's humanism proves to be qualitatively different from, and incompatible with, Feuerbach's anthropotheism.[21]

Whether one chooses to call Marx's position an extension or a rejection of Feuerbach's humanism may depend on whether one stresses the method or the content of Marx's critical approach. On first inspection, it would appear that Marx is simply carrying out the methodological implications of Feuerbach's critique of religion. Though Feuerbach eliminated God from his philosophy, he did not, as we have seen, completely concretize— secularize, radicalize—his concept of man. Marx would appear to be simply a consistent, thoroughgoing Feuerbachian whose aim is to complete the humanization process by eliminating all remnants of religious thinking about man.[22] Marx's anthropology on this view is simply the further radicalization of Feuerbach's own.

But Marx makes it equally plain that the decisive consideration for a radical critique of religion is that one can in no way find himself confirmed in religion, even if (or perhaps especially if ) the attributes formerly predicated of God are now applied to man or human society. For Marx, a radically secular anthropology can emerge only on the far side of the complete "suppression and transcendence" of religion.[23] If in this respect even Feuerbach's humanism is still fundamentally religious and preradical in its method of approach, then Marx's anthropology, far from being its extension, is its radical rejection.[24]

In summary, Marx agrees with Feuerbach's intention, via a critique of religion, to get on with the task of constructing a new and positive humanism, a "philosophy of the future." But Feuerbach's version of this new humanism never gets beyond the limits of the religious problematic. Marx's antihumanism—that is, his critique of Feuerbach's critique of religion—does not yet tell us what that alternative humanism might be. But, like atheism in the sphere of theological thinking, it is the necessary precondition of any genuinely radical approach to man.

## Radically Secular Metaphysics

In turning from Marx's critique of religion to his sketch of a positive anthropology, we must begin by clarifying what it means to say that Marx's philosophical alternative is a radically secular metaphysics. We may start with certain difficulties in the traditional distinction between the terms "secular" and "religious."

We usually think of a secular metaphysics as a philosophy which is nonreligious, either because it involves a critique of religion or because it simply contains no reference to any religious dimension whatsoever. We might also mean by a secular metaphysics a philosophy which involves the secularization— that is, the reformulation in secular terms—of certain elements of an earlier religious world view. Now the first thing to be said about Marx's metaphysics is that it is clearly intended, in distinction from that, say, of Hegel, to be a rejection of any attempt to secularize or express in nonreligious terms the basic elements of a religious world view. What is not so immediately clear is whether Marx's metaphysics may be taken to be secular in the first sense. For as Marx's critique of Feuerbach indicates, philosophies that are secular, in the sense of being explicitly atheistic, may nonetheless be conceptually determined by the onto-theological categories they claim to have overcome. This phenomenon appears especially in those types of secular humanism which, while denying God, introduce an ideal concept or program of deifying man in place of the traditional theological doctrine. And it is very clear that Marx does not view his philosophy as an atheism or humanism of that sort. Marx's metaphysics is neither an attempt to secularize religion or, on the other hand, to deify man.[25] Then in what sense may we say that his philosophy is a secular metaphysics?

One way that Marx expresses this further distinction within secular philosophy of different types of nonreligious secularity is by saying that a radical theory of man must be grounded in a positive and not merely negative superseding of religion.[26] It must be defined not by a negative relationship to religion but by its positive view of man.

This positive attitude toward the human world is not simply the opposite side of the coin from a negative attitude toward the alienated world of religion. Marx does not have in mind here some sort of affirmation of human autonomy that arises simply and automatically out of the death of God.[27] To be sure, Marx concedes that the criticism of religion is, given our historical situation, the first step toward the development of an authentic secular humanism. But if atheism is an historically necessary premise for a radically secular metaphysics, it does not by itself suffice to guarantee the possibility of the next step. In some ways, as the case of Feuerbach illustrates, it even represents a dangerous ideological obstacle to the creation of a radically secular view of man.

How so? The atheist's affirmation of man is ideologically mediated by its prior negation of God. Agreeing with the Aristotelian and Hegelian observation that contraries belong to the same genus, Marx views atheism as nothing more than an ideological contrary to religion. Hence it does not lead to a radical break with a religious way of thinking. Atheism looks more like a "last stage of theism, a negative recognition of God" than the theoretical foundation for a positive, this-worldly philosophy of man.[28] It gives rise inevitably to the desire to supplant the God thus denied by a correspondingly elevated or deified concept of man.

But there is another element in Marx's reservations about the capacity of atheism to provide the theoretical basis for a secular metaphysics. The belief that atheism by itself can offer such a foundation for humanism is itself an ideological or religious illusion. It is a piece of self-deception typical of philosophers who, as members of an intellectual elite, think that simply by overcoming theology on the level of thought they have overcome alienation in reality as well. In fact atheism, as an ideological position, is simply a "negation of the negation" (God) within the realm of alienation (the abstract existence of philosophers as a class).[29]

It is only by a second act of transcendence, by transcending the mediation of humanism via atheism, "which is, however, a necessary presupposition," that the possibility opens up of a "positive humanism, humanism emerging positively from itself."[30] The basis of Marx's atheism and of his secular metaphysics is not therefore a set of philosophical arguments or speculative disproofs of the existence of God. That would be an ideological foundation as theological in character as theology itself. It is, rather, an independently formulated humanism that stands in immediate or unmediated fashion on its own feet.[31]

For Marx, a radically secular metaphysics is therefore not

primarily an atheistic philosophy; it is the theoretical transcendence of atheism as well as theism. It marks a theoretical break with the entire genus of ontotheological or speculative metaphysics.[32]

With this we come to the other term in the phrase "radical secularity." What, more specifically, does Marx mean when he tells us that his philosophy is grounded not in a "mediated" humanism, an atheism that proceeds by way of God but in a direct or "immediate" humanism?

A radical humanism, says Marx, "no longer needs such mediation. It begins with the *sensuous perception, theoretically and practically,* of man and nature as *essential beings.* It is man's *positive self-consciousness,* no longer attained through the overcoming of religion."[33] Here, as we have noted, Marx appears to be following out in a more consistent manner the original Feuerbachian mandate to eliminate theology in favor of a naturalistic anthropology, to transcend the merely negative standpoint of metaphysical destruction with a doctrine which has its own positive metaphysical content.[34] The difficulty with Feuerbach's program, however, was that it stopped halfway in this radical secularization of philosophy. His positive humanism never got beyond its mediated status as an ideology that subtly reaffirmed the ontotheological way of thinking it claimed to have overcome.[35] His anthropology was not a radically secular one. It was simply a relocation of ontotheological predicates in the species being of man. It represented not the radical humanizing but the radical deifying of man. A radical metaphysics, on the other hand, in denying the logic of "God," must break as well with any atheism that would deify man instead. Here once again Marx views himself—correctly, I think—as radicalizing Feuerbach's critical polemic against the ontotheological nature of all previous modern metaphysics (including such speculative atheism or humanism as Feuerbach's own).

Now if, as Marx contends, his own attempt at a radical metaphysics really constitutes Feuerbach's called-for "new philosophy," then it follows, as Feuerbach pointed out in his critque of Hegel, that such a philosophy must differentiate itself totally, radically, from the older speculative philosophies of man in its method, its starting point, and the substance of its conclusions. Marx's task is to demonstrate that a radical perspective in metaphysics really does represent, as Louis Althusser puts it, "a new problematic, a new systematic way of asking questions of the world, new principles and a new method."[36]

### Radical Finitude: Marx's
### Humanistic Starting Point

The starting point of a radical metaphysics is man. Radicalism in philosophy, says Marx, means demonstration *ad hominem*. To be radical is to grasp things by their root. "But for man the root is man himself." Proceeding from "the decisive positive transcendence of religion," a radical metaphysics takes its start in "the doctrine that man is the highest being for man."[37] This man, however, is not to be understood as man in some abstract, idealized or ideological sense. "Man," for Marx, refers to real existing individuals at a particular stage in the historical development of their productive capacities and social relationships: "*Man* is not an abstract being squatting outside the world. Man is *the world of men,* the state, society."[38]

Already in his early critique of Hegel's philosophy of the state, Marx was pointing out this fundamental divergence in the starting points of speculative and radical metaphysics. Hegel, says Marx, fails to recognize "this actualization of the person as the most concrete thing possible."[39] He returns to this line of criticism in his "Critique of Hegel's Dialectic and Philosophy in General." Man is not to be approached as mind, thought, or spiritual self-consciousness. He is rather, after Feuerbach, to be understood as "a living natural being endowed with objective (i.e., material) capacities." He is "a corporeal, actual, sentient, objective being with natural capacities."[40] His fundamental mode of being is one of *sensuous human activity* or what Marx calls *praxis*—a notion which brings together the traditional materialist stress on the "actuality, sensuousness" of man's natural existence and the Hegelian-idealist insight into man's "active side."[41] The starting point of Marx's critique of the concept of man in speculative metaphysics is this concept of man as both an objective and natural (material) being and an independent and autonomous (self-subsistent) being, a practical agent in the world who, by means of his productive activity, owes his existence to himself. Through the activity of labor, man has not simply a spiritual but a real, objective capacity to create and determine the conditions of his own existence.[42]

One of the first consequences of this materialist interpretation of man as self-creating praxis is that it eliminates the need for a theistic view of man. Since "the *entire so-called world history* is only the creation of man through human labor and the development of nature for man, he has evident and incontrovertible proof of his *self-creation*."[43] Since history provides a sufficient demonstration of man's self-originative powers as a natural and social being, it is no longer necessary theoretically or practically to raise "the question about an *alien* being beyond man and nature (a question which implies the unreality of nature and man)."[44] In answer to the speculative (i.e., ideological or alienated) question, "Who created the first man and nature as a whole?" the radical metaphysician can only point out, as does Marx:

Your question is itself a product of abstraction. Ask yourself how you arrive at that question, whether it does not arise from a standpoint to which I cannot reply because it is twisted. Ask yourself whether that progression exists as such for rational thought. If you ask about the creation of nature or man, you thus abstract from man and nature. . . . I say to you: Give up your abstraction and you will also give up your question.[45]

Like Wittgenstein, the radical metaphysician does not try to refute the theist's question by offering a speculative counterargument of his own (say, atheism). That would be to play by the theist's rules, the rules of alienated abstraction, and hence to indulge in ideological speculation oneself. Rather, the radical metaphysician simply dissolves the entire controversy by refusing to accept the alienated standpoint from which such speculation proceeds.

This methodological and conceptual return to man's natural and self-originative being as the starting point of a radical metaphysics brings with it, or presupposes, an equally radical rethinking of such basic categories of ontology as finitude, infinitude, and transcendence. It is here that the revolutionary implications of Marx's metaphysics for traditional Western ontology begin to be apparent. For in opposing Hegel's and Feuerbach's efforts to deify man (whether as a vessel of absolute Spirit or as the infinite potential of a species being), Marx bases his own view of man on a radically finitist interpretation of being.

It was Feuerbach who pointed out that Hegel's ontotheological metaphysics constructed the predicates of the absolute by taking the predicates of finite, natural, or human things "in a sense that differs from their real meaning, that is, in an entirely reversed sense."[46] The attributes of God are taken by the speculative metaphysician to be the negation of the attributes of human finitude. Therefore, for Feuerbach, a positive or radical humanism will begin by reversing the procedure and interpreting the ontotheological predicates of speculative metaphysics in turn "in a sense that differs from their real meaning, that is, in an entirely reversed sense." The radical metaphysician begins with a methodological "negation of the negation" of his own—that is, by turning right side up again the ontotheological predicates of absolute being. A radical metaphysics involves the revolutionary inversion of the old metaphysical priorities, a return from heaven to earth, a return to that "self-subsistent positive positively grounded on itself . . . the actual, the perceptible, the real, the finite, the particular"[47]—a return to individual, sensuous, natural men in their productive activity and social interactions with one another. If, as Feuerbach observed, God is the negation of all finitude, then, for a radical metaphysics, the finite must be conceived as the negation of God—and the affirmation of independent, autonomous, finite, this-worldly man.[48]

In Feuerbach's case, however, this resulted in the simple transference of the ontotheological predicates from God to man conceived in the infinitude of his species being. To Marx, this was stopping the finitization of man or the radicalization of metaphysics halfway. It was a reintroduction of religion (the infinite predicates of divine being) into a positive humanism through the back door in the form of an "abstraction inhering in each single individual."[49]

To formulate a radical alternative to Feuerbach's elevation of finite man to infinite (species) being, Marx returns to Hegel's more sophisticated dialectical analyses, in this case, his analysis of the dialectic of the finite and the infinite. Despite his criticism of the speculative character of Hegel's thought, Marx clearly finds in Hegel a superior, albeit "concealed and mystified," analysis of the internal logic and complexity of what for Marx is the basic category of a radical metaphysics—man's finite-yet-self-transcending being. It was Hegel who, rejecting the Kantian antithesis of finite and infinite, first worked out a single, unified higher category, what Hegel called the "true infinite" (to distinguish it from the "bad infinite" of sheer theological transcendence), but which for Marx's purposes might just as easily and better have been called the "true finite" (to distinguish it from the "bad finite" of simple, undialectical limitation, immanence, or immediacy).

In contrast with the tradition before him, Hegel conceived of the finite not simply as that which is limited but as that which is at the same time self-transcending, related to itself as something negative, bearing a dynamic, internal contradiction that displays itself as a capacity for further development. Hegel saw the infinitude of finite being as consisting in its capacity for continually surpassing its past or present determinations.[50] Hegel's dialectical synthesis of these traditionally opposed or contradictory notions of finitude and infinitude results in a single, dynamic, internally restless higher category of infinity-in-finitude (or finitude-in-infinity, depending on whether one's perspective is man-centered or God-centered).[51] Hegel thus poses a radical challenge to the traditional metaphysical understanding of finitude, proclaiming instead that "this is just what it is to be finite, to set oneself aside":

> It is the nature of the finite itself, to pass beyond itself, to negate its own negation, and to become infinite. . . .
> . . . Finitude exists only as a passing beyond itself: the infinite, its own other, is therefore contained in itself. . . . The finite is not overcome by the infinite as by an externally existing might, but it is its own infinity, whereby it transcends itself.[52]

Already in Hegel, therefore, the concept of infinity no longer refers in traditional theological fashion to something having no limits (God, for example) but rather to "a thing as having it 'in it' to pass beyond any and every limit, and also as having the limits it has *in order* to have such an unlimited destination."[53] Findlay's interpretation of Hegel's dialectical reconstruction of this traditional conceptual polarity comes very close to being a statement of Marx's own interpretive use of Hegel (though it is of course questionable how far either one accurately portrays Hegel's real intent). As Findlay sums it up: "*True Infinity is, in short, simply finitude essentially associated with free variability.*" Or again, Hegel finds "the True Infinite in a self-understanding, freely variable finite which has simply forsworn the vain advance towards infinity."[54] In other words, as far as Marx is concerned, Hegel's analysis of infinity as the capacity of finitude for self-transcendence opens up the possibility, albeit in speculative and mystified form, of a metaphysics of radical finitude which, unlike Feuerbach's humanism, has once and for all forsworn the "vain advance toward infinity," forsworn, that is, the religious quest.

It is thus Hegel rather than Feuerbach, despite the latter's antitheological and positive-humanist rhetoric, who provides Marx with the conceptual resources for a radical—because radically finitist—metaphysics. It is from Hegel that Marx derives his basic metaphysical category of finitude as a capacity for self-transcending self-determination which resides not in the Idea but in *particular existence*.[55] It is Hegel rather than Feuerbach who stands behind Marx's view of finitude as the capacity of human existence to transcend itself immanently not in a theological direction above itself but by projecting ahead of itself new, objective, this-worldly possibilities of being. It is this new philosophical concept of radical finitude that makes it possible for Marx to declare that finite man is the ontological ground or source of his own being. It is therefore a radically finite interpretation of being that provides the starting point and the fundamental datum for a radically secular interpretation of man, the world, and being.[56]

Before concluding this section, we should note that while Marx disagreed with Feuerbach's interpretation of the infinitude of man's being, he agreed with Feuerbach in viewing the isolated individual as truly finite in the older, narrower sense of that term.

As did Feuerbach, Marx located the (potential) infinitude of man—that is, his capacity for real, this-worldly self-tran-scendence—somewhere else. Where Marx differed is that he located it not in the abstract species being of man but in the totality of man's collective self-activity or, as he put it, "the ensemble of social relationships." But I think we can take him to be in basic agreement with Feuerbach's intention when the latter remarked that, if solitude be taken to represent finiteness and limitation, then community represents the potential for human freedom and infinity. Whereas man "for himself," says Feuer-bach, is merely man in the ordinary (restricted, alienated) sense, man "with man" is "God," that is, men as together possessing the capacity for achieving what Marx called universal human eman-cipation.[57]

## Praxis and Transcendence

The concept of man's being as a process of finite self-tran-scendence brings with it a certain understanding of the dis-tinctively practical character or obligations of a radical meta-physics. Here once again, it was Hegel who was decisive in shaping Marx's conviction that the philosopher has the ad ditional, practical responsibility of promoting man's capacity for transcendence, particularly man's transcendence or overcoming of human alienation. In this latter connection, however, we discover a further, characteristically Marxian sense in which Marx's philosophy, in contrast to its speculative predecessors, is to be understood as a radical metaphysics.

In place of Hegel's concept of alienation as the contradictory relationship between man's consciousness and the external real-ity in which it is objectified, Marx proposes a concept of aliena-tion as the contradictory relationship between man's practical capacities and the inhuman way in which these capacities are objectified in a given social order. This distinction is grounded in the difference between Hegel's spiritualistic anthropology, which sees man as essentially defined by his consciousness and self-consciousness, and Marx's naturalistic or materialist an-thropology, which sees man as essentially a natural, practical, social being. The result of this difference in basic concepts of man and human alienation is a difference in respective prescriptions for transcending alienation and appropriating the essential capacities of man.

From the outset, Marx argues against the young Hegelians that since "concepts, thought, ideas, and all products of consciousness" have no real existence apart from their embodiment in and reflection of man's material life, they can no longer be regarded by philosophers as the "real fetters" of man (or, conversely, as "the true bonds of human society").[58] It is not in the realm of consciousness (Hegel) but in the sphere of our material activity (Marx) that alienation takes place, and hence it is to that practical, social arena that we must look for the genuine transcendence of alienation and the reappropriation of our natural, human capacities. For Marx, the concept of transcendence refers not to the overcoming of alienation in human consciousness but to the overcoming of those material conditions of alienation which are prior to, and the root of, the alienation that holds sway over man's spiritual life.

Transcendence, accordingly, is not some ideological activity or spiritual state that conducts us to a reality beyond the world of our own creation. It is rather an embodied, practical activity that takes place within, and at the very center of, an alienated world. It is another name for those efforts of men which open up new, this-worldly possibilities for the free exercise of our human capacities. It is the radical philosopher's way of talking about our capacity to overcome our alienated relations to man and nature and to construct new, unalienated relationships in their place.

*Transcendence* is an objective movement *reabsorbing* externalization into itself.—(This is the insight into the *appropriation* of objective being, expressed within alienation, through the transcendence of its alienation. It is the alienated insight into the *actual objectification* of man and his actual appropriation of his objective nature by the destruction of the *alienated* character of the world, by the transcendence of the objective world in its alienated existence, just as atheism which transcends God is the emergence of theoretical humanism, and communism which transcends private property is the vindication of actual human life as man's property, the emergence of practical humanism.)[59]

Transcendence for Marx is thus not the overcoming of the

objective world as such by its reabsorption into (or transcendence in) consciousness. It is, rather, the overthrowing of the alienated realization of man's natural capacities in the name of the unalienated appropriation of all of his capacities, not just his spiritual ones. In addition to its negative, destructive aspect, this activity of transcendence has its positive aspect as well—"the actual emergence and the actual, developed realization of man's nature as something actual"; or, again, "the vindication of actual human life" in the real, historical emergence of a "practical humanism" (i.e., communism).[60] Once again Marx explicitly acknowledges his debt to Hegel for having been the first to articulate the inner dialectical structure of this phenomenon of transcendence in terms of "the positive significance of self-referring negation" ("even if again in an alienated way"):

Hegel thus grasps man's self-alienation, the externalization of his nature, his loss of objectivity, and actualization as finding of self, expression of his nature, objectification, and realization. (In short, he grasps labor, within the realm of abstraction, as man's *act of self-creation*.[61]

For Marx, a radical metaphysics is thus the demystification and secularization or humanization of the religious and speculative-metaphysical concept of transcendence. Transcendence is now reinterpreted in radically finitist and humanistic terms as the ongoing, open-ended process of self-creative activity. In place of the traditional ontotheological concept of transcendence as a function of divine spirit, Marx substitutes a concept of transcendence as human praxis or labor.

Marx next draws out the practical implications of this reinterpretation of transcendence for philosophy. If it is not consciousness but material praxis which forges the real fetters or, conversely, the unifying bonds of men in society, then philosophy, which is chiefly an activity and product of consciousness, cannot offer itself as the weapon for overcoming real, social alienation. Any such claim on the part of philosophy must be regarded as a symptom of the alienation of philosophy and of the world order which it reflects. What Marx challenges in Hegel's philosophy is its claim that in it the alienation of consciousness and objectivity has been overcome. But if Marx's criticism is accepted, what other conception of philosophy could possibly be more valid? Is it not the peculiar nature of philosophy as such, even a radical metaphysics, that it confines itself to the realm of reflective self-consciousness? And yet an initial reading seems to suggest that for Marx there is something intrinsically inadequate about philosophy as philosophy. Or does Marx think there is some sense in which even philosophy, although it is a purely theoretical activity, can be understood in a more adequate way than it has been by the speculative metaphysicians? Is there some sense in which it can be seen as being a kind of praxis in its own right, a theoretical praxis as it were, capable of intervening in and transforming, of changing and not merely interpreting, the world of material praxis?[62]

It is clear that, despite the numerous passages in which Marx speaks of the abolition of philosophy, he is equally concerned about the realization of philosophy—a dialectically difficult notion which involves the idea that theory has a central role to play in the practical struggle to overcome the secular conditions of alienation. Here, as already mentioned, we find a second and distinctively Marxian sense in which Marx's philosophy is to be understood as a radical metaphysics. For as Marx points out in his gloss upon the term "radical":

As the resolute opponent of the previous mode of *German* political consciousness, the criticism of speculative philosophy of law does not proceed in its own sphere but proceeds to *tasks* that can be solved by only one means—*practice.*
The question arises: Can Germany reach a practice *à la hauteur des principes, that is, a revolution?* . . .
The weapon of criticism obviously cannot replace the criticism of weapons. Material force must be overthrown by material force. But theory also becomes a material force once it has gripped the masses. Theory is capable of gripping the masses when it demonstrates *ad hominem,* and it demonstrates *ad hominem* when it becomes radical. To be radical is to grasp things by the root. But for man the root is man himself. The clear proof of the radicalism of German theory and hence of its political energy is that it . . . ends with the doctrine that *man is the highest being for man,* hence with the *categorical imperative to overthrow all conditions* in which man is a degraded, enslaved, neglected, contemptible being.[63]

As this passage makes clear, for Marx a theory is radical only when it entails both (1) "the doctrine that man is the highest

being for man"—that is, radicalism on the level of philosophical
theory, and (2) "the categorical imperative to overthrow all
conditions,"—that is, radicalism on the level of "practical-
critical" or revolutionary action.

A radical metaphysics, as we have already noted, involves a
materialist reading of the relationship between a philosophical
theory and its material environment. It follows that, from a
radical perspective, it is not sufficient for a theory simply to
articulate a neutral or "correct awareness of an *existing* fact." The
task of theory also encompasses the struggle "to overthrow the
existing state of things."[64] Its task is to become genuinely
"practical-critical" theory, the theoretical edge of revolutionary
praxis.[65]

As an instance of theoretical praxis, radical metaphysics is
practical in two further respects. First, its critical activity is not
narrowly (technically, professionally) philosophical, but extends
to social criticism as well. Hence the peculiar mixture of description and evaluation, the unique concern for the dialectical interplay of theory and practice, that characterizes Marxism as a
philosophy.[66]

But second, Marxist theory also requires that the theoretician
become involved in the further practical question, "How is this
transcendence or overcoming of alienation to be accomplished?"
It is in response to this question that Marxism as radicalism on
the level of theory is forced out of its purely formal or abstract
role as a philosophy of man into the specific historical and social
situation of having to determine, through reflection upon its
practical circumstances, precisely at what places, by whom, and
in what ways the practical program of overthrowing the conditions of alienation is to be realized. At this point, Marxism, of
internal logical necessity, passes over from a general metaphysics
or philosophy of man in the traditional sense into a radical social
theory and program of revolutionary action.

It should now be clear why Marx considers a radical metaphysics to be the abolition of philosophy. All prior metaphysics
was nothing more than ideological reflection of human alienation. Its speculative concepts of man were not totally false, but,
like religion, they were unreal, distorted images of a world of

real, human suffering. It was therefore incapable of providing men with the necessary theoretical tools and guidance that would enable them to respond to the practical imperative for revolutionary change. But Marx's radical metaphysics may also be viewed as an attempt to realize philosophy—that is, to secularize and radicalize it by incorporating its capacity for free, rational, self-conscious universal criticism into the practical struggle for the liberation of men and the humanization of the world. Marx's radical metaphysics may therefore legitimately be viewed as the realization of Feuerbach's vision of a "philosophy of the future" which "possesses an essentially practical—and indeed in the highest sense practical—tendency without damaging the dignity and independence of theory, indeed in closest harmony with it."[67] And, in a strange way, insofar as Marxism is this lived unity of theory and practice, it also, though this time probably not in the sense Feuerbach intended, "takes the place of religion and . . . in truth . . . is itself religion."[68]

The Historical
Particularity of
Marx's Radical Metaphysics

We have noted that for Marx the union of theory and practice is not a regulative ideal that can be applied to just any philosophical system. Upon closer inspection, it turns out to be valid only for the relationship between an historically specific metaphysics and an historically specific praxis—namely, Marx's own materialist anthropology and the revolutionary struggle of the proletariat. Far from depriving metaphysics of its "dignity and independence (as) theory," it is this historical particularity which guarantees the integrity and relevance of theory as theoretical practice, while transforming praxis into "a practice *à la hauteur des principes,* which will raise it . . . to the *human level.*"[69] On this basis, Marx further distinguishes between the authentic historicity of a radical metaphysics and the alienated, unreal historicity of Hegel's speculative metaphysics.

One way to approach Marx's understanding of the historical particularity of radical metaphysics is to look again at his concept of the realization of philosophy in practice. Perhaps a better way of expressing what he intended with this phrase is contained in another term he uses in this connection: the secularization of philosophy. In a letter to Ruge in 1843, he says: "Philosophy has become secularized, and the most striking proof for this is the fact that the philosophical consciousness itself is drawn into the torment of struggle, not only outwardly but inwardly as well."[70] The inevitable outcome of a philosophy of radical secularity is the radical secularization of philosophy.[71] Marx's own work is an example of how a radical philosophy finds itself less and less oriented to disinterested description or speculation and becomes more and more, in Marx's figure, the head of passion—a method and metaphysics in the service of practical, revolutionary struggle.

Clearly, the secularization of philosophy means something quite different to the radical theorist than it does to the modern bourgeois spirit. It is not simply the antispeculative, neopositivist descriptive metaphysics of an existing world view. It is a dialectical critique of the existing world view and the revisionary construction of a new one which will more adequately reflect the specific sociohistorical struggles of its time. The difference between these two readings of the secularization of philosophy is the difference, finally, between the class perspectives which they reflect. The secularization of philosophy prior to Marx was the ideological reflection of the emancipation of the bourgeoisie and the modern political state from the religious institutions and ideologies of the feudal world. The radicalization of this process of secularization to which Marx refers is its extension or conversion from an ideology of the ruling classes, the beneficiaries of the modern political revolution, to the ideology of a new class, the proletariat, which is to be the vehicle of a total, social revolution. At the present stage of historical development, it would therefore be inaccurate to view the radical metaphysics of the working class as a universal metaphysics of man. It is rather the theoretical weapon of the proletariat.

As philosophy finds its *material* weapons in the proletariat, the proletariat finds its *intellectual* weapons in philosophy. . . .

Philosophy cannot be actualized without the transcendence of the proletariat, the proletariat cannot be transcended without the actualization of philosophy.[72]

Marx makes it clear that this specific historical link between philosophy and the proletariat is not just a programmatic one—it is an internal, logically necessary one. For Marx, both philosophy and the proletariat are universal in nature. What is more, they are linked in a uniquely historical manner in that the proletariat, like Israel in the vision of Isaiah, is summoned to play a concrete role in history as the bearer of universal human reason. The proletariat is that particular class whose historical mission is to become a universal class. By overcoming its existing status as a separate class which embodies the complete alienation and inhumanity of man with man, it will usher in a new era of universal human emancipation. It is the proletariat which is the incarnation of man's essential species capacities in the particularities of the historical process. Radical metaphysics, as the head of the proletariat, and the proletariat, as the heart or passion of philosophy, represent in their dialectical coming together the Hegelian realization of the concrete universal in history.[73]

Radical metaphysics is thus an historically particular ideology of revolutionary humanism. It takes its starting point in a concept of man as self-transcending praxis—it is a metaphysics of labor. But it also reflects the quest for universal human emancipation—it is a metaphysics of the proletariat. The specific historical function of a radical metaphysics is therefore to provide the philosophical foundations of communism, which is the attempt to realize this humanism in practice.[74]

As a part of this larger practical effort, radical metaphysics has a particular mission in the area of philosophy. Here its task is to help philosophy, which is to say philosophers, to overcome the alienated conditions of their theoretical work. Specifically, it is the task of philosophers, or radical intellectuals as a class, to integrate their theoretical labors with the practical struggle of the oppressed. By sharing in these struggles, philosophers can begin to see their own work as an effort to construct a theory of and for that practice.

To summarize our argument so far: What makes Marx's

philosophy a radical metaphysics has little if anything to do with his critique of religion. It has everything to do with its starting point in man's finite being-in-the-world. Further, by a radical metaphysics Marx understands not an abstract, transhistorical philosophy of men but a specific historical theory of a new social humanity. It is not an ideological humanism of man in general or man in the abstract, which, as we saw in Feuerbach, amounts to little more than a new theology in disguise. It is the metaphysics of one class in particular, that class of "degraded, enslaved, neglected, contemptible" beings whose life conditions represent "the complete loss of humanity." Radical metaphysics is not the privileged illusion of bourgeois intellectuals or semidivine free spirits; it is the theoretical weapon of alienated labor in quest of a more human life.

## The Phenomenological Basis
of a Radical Metaphysics

Marx states in his Eighth Thesis on Feuerbach, "All mysteries which lead theory to mysticism find their rational solution in human practice and the comprehension of this practice."[75] In the polemical context in which this statement occurs, it would appear to be a recommendation to surrender philosophy altogether in favor of, say, revolutionary action:

It is apparent how the resolution of theoretical antitheses is possible *only* in a *practical* way, only through man's practical energy, and hence their resolution is in no way merely a problem of knowledge but a *real* problem of life which *philosophy* could not solve because it grasped the problem as *only* theoretical.[76]

Nevertheless, it can also and perhaps more convincingly be argued that Marx's Eighth Thesis is in its own way a strong, positive reaffirmation of one of the fundamental insights which distinguish modern philosophy from its medieval Christian forerunners. For Marx may be seen as here drawing the logical and radical consequences of an insight first enunciated by Vico and later developed by such thinkers as Kant, Hegel, and, in our own day, Heidegger. This is the assertion, basic to a positive, practical humanism, that man comprehends fully only what he himself has made, that man is a field of possibilities, not simply actualities, that as such he is responsible for determining his own nature and reality, that his mode of being reflects, as it were, an "emptiness" or lack of purpose in the natural order which it is his job to fill in or constitute by his own self-creative activity.[77] In deriving from Hegel a concept of man as praxis, a being who in transforming his material world is simultaneously engaged in transforming and creating himself, Marx is simply transposing into materialist (sociohistorical) terms modern philosophy's insight into man's self-creative activity. In this sense, Marx's metaphysics, like Feuerbach's, is not an undialectical rejection, but an even more radical affirmation of the anthropological (antitheological) direction of modern philosophy.

Even so, the Eighth Thesis and the earlier passage from the Manuscripts of 1844 make it equally clear that Marx's anthropology adds something new to the content of modern philosophy. For, in contradistinction to previous philosophical humanism, Marx's practical or materialist humanism rests on an entirely different understanding of this basic category of praxis.[78] Merely ethical or political concepts of action (and hence of man) are in Marx's view hopelessly one-sided, abstract, and ideological. Though they reflect modern man's preoccupation with practical reason, they are the expressions of a philosophical viewpoint which is still mystified about the real nature of its practical foundations and thus blinded to the ideological nature of its basic concepts. Marx appeals to philosophers to look, instead, to praxis in its new, material or socioeconomic sense to find fresh conceptual resources for a rational solution to the traditional problems of philosophical anthropology. These problems will remain "puzzles," "riddles," or "mysteries"[79] as long as philosophical theory is not grounded in a comprehension of praxis in its fundamental, nonideological, material sense.

Marx's point is therefore not that philosophers should abandon philosophy, but that they should reinterpret it as an analysis of human existence that begins from the phenomenon of material praxis. In contemporary terms, Marx's materialist anthropology may be viewed as a phenomenology or descriptive metaphysics of man as a practical being-in-the-world. As Roger Garaudy explains:

> *Marxist materialism* gives us the key to the problem of *phenomenology* by working out a concrete method for going back from the constituted object to activity, to the subject in the process of being constituted; a materialist method enabling us to grasp again the "meanings" of things and the "intentions" of men—and their interconnections. The grasp of "meaning" is at one and the same time the grasp, through historical analysis, of the purposive operations of creative, productive man and the ideational reproduction of the diverse moments of the creation of products or of institutions in their origins and systematic interconnections.[80]

In this perspective, Marx's materialism is not so much a science of history as it is a new philosophical approach to man. Material praxis is the phenomenological and conceptual basis of that total theoretical revolution which Marx's metaphysics signals in the history of modern thought.

## Marx's Ontology: Some Provisional Generalizations

Our final task is to indicate briefly some of the more general ontological implications of this metaphysics of praxis.

Marx's materialist inversion of the categories of Hegelian metaphysics was made possible by Hegel himself. As Avineri points out, an astonishing and profound rehabilitation of matter had taken place already in Hegel's ontology, albeit in an idealist framework. Once the realm of nature came to be viewed as an expression of spirit in its self-alienation, as it was in Hegel, matter was perceived in terms qualitatively different than those of Cartesian philosophy with its lifeless, spiritless, mechanical matter in motion. It is no longer viewed as the absolute negation, absence, or unbridgeable opposite of spirit. When, as in Marx, the humanistic secret of Hegel's absolute spirit is disclosed, the movement of matter in nature and history acquires a profoundly human significance. In Marx's materialism, matter is no longer the negation of spirit, but the necessary vehicle of spirit's—that is, man's—self-objectification. Marx's materialism is the vehicle of a radical humanism, because in it matter is no longer the direct descendant of the school of traditional materialism, but has been passed "through a transforming contemplation of the principles of German idealist philosophy itself." Marx's materialism represents the conceptual liberation of the natural-humanistic and sociohistorical truth of Hegel's idealist ontology.[81]

But the philosophical key to Marx's historical, humanistic interpretation of matter lies elsewhere. For Marx also pushes through an inversion of conceptual priorities in the very notion of being itself. Behind Marx's materialist interpretation of praxis and history lies a radicalization—that is, a radically temporal reconstruction—of Hegel's concept of being. It is here that we arrive at the most original element in the theoretical revolution inaugurated by Marx's metaphysics.

To go back a step: Between Hegel's death in 1831 and Marx's *Manuscripts* of 1844, "the most brilliant and the most important single text published" was not, as far as the origins of a radical metaphysics are concerned, Strauss's *Life of Jesus* but Cieszkowski's *Prolegomena zur Historiosophie* (1838).[82] It was Cieszkowski's special achievement to have initiated a central debate among the left-wing Hegelians about the relationship between Hegel's apparently closed system and the open-ended character of the future as the decisive dimension of man's historical being. The left-wing criticism of the Hegelian system was that reconciliation in the world of thought now had to be completed by reconciliation in the real world. For Hegel, philosophy, as a retrospective interpretation of the world, looked to the past for its material. But for anyone concerned not simply to comprehend the world but to change it through practical activity, it seemed clear that the future was far more important than Hegel had ever believed.[83]

Why? According to Cieszkowski, Hegel's system, methodologically oriented to the past, was inevitably weighed down by necessity. Everything belonging to the past, particularly that which was not produced by the conscious activity of man, appeared to have happened by necessity. Freedom, accordingly, could be achieved only through, and was equated with, (absolute) knowledge—that is, contemplative reflection or after-the-fact interpretation of that necessity. But for philosophers who desired to translate reconciliation in thought into reconciliation in reality—that is, the realization of philosophy in practice (the motto of the young Hegelians)—the future was the only place where someday such a program might be realized. Such reconciliation was possible only if men could overcome the necessities of the past and present and project themselves toward the future through self-conscious action. This, at least, was the practical conclusion drawn from Cieszkowski's historiosophy by none other than Marx's teacher, Moses Hess. The concept of action or praxis, concrete practical activity to bring about the future liberation of men, thus represented for the young Hegelians the "synthesis of self-consciousness and the future."[84]

It is this attempt of the young Hegelians to spell out the logical connections between the concepts of praxis and the future that provides the clue to Marx's radicalization of Hegel's concept of being. As Avineri notes, "Hegel very emphatically denied any possibility of recognizing the future prior to its becoming the present, or rather the past."[85] Or, as it is perhaps more accurate to say, to the extent that Hegel did recognize the future as prior to its present or past objectification, it was only because the future was grasped as a dimension already determined by the intrinsic teleological logic of the historical process as a whole. What was to be was already there *in nuce* in the logical beginnings of the system. There was in a profound sense nothing radically new to be expected from history. The historical process was merely the necessary unfolding of a form and content already contained in its logical or ontological beginnings.

But a materialistic concept of praxis, a concept of human activity as capable of freeing man in reality and not just in thought from the necessities of the past, requires a different concept of the future and hence of being. It requires a concept of the future as a realm that is open to the possibility of something new, possibilities which can free men from the givens of the existing order of things. It requires a concept of being as a process that does not already contain a priori the determinants of the future, a process that is unfinished, open-ended, capable of that which is new. It requires a radically temporal, finitist concept of being.[86]

Along with its more immediate practical implications, in other words, Marx's radical humanism also opens the way to a revolution in the traditional Western understanding of the most general categories of being. Marx's materialist inversion of the categories of Hegel's ontology represents, if only implicitly, a revolutionary reversal of the traditional priorities of being over becoming, past over future, necessity over freedom, eternity over time, absolute over contingent, infinite over finite. It is here that we begin to see what is involved in breaking with an alienated, theological perspective on being and moving toward a new, radically secular perspective on being. It is in Marx's metaphysics that we take the decisive step beyond the old ontology of transcendent being toward a new ontology of radical secularity.

# 5     The Radical Perspective
        in Contemporary
        Metaphysics

Secular existentialism may be viewed as an attempt to develop and make explicit the radical perspective that was struggling for birth in the philosophical notebooks of the young Marx. In such philosophers as Heidegger, Sartre, and Merleau-Ponty, we see the formulation of an ontology of finitude that offers a radically secular and non-theistic alternative to the theistic way of thinking that characterizes the efforts of even the most radical theologians.

Theologians have understandably had some difficulty in making sense of the radical perspective of secular existentialism. Where existentialism has resisted assimilation to the apologetic efforts of theology, it has been regarded as an updated version of traditional atheism. When it has refused to go beyond an affirmation of man's being in the world, it has been regarded as an incomplete, truncated humanism and hence fair game for a theistic rounding off. To defend the thesis that existentialism provides the elements of a radical metaphysics, therefore, we must first counter unwarranted theological criticism by clarifying the sense in which existentialism proceeds from a perspective that is post-theistic and radically secular.

The first difficulty theologians have had with secular existentialism is in understanding the latter's claim that it is a post-theistic rather than an antitheistic philosophy. The death of God in secular philosophy has been understood by the theistically inclined for the most part in negative terms. As noted in an earlier chapter, theologians, even radical theologians, tend to see

Marxism and secular existentialism as examples of an antitheistic
humanism. Radical humanism of this sort is doomed by its own
covertly anthropotheistic logic to issue in a series of self-
contradictions (example: Sartre's man as "useless passion"). If
contemporary philosophers are to be credited with understanding their own intellectual efforts, however, this theological reading represents a serious misinterpretation of their intentions
and, at least in some cases, their actual achievements. Feuerbach
was the first to warn us against this line of criticism: "The individual who knows and says nothing more about me than that I am
an atheist, knows and says nothing about me."[1] Marx too, as we
have seen, rejected the attempt to place a theological interpretation on his radical humanism. Among the secular existentialists,
it is perhaps Merleau-Ponty who most directly addresses himself
to this stubborn reluctance of the theological mind to admit the
possibility of a philosophy which is post-theistic but not antitheistic.

   In his book *In Praise of Philosophy,* Merleau-Ponty argues that
there is a fundamental difference between the finitist,
nonspeculative attitude of contemporary philosophy and the
ontotheological, speculative posture of both theism and atheism.
He agrees with theologians like de Lubac and Maritain that there
is indeed a species of atheism which can be called "antitheism"
and which can best be understood as an "act of inverted faith," a
"refusal of God," or a "defiance of God." But while such antitheism exists and is "an inverted theology," nevertheless "it is
not a philosophy." At best antitheism is an intermediate step on
the road from a theological to a secular way of thinking, but it
is not yet the expression of a radical perspective in philosophy.
Its intellectual motivation is still determined by the perspective
of theology. It is here that Merleau-Ponty and the theologian
part ways. For the theologian, there is no possibility of a further
distinction between atheism and a post-theistic perspective in
philosophy. For the theologian, "philosophy, when it is not
theological, is reduced to the negation of God." For Merleau-
Ponty, on the other hand, one fails to understand the radical
perspective of contemporary philosophy "when one *defines* it as
atheism. This is philosophy as it is seen by the theologian."[2]

Like Marx, Merleau-Ponty views the radicalism of philosophy as originating from another perspective. It does not derive from the inverted theological perspective of atheism. Nor, what amounts to the same thing, does it reflect a belief in an alternative religion of humanity. It is the expression of a finitist perspective on being that bypasses the speculative controversy between theism and atheism, and offers, instead, a self-grounded and self-sufficient metaphysics of man's being in the world. As at least one theologian has seen, the secular existentialists, like their predecessors Feuerbach and Marx, confront us with an entirely different option, a positive humanism which "is no longer an explicit negation of faith or primarily a system built in opposition to faith," but one "which offers itself rather as a positive possibility of human existence, an integral way of being human without faith."[3] Seen from this perspective, a radical metaphysics is not only post-theistic but post-atheistic as well.

Most theologians, radical or otherwise, must of course reject any assertions on behalf of a radical, nontheistic perspective in philosophy. They must, that is, unless it can be shown that it is possible to formulate an ontology of finitude that is logically coherent and self-sufficient and that speaks to men's existential needs without secretly feeding upon the logic and psychology of an ontotheological or anthropotheistic way of thinking. If this cannot be done, then it would seem that the theistic or broadly religious argument must prevail, that any kind of atheism or humanism must inevitably present itself as the functional (logical and existential) equivalent of a theistic perspective. Sartre's early existentialism would, according to this argument, be a dramatic confirmation rather than a refutation of the theist's counter-assertion. In his dialogue with Merleau-Ponty, the theologian de Lubac argues that a nontheistic philosophy which pretends to have transcended the human problematic which gives rise to the consciousness and need of God has in fact merely succeeded in suppressing it; it must inevitably resurface in such a philosophy in the form of the self-deification of man or in stances of defiance or despair. Merleau-Ponty's reply is that a radical metaphysics, far from ignoring such a problem, in fact "radicalizes it, and places it above the 'solutions' which stifle it."[4] In Merleau-

Ponty's comment lies the clue to a radically different way of
thinking.

The second difficulty theologians have had with secular existentialism is in appreciating the sense in which it is a radically
secular metaphysics. This is simply another and more direct way
of approaching the question we have already been considering.
What, in contrast to a theological or theologically dependent
view of philosophy, is a philosophical perspective that is radical
or radically secular?

The concept of the secular has been interpreted in a number of
ways in the modern period, but all these interpretations receive
their meaning from the contrast of this term with corresponding
notions of religion or the sacred. Like atheism, though perhaps
less negatively, the secular is understood within a larger
framework of meaning established from the perspective of religion. In its original and most general sense, the secular world is
that sphere of life whose primary concern is with nonreligious,
mundane, temporal, penultimate matters—the world of public,
economic, social, legal, and political concerns. It is distinguished
from the world of religion—the realm of specific religious in-
stitutional activities or individual, ultimate concerns. Increasingly the term has also come to refer to systems of secular
meaning which officially pride themselves on their autonomy
and independence of religious ideology. Here too, however, the
religious connotation remains implicit, for in such cases, the
secular is understood as a realm of meaning that was at an earlier
time liberated from, or carved out in defiance of, the dictates of a
religious way of thinking, and that historical fact remains a part of
their self-understanding. On whatever interpretation, it would
therefore seem that the concept of secularity can never really be
freed from a hidden determination by its original religious frame
of reference.

This somewhat troublesome dialectical fact about the concept
of secularity fits right in of course with the apologetic claims of
the theologian. We mortals will always have ultimate concerns,
and if we try to deal with them in nonreligious or secular ways,
we shall inevitably do so in ways that are functionally equivalent
to the solutions traditionally provided by religion. Even in the

case of the radical theologians, we see that the theological affirmation of secularity does not go so far as to deny the transsecular dimensions of ultimate concern, nor does it permit modern men to suppose that secular philosophy or human resources can do what only a transsecular power and perspective can do. Even for the radical theologians it is the traditional—that is, theological—interpretation of secularity that remains, if only implicitly, normative for the modern world as well. Given the intellectual history and existential problematic surrounding the phenomenon of secularity, how could any other conclusion be possible?

And yet Merleau-Ponty suggests in his enigmatic remark that there is an alternative, a philosophical perspective which, far from ignoring this problematic, radicalizes it and places it beyond the reach of every theological solution that would stifle it.What could Merleau-Ponty possibly mean? I take him to be saying that the concept of secularity must be freed from every meaning that is determined, whether negatively or positively, by reference to an earlier and more fundamental religious sense and, instead, be provided with a meaning that is independently and originally its own. As things stand, the term "secularity" is not enough. If it is to free itself of its past history and logical status, it must become a *radical* secularity; it must reach down to roots, to philosophical origins, that are original not only in a history-of-ideas sense but, more important, in an ontological sense. A radical secularity will be rooted in metaphysical foundations which are themselves logically original—that is, fundamental categories of being which are not themselves in turn derived from some prior, deeper ground. If the surface meaning of the concept of secularity is "self-grounded and self-sufficient, having no source or goal in any transcendent realm,"[5] then it must be rooted in an ontology which is likewise "self-grounded and self-sufficient, having no source or goal in any transcendent realm." But that can only be an ontology of radical finitude, a philosophical perspective in which man's finite being in the world serves as the phenomenological basis for a metaphysics of radical secularity, a metaphysics which in turn is no longer derived by way of an antitheistic negation from a prior ontotheological perspective. It is in an ontology of finitude that Merleau-Ponty proposes to find the resources for a radical concept of secularity that will put it safely beyond the reach of theologians.

A radical perspective on secularity does not of course do away with the former, contrastive sense of the term. But it does mean that the relative positions of the secular and the religious have now been reversed. For a radical secularity is, after all, a revolutionary secularity. It stands the theological perspective on its head. No longer is the secular to be understood in terms laid down by religion. Rather, as Marx already saw, it is religion that is henceforth to be understood as an inverted and alienated mode of secular existence. No longer is man's finite being to be regarded as an incomplete or penultimate mode of being while ultimacy is reserved as a predicate for transcendent being. Rather, religion is now seen as a penultimate and less than wholly satisfactory attempt to free man to be a finite, human being. The radical metaphysics of the secular existentialists is thus the logical extension and fulfillment of the promise which first appeared in Marx's critique of the "critique of religion."

With these preliminaries behind us, let us look at the specifics of the ontology which in Heidegger, Sartre, and Merleau-Ponty has emerged as an alternative to ontotheological thinking about being, man, and the world.


The Finitude of Being

The key to a radical alternative to the traditional metaphysics of transcendent being lies in a reversal of our previous understanding of the concept of the finitude of being. Two of the most important elements in that concept are the notions of contingency and temporality. These categories are as old as metaphysics itself. What has changed is their relative position within the overall logic of being. The revolutionary achievement of the secular existentialists is to have reinterpreted the categories of infinite, absolute, eternal being in terms of the categories of contingency, temporality, and finitude. It is this inversion of the categorial priorities of traditional ontology that

provides the basis for the definitive overcoming of ontotheological thinking and the creation of an ontology of radical secularity.

## Contingency

Whatever one makes of the final coherence or consistency of
Sartre's ontology, it has the virtue of affirming in a clear and
direct manner the radical or irreducible contingency of being.
Already in his early novel *Nausea,* Sartre exposes the logical and
psychological deception inherent in the fundamental question of
traditional ontotheology: "Why is there something rather than
nothing?" As others, such as Hume and Kant and in our own day
the linguistic analysts, have also shown, this question is parasitic
for its meaning and apparent legitimacy upon questions of a
similar sort which can be raised about various phenomena
within the world. One runs into insurmountable logical difficulties, however, when such a question is extended beyond its
normal, inner-worldly use and asked of experience or the world
as a whole. There is no answer to this question; in fact, it is not
even a proper question to begin with. For Sartre, therefore, this
means that there is no ultimate reason or ground for the being of
things. Being is ultimately contingent; it cannot be derived or
deduced from anything higher or other. Things, as it were, just
are.[6]

God, a transcendent ground or first cause of contingent being,
thus becomes for Sartre a self-contradictory idea and a superflu-
ous hypothesis. To posit the existence of God is to posit "the
baseless existence of God over against the baseless existence of
the world."[7] It is to engage in an unnecessary duplication of one's
metaphysical effort. Sartre's conclusion is even more radical than
that of the secular theologian: "God, if he exists, is contingent"
—which is to say, the being of God, if there is a God, is no more
of a reason for things than is the irreducible mystery of the world
itself and hence adds nothing to what we already do not know.[8]

The traditional Christian doctrine of God as the Creator of the
world *ex nihilo* is seen from this perspective, as it was by Marx, to
be an inverted mythological expression of the radical contingency of the world, what Merleau-Ponty refers to as the

"caryatid of the void."[9] The statement "God exists" is not an
Anselmian clue to the one instance of a necessary being; it is,
rather, an indirect way of affirming the ultimacy of contingency.
From a radical perspective, it is contingency, not openness to
some transcendent source, that is the ultimate mark of finitude.[10]

## Temporality

The affirmation of the ultimacy of contingency does not by itself
explain the radical nature of finitude in contemporary ontology.
As important as contingency is the existentialist insight into the
temporality of being. As the title of Heidegger's major work
indicates, the concept of time has come to play a central role in
the contemporary reinterpretation of being. In fact, as we shall
see, it is the temporal nature of being which opens up the
possibility of affirming the ultimacy of contingency.

There are many ways to demonstrate the importance of the
concept of time for an understanding of the finite, contingent
nature of being. The phenomenon of perception offers one
example. Ever since Kant's first *Critique,* philosophers have
recognized the irreducibly temporal structure of the activity and
objects of perception. The objects of experience do not present
themselves as raw sense data existing in a hypothetical state of
sheer temporal immediacy. They appear before us bringing their
past determinations and contingencies with them and, what is
more important, projecting their unfinished possibilities ahead
of them.[11] The objects of experience are radically temporal
phenomena, eventlike structures stretching backward into the
past and forward into the contingent future. On the side of the
subject too, time conditions our perception of being. The logical
features of our acts of seeing are not unchanging structures,
except at a very high level of descriptive generality. They are,
rather, little hypotheses, practical guides, imaginative projections of future possibilities, and anticipatory expectations of
future confirmations of that which confronts us in our present
experience.[12] The contingency of being, as the example of perception suggests, is grounded in the temporal conditions of our

experience, particularly in the openness of the future to possibilities of experience and being which go beyond the determinations or expectations of the present or the past.[13] It is the future which prevents the realities of the past or present from being transformed into fixed and absolute determinants of being. It is the ontological priority of the future which guarantees the radical contingency of being and thus the ontological ultimacy of finitude.[14]

But the concept of time could not play the central role it does in a finitist ontology if the reverse propostion were not also true. A radical perspective on the temporality of being is possible only if time is in turn understood in terms of the phenomenon of contingency. The "temporalization" of time must itself be understood in a finite way.[15]

What Heidegger means by the "finitude of temporality" will perhaps become clearer if we compare his analysis of time with the concept of time in classical metaphysics. Take, for example, Artistotle's doctrine of *entelechy*, the doctrine that things contain within them the determinants of their future development. Here it is clear that the outcome of the future is already present in the beginnings of a thing. The future is predetermined by the past. The temporal process of being, or what Heidegger calls the temporalization of time, is thus only the unfolding of a goal which has already been determined. But this means that in Aristotle the temporal process as a whole is conceived in *atemporal* terms. The process of temporalization has already been determined for all times by the timeless presence of its origins in all of its subsequent stages.

Aristotle's concept of time presupposes a similarly timeless and noncontingent concept of the essence or being of things as that cause which must already be somewhere in the past.[16] But here we discover a curious fact. This concept of the timelessness of being, its timeless presence in every stage of the temporal process, is itself an implicitly *temporal* notion. The timelessness of being is in fact an inverted expression for the ontological priority of the past. Aristotle's formula for the essence of things makes this very clear: *to ti ēn einai,* the "what-it-was-ness" of a thing. The timelessness of being is conceived by classical ontology in terms of past origins which continue in an unchanging way to be determinative throughout all subsequent times. Classical metaphysics arrives at its concept of infinite, eternal being by absolutizing one particular mode of finite, temporal being—the past.

Classical ontology is thus an alienated ontology; it is based on the ideological inversion of the categories of finite being and time. Time is deprived of its ontologically fundamental status, and reduced to a derivative, penultimate mode of being. Time is but the moving image of eternity. Priority is accorded instead to the concept of timeless, unchanging, infinite, necessary being. But with the discovery of the hidden temporal secret of classical ontology, everything is changed. It now becomes possible to replace the alienated concepts of classical ontology with a new and positive understanding of what Heidegger calls the finitude of the temporalization of time.

To affirm the finitude of temporality, and hence of being, is not to say that time and being eventually come to an end; nor would its denial mean that time and being are endless. Such statements would represent the propositions of a speculative metaphysics, illegitimate attempts to talk about being and time from some Archimedian standpoint beyond them. To say that time is finite is rather to make a statement in the context of a descriptive metaphysics. It is an attempt to say something from within the process, as it were, about the way in which time "temporalizes" itself.[17] It is to say, in opposition to the classical doctrine of temporality, that time does not realize itself in a necessary or noncontingent way. The future is not timelessly predetermined by its origins in the past. Time and again the future goes beyond the determinations of the past and offers us possibilities that are unexpected, surprising, and genuinely new. Neither the past nor the present is capable of completely overcoming this fundamental contingency which the future introduces into the heart of the temporal process. Time is therefore finite, not simply in the sense that the possibilities of the future are limited by the realities of the past and present but also in the sense that these realities can never completely determine these future possibilities. Time is always surpassing itself, transcending the givens of the past toward the openness of an ever-outstanding future. As in Hegel, so in Heidegger, the finitude of time is equated with this phenomenon of self-transcendence.

To summarize, it is an affirmation of the ultimate contingency of being which makes possible this insight into the radical temporality of being. To say that being is contingent is to say that its past never completely determines its future, that its future is always capable of going beyond its past and present. It is this circular dialectic of the concepts of contingency and temporality that provides the logical basis for a finitist interpretation of being.

An ontology of radical finitude represents an inversion of the categories of classical ontology. It does not eliminate the older predicates, however, nor does it leave them in a state of suspended alienation. Instead, it radicalizes them. It reinterprets them as absolute qualifiers of finite, temporal being, as legitimate, unalienated ways of pointing to and safeguarding the irreducible contingency of being.

The concept of the being of things, for example, is no longer interpreted as their timeless *to ti ēn einai,* their "what-it-was-ness," but as their open-ended future possibilities. Their essence or substance is always contingent and provisional, not something already definitive, fixed, and unchanging. The being of things is something which reaches before or ahead of them, not something which is already within or behind them.

Given this temporal and finitist concept of being, negative qualifiers such as "absolute," "infinite," and "eternal" undergo a similar transformation. They no longer qualify entities or states which transcend the logical limits of temporal, contingent being. Rather, they are used to invoke the unqualified contingency and temporality of being, the eminent openness of finite being. That which is absolute or infinite is that which is unqualifiedly open; hence, the absolute future is the unqualifiedly open future. Similarly, that which is eternal is that which is eminently temporal, that which is true at every point in time. To speak of the eternal being of God, for example, is simply an inverted way of saying that at every point in time the future remains open. To affirm the power of the eternal is to affirm the eminent openness of time itself.[18]

Finally, the phenomenon of transcendence does not refer to a
dimension of infinite, unchanging being that lies outside or
beyond the limits of finite, temporal being. It stands, rather, for
the eminent openness of finite being, its capacity to transcend
itself in the direction of the future. To celebrate the power of
transcendence is to celebrate the ultimate contingency of being.

When reinterpreted in temporal terms, the traditional predicates of the absolute, infinite, eternal, or transcendent therefore
become ways of pointing to the positive significance of finite
being—the irreducible openness of being—rather than the negative qualifiers of a way of thinking that is alienated from the
conditions of its being. This ontology of radical finitude has
equally liberating consequences for a post-theistic way of thinking about man and the world.

## The Finitude of Man

A radically secular perspective on man is one that views man's
being as essentially finite and rules out a theistic interpretation of
the meaning of that being. The critical question for such an
anthropology is whether in fact it can eliminate man's theistic
need. Merleau-Ponty asserts that it does. He argues, it will be
recalled, that contemporary philosophy so radicalizes the concept of human finitude that it puts it beyond the reach of theistic
solutions. The concept of God only stifles attempts to grasp the
true, positive significance of the finitude of man.

In trying to make sense of Merleau-Ponty's assertion, the first
thing to be noted is that for the existentialists the notion of the
finitude of man does not refer to the empirical fact that all men
are mortal, that at some point in time our earthly lives inevitably
come to an end. By itself this fact has no significance one way or
the other for the question whether the nature of man is such as
to require a theistic guarantee. That man is finite means rather
that the categories upon which man draws to understand reality
as a whole, and hence to understand his own mode of being, are
those of temporality and contingency. As in the case of Heidegger's phrase, the "finitude of temporality," the term "finite"
refers not to the fact that something comes to an end but rather

to the way in which things in general, and men in particular, exist.[19]

Insight into the mode of man's being tells us something, in turn, about the nature of men's needs, capacities, and aspirations. It gives us some general logical or ontological criteria for deciding what is legitimate and what is unwarranted in man's quest for meaning. The assertion that man's mode of being is finite entails the parallel assertion that his need and capacity for meaning must be interpreted in finitist terms—that it must be radicalized and placed beyond the reach of those answers that would infinitize and hence alienate or distort it. Merleau-Ponty's position thus has two parts: first, that the concept of the finitude of man refers to the mode of man's being, the way he exists; and second, that a finitist interpretation of man's being makes possible a radicalization of man's quest for meaning, which means, among other things, the overcoming of man's theistic need.

A new, radically finitist perspective on being brings with it the need for equally new ways of talking about the nature of man's being. In the case of the existentialists, this has resulted in a rather strange and difficult terminology. Man is understood in terms of the new metaphysical concept of *ek-sistence*. Man's mode of being is "ek-sistential"—that is, he exists by "standing out from" himself and "standing out toward" the world in which he is practically engaged. He does this primarily by "pro-jecting" new possibilities of being forward into the future, thereby "standing out from" those conditions or already realized possibilities which determine his present situation. Man's mode of being, or ek-sistence, is thus defined as a process of finite self-transcendence. The old metaphysical terminology which erected an insurmountable barrier between the phenomena of existence and transcendence, the immanent and the transcendent, no longer fits this finitist perspective on man.[20] The existentialists, following Hegel, have built infinitude, the capacity for self-transcendence, into their concept of man as a finite being.

This concept of man's being, like the general notion of being iself, is grounded in the temporal priority of the future. The existentialist emphasis upon the future is, we have seen, another way of stressing that being is finite, that it is a phenomenon of

open-ended contingency. Similarly, it is the openness of the
future which guarantees that man's essence is to ek-sist, that man
is at every point in time capable of transcending his present
nature and creating himself anew. For these philosophers, man's
true humanity, his being as *homo humanum* rather than a creature
of God, is not something already there or given (cf. Aristotle's *to
ti ēn einai*). It is something that is not yet, something that is
coming to be. More exactly, it is his enduring capacity for pro-
jecting new possibilities of being that transcend what he already
is or was.[21] Just as it is the future which characterizes the transcendent dimension of being in general, so it is man's openness to
the future which represents the reality of transcendence for
him.[22] By focusing our gaze ahead rather than above, the secular
existentialists, like Marx, provide us with a radicalized understanding of transcendence which no longer needs to be justified
on alienated, theological grounds.

Given this finitist perspective on man's being, what follows for
our understanding of man's quest for ultimate meaning? Since
human existence is ultimately qualified by the categories of
temporality and contingency, a religious or ontotheological interpretation of his needs and hopes must obviously be ruled out.
Even the theologian can admit that man ought no longer to be
looking for "an absolute confirmation of himself in the apo-
theosis of what always is." As a process of finite self-transcendence, man's projection of meaning can only succeed if
at the same time it is exposed to "the uncertainty that lies in the
contingent experience of reality and in the contingency even of
one's own constructing."[23] Man can find or create meaning only
by enduring this lack of absolute certitude. Why? Because it
makes sense to talk about the possibility of transcending the
limitations of one's present circumstances only if one first accepts the finitude of one's being which this capacity for self-
transcendence implies. To exist in such a way as to be able to
liberate oneself from the meaninglessness of the past and create a
new, more human future is to exist finitely. To act meaningfully
is therefore to live through, and stand forth in, one's finitude.

Heidegger concludes that it is only by accepting the radical
finitude of one's being that one is set free to appropriate the

possibilities of an unalienated, authentically human way of being. This much-misunderstood argument must of course be taken in its positive, post-theistic sense and not in a nihilistic or antitheistic sense. It is a positive affirmation that, however paradoxical it may sound, it is the radical finitude of man's being which provides the ontological basis and guarantee for his sense of the eschatological urgency of life. It is because of man's sense of an irreducible need and capacity to create the conditions and possibilities of his own existence, an exigency that is never fully satisfied and an initiative that is always open-ended, that he is able to project a wholeness and a meaning that rescues him from "the absurdity or triviality that characterizes a mere coming-into-being and passing-out-of-being."[24]

We can further illustrate this radicalization of man's quest for meaning by noting certain contrasts between Merleau-Ponty's and Sartre's approach to the problematic of man's finitude. Sartre's humanism is self-admittedly "an attempt to draw all the consequences of a coherent atheistic position."[25] It defines itself in antitheistic terms as a humanism which is capable of taking over the place vacated by the death of God. It is man, not God, who precedes every attempt at definition or determination and who bears as a consequence the burden of radical (absolute) freedom. It is man, rather than God, who is now responsible for the ideal value of "infinite and perfect consciousness."[26]

In the absence of God, these predicates of absolute freedom and consciousness must somehow be grounded in man's own being. But man is a radically finite being, "a hole of being at the heart of Being."[27] Ontologically speaking, there is an unsurpassable hiatus between the nothingness of man's being and the Parmenidean plentitude of Being. Far from being incompatible with these quasi-theological predicates of absolute freedom and consciousness, however, this finitude of man's being is what gives them their sense. Man's freedom and consciousness are as absolute and unconditional as is the radical nothingness that separates him from the fixed determinants of the unbroken plenum of Being.

For our purposes, it does not matter that, for Sartre, man's quest for absolute meaning is doomed, because of his finitude, to

perpetual failure.[28] What is more important is that Sartre does
not regard this quest as incompatible with man's finitude. Quite
the contrary, he takes it to be the very essence of its ontological
meaning. In other words, despite his philosophical radicalism,
Sartre gives us an ontotheological interpretation of the significance of human finitude. If we tend to miss this fact it is because,
within that overall perspective, he himself chooses the atheistic
option of defiance or despair. It is no wonder, therefore, that
Sartre's radical humanism is so often selected by theologians to
illustrate the allegedly inescapable necessity for a theistic view of
man's finitude.

When we turn to Merleau-Ponty, we find a different reading
of the matter. For Merleau-Ponty, the concept of man's finitude
entails a radicalization of the human problematic. It means, as we
have already noted, going beyond the sphere of ontotheological
thinking altogether and thus beyond Sartre's quasi-theological
predicates of absolute freedom and consciousness as well. For
Merleau-Ponty, Sartre's concept of man as absolute freedom is
simply theism in another guise—a criticism which, interestingly,
parallels the Marxist critique of Sartre's notion of freedom as
being too abstract and theological.[29] Merleau-Ponty calls, instead, for a way of thinking that offers a positive interpretation of
the ambiguity at the heart of man's quest for meaning. For
Merleau-Ponty, man's ability to discover and create structures of
meaning, whether through knowledge or through action, implies
a radical contingency, a necessary unclarity and uncertitude, that
is destroyed as soon as anything absolute is presupposed,
whether that absolute takes a theological or, as in Sartre's case, a
humanistic form.[30]

Perhaps we can get a better idea of what Merleau-Ponty means
by this concept of ambiguity if we compare the models which he
and Sartre use to describe the nature of human reason:

For Sartre the model is knowledge, and the attitude one of great
confidence in reflection and in its lucidity. In *L'Imaginaire,* for
example, he said that "we must repeat here what has been known
since Descartes: a reflective consciousness gives us absolutely
certain data." But for Merleau-Ponty the decisive experience is
perception, and reflection is never allowed to be sure of itself. A
remark by Sartre reflects, as much by its tone as by its content, the

difference in style that has grown out of these two developments:
"I have always thought, I still think that the Truth is one . . .
Merleau-Ponty, on the other hand, found his security in the
multiplicity of perspectives."[31]

If, as Merleau-Ponty suggests, it is the ambiguities of perception
rather than the certainies of reflection which provide the foundation and model for human reason, then our ideal of rationality
must not be conceived in absolutist terms. If our mode of being is
that of an entity whose nature is fundamentally incomplete and
whose future is never completely certain, then another kind of
thinking is called for. It must be one that takes the ambiguity of
our situation—the seeming irrationality or incompleteness of
things and the obscurity of our finite awareness of them—into
itself in a direct and positive way.

What is of decisive importance is that this move be understood
as representing not an impoverishment but an enlargement of
human reason. The finitude of man's thinking is a positive phenomenon, not a lack to be deplored and someday, it is hoped,
overcome. The ambiguity inherent in the objects and activities
of human reason is not a limitation placed upon man's potentially
infinite or perfectible capacities. It is the necessary condition for
the free and creative exercise of those capacities.[32] Ambiguity is
not something that is provisionally admitted alongside certainty
pending the advent of absolute knowledge. That is to put things
the wrong way around. It is to read the lesson of Socrates
through inverted Platonic spectacles. "Socrates . . . knows only
that there is no absolute knowledge, and that it is by this absence
that we are open to the truth."[33] From a radical perspective,
man's finitude is not a limitation but an openness to being. The
ambiguity of his situation is not an obstacle but an invitation
to the adventure of meaningful thought and action. If this is so,
then Merleau-Ponty's radicalizing or deabsolutizing of man's
quest for meaning expresses not a truncated or tragic view of
life but an enlarged and humanizing vision of what it means to be
a finite being.

Merleau-Ponty's argument, in opposition to both de Lubac
and Sartre, is that the loss of the ontotheological dimension of
being in contemporary philosophical anthropology is not an

occasion for despair or surrender to absurdity. It is, rather, the necessary and final step in the process of radically secular, or human, emancipation. Sartre had already argued that the concept of God is a logically impossible or self-contradictory notion. But a concept of man which is dependent upon theistic metaphysics is also the concept of an impossible being, as proved by the futility of Sartre's attempt to substitute man for God while retaining the absolute predicates of an ontotheological way of thinking. As Marx had already argued against Feuerbach, so Merleau-Ponty now argues against Sartre that, on the terms set by the logic of ontotheology, not only God but also man becomes an inverted, alienated, nonhuman being.

But there is another way of looking at man. An ek-sistential interpretation of man's being is not, Heidegger tells us, simply a secular vehicle for theological attempts to talk about man in a contemporary vocabulary (for example, Bultmann or the radical theologians). Nor is it, on the other hand, a radical secularization of the traditional attributes of God and their transferral to the realm of man (for example, Feuerbach or Sartre).[34] It represents, rather, something which the older metaphysical and theological tradition would not allow and could not conceive. It is a brand-new idea, one that may be put in the form of a simple tautology (which nevertheless speaks volumes): man is neither a creature of God nor a rational animal, but simply man, *homo humanum*.[35] A radically finitist ontology of man does not propose, as theistic rumor might have it, a burial of the real problem of man by a divinization or alienation of man. Marx's critique of Feuerbach and Merleau-Ponty's critique of Sartre ought to have laid that rumor permanently to rest. What it attempts is something rather different and far more daring, something truly radical—namely, the acceptance and affirmation of man as simply man.

## The Finitude of the World

This affirmation of the finitude of man and the end of his theistic need acquires its large-scale metaphysical significance only in the setting of an equally radical and post-theistic way of thinking about man's being-in-the-world. Here once again, we find in the

philosophies of Heidegger and Merleau-Ponty an illustration
of the thesis that a finitist ontology, this time directed to our
concept of the world, brings with it a radicalization of man's sense
of the meaning of his being. Before we turn to the positive details
of this thesis, however, we must first clarify some typical misunderstandings of the existentialist concept of the world.

Heidegger's basic term for the way in which man exists is
*being-in-the-world.* One of the most common misunderstandings
of this concept, especially among the theistically inclined, is that
it refers to the totality of entities, activities, and concerns that
characterize mere this-worldly being. Man's secular (worldly)
being, on this theistic interpretation, "only admits the this-
worldly, thereby negating the other-worldly and renouncing all
'transcendency.' "[36] As Heidegger makes clear, however, a
genuinely radical concept of secularity has something quite different in mind when it defines man's being as "in-the-world":

> To refer to "being-in-the-world" as the basic trait of the *humanitas* of
> the *homo humanus* is not to claim that man is simply a secular being,
> in the Christian sense, and so turned away from God and devoid of
> "transcendency." What is meant by this last word might be more
> clearly called: the Transcendent. The Transcendent is the
> super-sensual being. This is valued as the supreme being in the
> sense of the first cause of every being. God is thought of as this
> first cause. "World," however, does not in any way signify, in the
> term "being-in-the-world," the earthly being in contrast to the
> heavenly, nor does it mean the "secular" in contrast to the
> "spiritual." "World" does not signify in this determination a being
> at all and no realm of beings, but the openness of being.[37]

The world, viewed as "the openness of being" rather than as a
"realm of beings," is thus to be understood not as a term referring to the totality of the finite, created order over against a
transcendent Creator but as a general descriptive term for the
way in which man exists. Man exists as a being who ek-sists, who
"opens out toward" or stands in relationship to the various items
of his environment. As Heidegger adds, "Thought of from the
point of view of ek-sistence, 'world' is in a way transcendence
within and for existence."[38] Man ek-sists or goes beyond himself
by opening himself up to that which is around him. More exactly,
like time and the future, the concept of the world is a limiting

concept in a descriptive metaphysics of man's being. It stands for the a priori or structural feature of man's being which makes possible, logically or ontologically, man's relationships to objects and persons within the world. The term "world" points to that primordial openness to being which provides a logical space or "between" within which the logically derivative relation between subject and object can arise and be.[39]

This leads directly into a second misunderstanding of an existentialist view of the world—one that is not confined to theologians. As the catch phrase "world view" suggests, this is the notion that, with the elimination of a theistic, or some other objective metaphysical, foundation of man's being-in-the-world, the status of the world is reduced to a mere predicate of human subjectivity. Has not Heidegger just told us that the world is a predicate of man's being? The necessary corollary of reducing the world to our view of it is absolutizing the subject or our subjective perception of it. As Heidegger notes, "That the world becomes a view is one and the same process with that by which man, within that which exists, becomes a *subjectum*."[40] The world is interpreted dualistically as the sum total of objective reality over against the subject (it can even include the subject viewed as an object) and, at the same time, as our subjective picture or representation of the world as it exists for us. The result of this distinctively modern ontological reduction and subjectivization of the world is, as Heidegger reminds us, that today we find ourselves torn apart by the conflicts of competing world views or ideologies.[41] Corresponding to the alienation of man's actual being-in-the-world is a metaphysical view of the reality of the world which reduces it to our distorted, ideological interpretations of it.

Heidegger wishes to argue, however, that there is a deep and fundamental cleavage between this one-sided, subjective interpretation of the world as our view of it, and the ek-sistential interpretation of the world he is offering in its place. As the hyphenated structure of the term suggests, the notion of being-in-the-world points to a unitary but many-sided phenomenon, a complex dialectical or relational totality of man and the world which precedes the analysis of its several constitutive elements (for example, man-as-subject and entities-within-the-world as objects) and which cannot be reduced to a predicate of any one of them (for example, man-as-subject taken in an isolated, one-sided way). It is this multisided but logically primitive category of being-in-the-world which provides the conceptual framework for interpreting such central anthropological terms as ek-sistence and trans-cendence.[42] This cosmological setting of man's ek-sistence does not rob him of his subjective freedom or historical initiative. Rather, it places it in proper metaphysical perspective and provides it with the necessary conditions of its true, radically secular significance. Neither one-sidedly subjective nor one-sidedly objective, being-in-the-world is the phenomenological basis and limit of man's existence behind which or beyond which he cannot go.

Where do these initial clarifications leave us concerning the ontological status of the world? Do they entail its radical finitude, or do they leave room for the possible existence of God? According to Heidegger, nothing is necessarily decided one way or the other concerning this question.[43] A description of the general features of man's being (a descriptive ontology of the world) is not to be confused with an explanation of how man or the world came into being (an ontic account of the world, whether scientific or theological). However, enough has already been said concerning the speculative status of theological propositions masquerading as explanatory accounts to render Heidegger's official neutrality at this point philosophically unnecessary. The fact is that when we conjoin Heidegger's concept of the world with an interpretation of being as temporal and contingent, a radically finitist, nontheistic cosmology follows.

Here Merleau-Ponty has been more consistent and explicit than has Heidegger. To begin with, he says, it is no accident that our primordial relation to the world has often been designated by philosophers, and not only religion, as one of faith (opinion, natural belief). "Each of our perceptions is an act of faith in that it affirms more than we strictly know, since objects are inexhaustible and our information limited."[44] The first question for a radical philosophy, as for the theistic perspective, is what ontological sense it can make of this contingency which characterizes our initial and basic contact with the world. What distin-

guishes the radically secular perspective from its theistic counterpart is that whereas the latter offers a solution to this problem,
thereby in effect undermining its original force, the former
accepts and abides in the problematic nature of this contingency,
thereby in effect putting it beyond the range of all attempted
solutions. The irreducible facticity or contingency of the world
and my perception of it is part of what it means to be in the world.
To try to eliminate that contingency by reducing it to rationally
transparent and necessary grounds is to try to eliminate what it
means for me to be in the world. As Merleau-Ponty puts it:

> The world is not what I think, but what I live through. I am open
> to the world, I have no doubt that I am in communication with it,
> but I do not possess it; it is inexhaustible. "There is a world," or
> rather: "There is the world"; I can never completely account for
> this ever-reiterated assertion in my life. This facticity of the world
> is what constitutes the *Weltlichkeit der Welt,* what causes the world
> to be the world. . . . There is behind it no unknown quantity
> which has to be determined by deduction, or, beginning with it,
> demonstrated inductively. We witness every moment by miracle of
> related experiences, and yet nobody knows better than we do how
> this miracle is worked, for we are ourselves this network of
> relationships. The world and reason are not problematical. We may
> say, if we wish, that they are mysterious, but their mystery defines
> them: there can be no question of dispelling it by some "solution,"
> it is on the hither side of all solutions.[45]

In other words, for Merleau-Ponty, the contingency of the
world cannot itself be accounted for, since it lies at the root of the
sorts of reasons, deductive and inductive, we give for the existence of things; hence it lies at the root of any explanations we
might wish to give for it as well.[46] Heidegger has a linguistically
peculiar but conceptually effective way of making the same
point: *die Welt weltet.* The concept of the world is an ontologically
ultimate or limiting concept about which nothing further can be
said, at least in the sense of "giving reasons for the existence" of
something. The being of the world is in this sense ultimately
contingent. To say that it is mysterious is simply another way of
saying the same thing. A theistic solution of the radical contingency or mystery of the world's being would have the logical
effect of contradicting the secularity or worldliness of the world
in the very moment that it claims to be grounding it.

There is a second point that Merleau-Ponty wishes to stress.

To point to the ultimate contingency of the world is not to indicate an ontological deficiency in reality or a logical deficiency in our ability to think about the world. The contingency of the world is, rather, the logical and ontological basis for whatever positive significance our being or thinking has.

Finally, the contingency of the world must not be understood as a deficiency in being, a break in the stuff of necessary being, a threat to rationality, nor as a problem to be solved as soon as possible by the discovery of some deeper-laid necessity. That is ontic contingency, contingency within the bounds of the world. Ontological contingency, the contingency of the world itself, being radical, is, on the other hand, what forms the basis once for all of our ideas of truth.[47]

It is because our being-in-the-world is ontologically contingent, or, put in another way, because it is characterized by a primordial and irreducible openness to being, that we are able both to build upon our former perceptions and to construct newer, more satisfactory ways of seeing. The contingency of the world is therefore "not an imperfection in itself, but rather what assures me of my existence."[48] The biblical doctrine of Creation, when viewed from this perspective, is not a theistic-metaphysical explanation of the existence of the world, but an inverted, alienated way of expressing the double insight of a radically secular ontology: that the phenomenon of the world, like being itself, is ultimately and radically contingent, and that this fact has positive rather than negative significance for the way in which man exists in the world.

Merleau-Ponty's defense of the contingency of the world brings us to the second part of our opening thesis—namely, the claim that a finitist ontology makes possible a radicalization of man's sense of the meaning of his being. The theist's position is that a finitist ontology cannot provide the ontological support necessary for a belief that human life has an ultimate meaning. The question we must consider is whether the theist's charge is true or, rather, if it is true, whether it leads to the sort of conclusion the theist has in mind.

The theist's charge is grounded in the tendency of theologians to equate the choice between theism and atheism on the level of theory with the choice between meaning and lack of meaning on the level of lived experience. To think of ultimate reality as divine, to call it "God," is to say that being is worthy of trust and confidence or that being is the source of meaning and grace. To be an atheist, on the other hand, is to say that being is alien and indifferent, that is is devoid of meaning and grace. For the theist, therefore, talk about the contingency or openness of being simply transfers the old dispute between theists and atheists into a new conceptuality. Whatever one's choice, the underlying existential options are the same: either one chooses the stance of defiance or despair (Sartre) or one chooses the stance of confidence and trust (Heidegger).[49] Beneath the surface drama of linguistic innovation, the underlying life issues remain unchanged. What is important is one's existential stance, not one's theoretical beliefs. However, if one's thinking is consistent with one's stance in life, then existential faith must find corresponding expression at the level of theoretical belief. For the theist, existential trust must inevitably be expressed in terms of belief in God.[50] On the other hand, an ontology of radical finitude, a metaphysics which does not ground the contingency of the world in the being of God, will prove less than satisfactory as a basis for confidence in the openness of being.

There are, however, several difficulties in this line of argument. To begin with, despite its sensitivity to the distinction between existential and intellectual levels of belief, it presses too hard for a necessary link between existential trust and a specifically theistic formulation of belief. The theist can reply that the existential issues remain the same nevertheless and that this is sufficient to establish his case. However, there is a close enough link between our theoretical beliefs and our life stance so that a radical change in one must have a significant effect on the other, and vice versa. The theist has failed to consider the possibility that, along with the shift to a radical metaphysics on the level of our theoretical understanding of the world, there goes a parallel shift in our prereflective, existential understanding of our being-in-the-world. If on the level of theory a radical metaphysics dissolves the traditional dispute between theists and atheists, it is quite possible that it also radicalizes the problem that brings God to mind on the level of our lived experience, that

it so redescribes our prereflective encounter with that problem
as to place it beyond all solutions, whether existential or theoretical. Once again, therefore, the battle lines are drawn between a
finitist and a theistic perspective on the implications of the
finitude of the world for man's sense of the meaning of his being.

How, then, does Merleau-Ponty describe the phenomenon of
faith? Faith is another name for our natural, prereflective mode
of engagement in the world:

> Faith—in the sense of an unreserved commitment which is never
> completely justified—enters the picture as soon as we leave the
> realm of pure geometrical ideas and have to deal with the existing
> world. Each of our perceptions is an act of faith in that it affirms
> more than we strictly know, since objects are inexhaustible and our
> information limited.[51]

Our primordial openness to the world is also an unreserved
commitment to the world, an affirmation of the various structures of meaning into which we are born and which forever
transcend our ability to grasp them completely. Faith is the
appropriate name for the world of a being who is, as Merleau-
Ponty puts it, condemned to meaning. We find ourselves open to
the world, we find the world open to us, but we are unable to
possess either ourselves or the world. Our being-in-the-world is
a phenomenon whose potential for meaning proves ever-
changing and inexhaustible.

The radical contingency of our initial contact with the world,
in turn, provides the lasting matrix for all higher or reflective
expressions of our being-in-the-world. In philosophy,
Merleau-Ponty says, a radical perspective on man's existence is
one which is characterized by "a consciousness of its own dependence on an unreflective life which is its initial situation, unchanging, given once and for all."[52] Philosophy cannot therefore
require either of itself or of lived experience the sort of absolute
certainty that applies to the realm of geometrical ideas. Our
primordial way of being-in-the-world is neither capable of nor in
need of assurances of an absolute sort. It is rather the contingency, the openness, of our being-in-the-world which "assures me
of my existence."[53]

This radicalization of the question of meaning does not there-

fore involve a shift from one conceptuality to another which is its
logical equivalent nor does it entail a replacement of proposi-
tional with existential certitude. It involves recasting the issue in
entirely different terms. In place of a quest for absolute meaning
or absolute meaninglessness, a radical metaphysics speaks of our
inescapable commitment to partial, shifting, contingent meaning.
In place of unqualified trust in the ultimate goodness of being or
an attitude of defiance in the face of an indifferent universe, it
speaks of the risk and adventure of bringing meaning into existence out of our dialectical interchange with the world. In place
of optimism or pessimism about our ultimate destiny, it speaks in
melioristic, Jamesian terms about our struggles to create a more
human future. It grounds its hope not in that which already is or
is inevitably to come but in that which is not yet and which can
never simply be.

Philosophy works itself out in another order, and it is for the same
reasons that it eludes both Promethean humanism and the rival
affirmations of theology. The philosopher does not say that a final
transcendence of human contradictions may be possible, and that
the complete man awaits us in the future. Like everyone else, he
knows nothing of this. He says—and this is something altogether
different—that the world is going on, that we do not have to judge
its future by what has happened in the past, that the idea of a
destiny in things is not an idea but a dizziness, that our relations
with nature are not fixed once and for all, that no one can know
what freedom may be able to do, nor imagine what our customs
and human relations would be in a civilization no longer haunted by
competition and necessity. He does not place his hope in destiny,
even a favorable one, but in something belonging to us which is
precisely not a destiny—in the contingency of our history.[54]

For Merleau-Ponty, the ontological basis of our sense of meaning is to be sought elsewhere than in the alleged necessities of
either history or divine being. It is provided by our initial and
lasting awareness of the contingency of our being. Here we
arrive at the fundamental difference between the perspective of
a radical metaphysics and that of theology. In his essay on
Bergson, Merleau-Ponty refers to the latter's attempt to provide
an experiential interpretation of the meaning of God: "Everything happens . . . as if man encountered at the roots of his
constituted being a generosity which is not a compromise with
the adversity of the world and which is on his side against it."[55]

Though Merleau-Ponty speaks approvingly of this conception, he is also concerned that we see its fundamental ambiguity. For the radical metaphysician, the notion of a generosity which man encounters at the roots of his being and which remains uncompromised by the particular resistances of the world does not point beyond us to a realm of noncontingent being. It does not refer to a power of absolute being which perpetually absorbs the threat of nonbeing into a higher necessity. It refers rather to the absolute power of contingency, or, put another way, to the "infinite weakness" of being. As Sartre says in summarizing Merleau-Ponty's vision of radical contingency: "He lets transcendence flow into immanence, there to be dissolved at the same time as it is protected against annihilation by its very impalpability. It will be only absence and supplication, deriving its all-encompassing power from its infinite weakness."[56] It is because the being of the world is radically contingent that we are able in our finite ways to transcend the givens of previous experience and bring forth new possibilities of being. But this generosity of being does not secure us or our projects from, in James's term, the possibility of final shipwreck. The world assures me of my existence, but not in a noncontingent way.

The fatal ambiguity in a theological interpretation of the contingency of being is that in the very moment in which it grounds this contingency in a deeper necessity it cancels its original meaning. As Merleau-Ponty observes: "Theology recognizes the contingency of human existence only to derive it from a necessary being, that is, to remove it. Theology makes use of philosophical wonder only for the purpose of motivating an affirmation which ends it."[57] Theology either explains contingency away or it affirms it in an indirect and alienated way by positing the equally inexplicable being of God. The task of a truly radical, finitist perspective in philosophy, on the other hand, is to preserve our original sense of the wonder and mystery that something exists rather than nothing. To say that the being of the world is radically contingent is to say that it lies beyond the range of every explanatory solution. It is not to issue an invitation to theologians to solve—that is, dissolve—this mystery by providing it with a noncontingent ground.

A radical perspective in philosophy, one that presents itself as an alternative to the traditional ontotheological way of thinking, takes seriously its grounding in the contingency of our experience of the world. It does not assume that its task is to provide an absolute perspective on the world or an absolute answer to its problematic status. It begins, rather, with the admission and self-reminder that it itself becomes a problematic enterprise the moment it abandons its roots and gives voice to these absolutist assumptions.

> A philosophy becomes transcendental, or radical, not by taking its place in absolute consciousness . . . but by considering itself as a problem; not by postulating a knowledge rendered totally explicit, but by recognizing as the fundamental philosophic problem this *presumption* on reason's part.[58]

Philosophy, when it becomes radical, is no longer a vehicle of absolute knowledge; it is the expression of a secular faith.

It could be argued at this point that a radical perspective in philosophy is strangely akin to the original perspective of biblical faith. Its critical stance could be regarded as the logical outcome of "that criticism of false gods which Christianity has introduced into our history."[59] An all-important difference remains, however. The biblical perspective is grounded in the being of God; hence it still requires a heteronomous or alienated attitude toward our contingency. A radically secular perspective, on the other hand, is directly grounded in that contingency and is identical with its autonomous self-affirmation. From a radical perspective, therefore, it is faith in the problematic being of man and the world rather than faith in the absolute being of God which most adequately reflects and preserves the original wonder and mystery of being.

This perspective in contemporary metaphysics is more radical in its affirmation of the contingency of being than even the most secular of theologies, but it is more mindful of its own limitations than either the theistic or antitheistic doctrines of the past. Merleau-Ponty's motto for Socrates might well be an emblem for his own radical perspective in philosophy and at the same time an ironic rejoinder to the theologian's eschatological claims: "He believes *more* than they, but also he believes in another way, and in a different sense."[60]

III    *Post-Theistic
Thinking*

# 6

# The Metaphysics
of Marxist Humanism:
Being and Man

Having sketched the origins of a radical metaphysics in the philosophical writings of the young Marx and described the efforts of contemporary metaphysicians to articulate a radically secular perspective on being, man, and the world that could take the place of traditional ontotheology, we must now determine whether it is possible to use this new metaphysics to work out post-theistic alternatives within the two traditions we have been considering. In this chapter and the next, we shall look at what happens when a radical metaphysics is used to rethink the philosophical possibilities of the Marxist tradition. In two following chapters, we shall ask whether a similar undertaking is possible in a Christian setting.

There are a number of reasons why Marxism could be regarded as the contemporary world view which most adequately expresses, theoretically and practically, the insights of a metaphysics of radical secularity. We have already seen that historically Marxism, along with Hegelianism and the traditions to which it gave rise (e.g., pragmatism), serves as one of the most important philosophical resources for the contemporary development of a radically secular metaphysics. The influence of Marxism on Sartre and Merleau-Ponty testifies to this fact. Further, as recent developments in Eastern Europe have shown, Marxism appears to contain within it the social and ideological resources necessary for constructing a "socialism with a human face." Our concern in these chapters is, however, not with the history of ideas or the chances for reform in the socialist states.

The latter in particular involves considerations of an economic, social, and political sort which fall outside the scope of this study. Our interest here is, rather, with the thesis advanced by contemporary Marxist philosophers that their tradition has the theoretical capacity to appropriate an ontology of radical secularity which has developed subsequent to, and in large part independently of, their own tradition. It is this assertion made on behalf of the continuing vitality and ideological superiority of the Marxist philosophical tradition that will occupy the center of our attention.

In considering this claim, we shall draw primarily on the philosophical writings of Western and Eastern European Marxists, such as Roger Garaudy, Ernst Bloch, Milan Prucha, and Gajo Petrovic, philosophers who, by drawing on the work of the young Marx as well as on the secular existentialists, have succeeded in fashioning what I shall be calling the new Marxist humanism.

The first thing to be said about this new Marxist humanism is that it is not simply a revival of exegetical interest in the early writings of the founder. Nor is it the isolated effort of a few figures on the periphery of Marxist thought. As the number and character of the contributions to Erich Fromm's volume *Socialist Humanism*[1] convincingly demonstrate, we are dealing here with the mainstream of a philosophical movement which is aimed at redesigning the face of contemporary Marxism and which, in turn, reflects a reawakening and revitalization of Marxism that goes far beyond the confines of theory alone.

The most apparent and striking feature of this movement of post-Stalinist Marxism is its recurring emphasis upon the centrality of man. Typical in this regard is the comment by the Yugoslav philosopher Gajo Petrovic, that "man, who was excluded from the Stalinist version of Marxist philosophy as an abstraction, is in the center of authentic Marxist thought."[2] For Eastern and Western European Marxists alike, the new Marxism is seen as a philosophy of human existence as a whole. It is a reassertion of the total humanism of the original Marx over against the truncated economism or reductionistic materialism of Marxist scholasticism. It is an explicit and deliberate repudiation of the

traditional Marxist attempt to interpret man primarily in
socioeconomic categories to the exclusion of those moral and
uniquely existential questions which belong to man's existence
as a whole.[3] In the hands of Marxist orthodoxy, Marx's original
concern for complete human emancipation was converted into
an ideological sanction for opportunistic and oppressive state
power. Marxist philosophy was reduced to the abstract banalities
of dialectical materialism, and socialist society was made the
object of political manipulation. The Marxist humanists see their
task as that of restoring Marxism's social and economic concerns
to their original setting within a broader and deeper search for a
new type of human existence. Like their radical religious counterparts, they are engaged in the task of demythologizing and
"secularizing," or radically humanizing, Marxism itself.[4]

The chief difficulty in this attempt to rethink Marxism along
more fully humanistic lines is that, though most of its exponents
talk about it as if it were a restatement of the insights of the
original Marx,[5] in fact, as we have seen, Marx himself never
really systematically elaborated a philosophy of man. For all their
references to the early Marx, however, contemporary Marxist
philosophers are quite aware of this fact and thus of the mag-
nitude of the task they confront.[6] Petrovic notes, for example,
that whatever their faults as original thinkers, Engels, Plekhanov,
and Lenin were at least correct in feeling "the need to develop
more explicitly and fully the ontological foundations of Marx's
philosophy."[7] For the Marxist humanists, however, the
metaphysical tradition of classical Marxism has proved to be
inadequate to the humanistic elements more recently discovered
in Marx's earlier writings. The development of the metaphysical
foundations of Marx's humanism therefore confronts these new
Marxists as a job that still needs to be done.[8]

There is a further difficulty. The job of constructing a
humanistic metaphysics for contemporary Marxism also cannot
be understood as simply an unfolding of something already there
implicit in Marx's own sketchy anthropology. In the first place,
there can be no true account of Marx's original philosophy as it
was in itself. As Petrovic explains, "The exposition of the 'true'
Marx is possible only as interpretation"; hence "it is illusory to

think that we can give an absolutely objective account of Marx's thought as it is in itself."[9] In the history of philosophy at least, every reading of a text is at the same time a further bit of philosophizing as well. Second, despite the legitimizing references back to the early Marx, the development of an ontological foundation for a Marxist humanism is something that has become a real philosophical possibility only in our own time. It would therefore be a mistake to criticize the efforts of these contemporary Marxists for failing to adhere to the criteria for an historical reconstruction of the real intentions of the young Marx. Their thought must be viewed and judged as an attempt to extend the possibilities of the Marxist tradition. Marxist humanism is not an exercise in textual exegesis, but an endeavor at original philosophical thought. As Petrovic points out:

The essence of Marx's philosophy cannot be reduced to what Marx's or Marxist philosophy has been so far; nor to an empirical description or summing up of what Marx or some Marxist wrote about philosophy. The question of the essence of Marx's philosophy aims at discovering what makes Marxist philosophy what it is: the fundamental ideological possibility of our times, the critical humanistic thought of modern man about himself and his world. Therefore the answer to this question cannot be a report on what has been or is still going on, but rather participation in the creation of something that can and should be. A correct answer cannot be obtained by a detailed comparison of quotations from Marx, but only by creative thinking in the spirit of Marx, by co-thinking with Marx and by thinking through Marx's guiding ideas.[10]

Contemporary Marxist philosophy is therefore quite consciously an effort to create something new.

There is another aspect to the humanist reinterpretation of the Marxist tradition, one that both radicalizes this philosophy and reflects its openness to a different way of thinking in metaphysics. Marxist humanism does not view itself as a rationalistic system or deterministic doctrine of historical inevitability—that is, it no longer views Marxism theologically. The Marxist world view, from this new humanist perspective, presents itself "not as the *result* of a particular transitory historical situation, but as a *task,* the fulfillment of which is not guaranteed by the inevitability of a happy 'end of the story.' "[11] As a

radically secular and humanistic approach to man, contemporary
Marxism sees itself as "not only and not so much a set of *answers*
as a structure of *questions* and *tensions* that problematize man."[12]
Contemporary Marxist humanism is thus not only a critique of
Marxist orthodoxy and a creative extension of the philosophy of
the original Marx. It is also and, more important, an expression
of that activity of permanent self-criticism which the modern
world regards as essential to the humanizing of man.

Because of these self-critical and humanizing tendencies, contemporary Marxist philosophers have felt free not only to return
to the earlier sources of their own tradition or to draw on the
resources of contemporary non-Marxist philosophy but also to
acknowledge their indebtedness to the Western religious tradition and contemporary theology as well. They have reaffirmed
the ideological validity of prophetic, heretic, and revolutionary
movements within the Jewish and Christian traditions. They
have also demonstrated a willingness to incorporate the traditional insights of religion into the more subjective and transcendental dimensions of human existence.

Given these new initiatives in contemporary Marxist thought,
the religious thinker who is serious about coming to terms with
this alternative view of man must consent to put his polemical
weapons aside for a moment and first look more carefully at what
these philosophers are trying to do. Otherwise, he risks having
his usual criticisms—for example, that Marxism does not or cannot speak to the whole man—simply rejected as uninformed.
The orthodox Marxist, for his part, must consider whether he is
really prepared to answer the revisionary Marxist's question,
"Why should a living Marxism be weaker than a dead one?"[13]
Since it is the continuing vitality and validity of the Marxist
tradition which are at stake, for him to adopt any other attitude
toward this impetus for humanization is to condemn Marxism to
the fate reserved for it by its secular and theological critics. From
both sides of this dialogue, it is therefore necessary to look at
how these new Marxists go about putting a metaphysics of radical
secularity to work in the context of a specifically Marxist
perspective on being, man, and the world. Only when this has
been done will we be in a position to ask whether the radical

religionist has something more to say that cannot be said just as well by the philosophers we shall now consider.

## An Ontology of
## Not-Yet-Being

The most systematic attempt to work out the metaphysical foundations of a new Marxist humanism is Ernst Bloch's ontology of "not-yet-being."[14] Bloch's metaphysics aims at a revolutionary reversal or categorial inversion of the conceptual priorities of classical and early modern ontology. As in the ontologies of such non-Marxist thinkers as Heidegger, James, and Dewey, in Bloch too, concepts such as possibility, temporality, and contingency no longer refer to inferior modes of being, but have become the fundamental elements of a new interpretation of being. While it is thus in harmony with the achievements of contemporary non-Marxist metaphysics, Bloch's ontology may also be seen as the further carrying out of the young Marx's humanistic inversion of the categories of Hegelian ontology. It follows, as we shall see, that Bloch's ontology represents a radical alternative not only to traditional theological thinking but also to the quasi-theological metaphysics of classical Marxist materialism.

### Possibility

Bloch begins by arguing the need for a concept of being that goes beyond the traditional connotations of the concept of reality. The being of things is something more than just their actuality or presence-before-us (cf. Heidegger's *Vorhandenheit*). The reality of a thing, narrowly understood, is itself surrounded by the much greater realm of its real and objective possibilities. We live, says Bloch, "surrounded by possibility, not merely by presence." This invocation of a quasi-substantive domain of possibility is not just another instance of ontological mystification. Possibility, argues Bloch, is "an exactly definable concept; namely partial conditionality. The world is not yet completely determined, it is still somewhat open: like tomorrow's weather."[15] Or again:

"Possibility is the partial present existence of conditions, though a givenness that is never sufficient for their realization."[16]

Bloch traces this larger notion of being as inclusive of possibility back to Aristotle. But for Aristotle, says Bloch, being is conceived as passive possibility, whereas Bloch envisages another, more active connotation of the term. In the Aristotelian left and again in Spinoza's *natura naturans,* we see the development of this more active concept of possibility into an understanding of the being of the world "which meets man halfway and gives him a well-founded direction so that he can act creatively in a confident manner and in complete seriousness—not with confidence, for that would be based upon a determined world, but with fear and hope which are based on the not yet determined."[17] In Bloch's own version of this ontology of possibility, his concept of being as "not-yet-being," we find a new understanding of reality as that which comprehends "actuality together with its possibilities, and matter together with its future."[18]

### Temporality

An ontology which incorporates the dimension of the not-yet into its concept of being is also a doctrine which conceives of being in temporal terms. There are different ways of conceiving the temporality of being, however. According to Aristotle and Hegel, for example, temporal development is seen as merely the evolution of what, in the ontologically important sense, already is. Hegel's outwardly dynamic or processive understanding of reality is in fact, says Bloch, a doctrine of mere appearance, not of being: "What has already existed eternally is being unrolled."[19] Bloch's concern, on the other hand, is for concepts of being and temporality which allow for the possibility of something that is, in the ontologically important sense, not yet—that is, for possibilities of being that are entirely new. Accordingly he conceives of the ontology of not-yet-being as a doctrine of the temporality of being which emphasizes the openness of the future rather than the priority of that which already or eternally is.

In fact, says Bloch, the choice is not between an ontology for which time is of the essence and an ontology for which time is

mere appearance. The hidden secret of the Aristotelian and
Hegelian doctrines of the transtemporal or eternal essence of
being is the priority of the temporal dimension of the past. That
which eternally is is that which already exists and has always
been. Harvey Cox reports an incident which sheds light on
Bloch's claim. Once when Bloch was asked to summarize his
philosophy in a single sentence, he replied: "S is not yet P."
Bloch was calling attention to the fact that when one rests one's
understanding of being, as thinkers since Parmenides have done,
upon the identity principle of "S = S," one falls into a static and
nontemporal or, more precisely, a past-temporal, deterministic
view of reality. In Plato, for example, "That which has been
enjoys primacy over that which is to come; indeed, very being (or
essence) itself is identical with having-been-ness. . . . The dialectical cosmology of the disciplines is therefore only a journey-
*anamnesis* to logic-ontology *ante rem*."[20] The ontology of eternity
turns out to be an ideological disguise for an alienated concept of
temporality in which the possibilities of the future are predetermined by the givens of the past.

By emphasizing the priority of the future, on the other hand,
Bloch's ontology of not-yet-being is an effort to liberate us from
the ontotheological myth of transtemporal, eternal being and to
free us, instead, for an ontology of radical temporality, an ontology of the finitude of being viewed as the unconditional openness of the future. Bloch's ontology of not-yet-being is designed
not to accommodate the alienated unfolding of that which already or eternally is but to assist in the revolutionary overthrow
of those existing structures of reality which prevent the
emergence of that which is liberating and new. As Cox points
out, Bloch's ontology of not-yet-being is an onto-logic of radical
change, "a new logic appropriate to a time when we have discovered at last that change is the only permanent thing we have."[21]

*Contingency*

Bloch's analysis of the concepts of possibility and temporality
brings us to what is perhaps the most paradoxical aspect of his
inversion of the categorial priorities of traditional ontology.

Along with philosophers like Heidegger and Merleau-Ponty, Bloch insists upon the radical contingency of being without rejecting altogether a sense for that which is unconditional. The secret of course is that the idea of the unconditional is no longer to be interpreted in the ordinary philosophical way in terms of a reference to the Absolute. Rather, when approached from the perspective of an ontology of not-yet-being, the unconditional may still be interpreted in a positive sense as an idea set up in opposition to the idea of a world that is totally (already, eternally) conditioned. The idea of unconditional or absolute being is the idea of a reality that is not yet conditioned rather than of a reality that is beyond all conditions whatsoever. The idea of a reality that is in this sense unconditional is thus not the idea of something that transcends the realm of contingent being. It is another way of emphasizing that very contingency. A concept of being as permanently not-yet-conditioned is an idea of being as radically, irreducibly contingent.[22]

This approach to the contingency of being also requires, says Bloch, a reevaluation of the traditional concept of nothingness or nonbeing. By itself, the term "nothingness" is, like "possibility," a clearly definable concept—namely, the partial or total absence of something: the world is not this nor yet this. Traditionally, however, this concept has been defined relative to the Parmenidean concept of being as a plenum of substance and value. It has thus stood for an absolute vacuum of being and meaning—the threatening void. When being is reinterpreted in terms of possibility, temporality, and contingency, however, then the concept of that which is not must be brought into a different and more positive relation to the concept of that which is. Thus for Bloch, nothingness is "ontologized into 'not-yet.'"[23]

What is particularly interesting about this reinterpretation of nothingness is that it offers clear evidence that Bloch's neo-Marxist ontology of not-yet-being does not hold out as much promise for theology as may have initially appeared. For Bloch, the phenomena of contingency and nothingness are ontological ultimates. There is no God to pick up the pieces on the far side of the finitude of things. This is to attack the theological perspective at its very root. To the theologian, Bloch must inevitably appear to have evaded the question of the ultimate significance of the threat of nonbeing. By "interpreting the destructive power of nothingness as a 'not-yet' of that which is possible, but as yet unrealized," Bloch in effect ignores "the regions over which nothingness holds sway and where human beings experience suffering and death." His ontology therefore "comprehends nothingness only to the extent that the courage to hope can 'do something'; it cannot apply hope to no-longer-being."[24] As Cox and Moltmann are forced to conclude, Bloch's ontology, though profoundly illuminating and suggestive, is ultimately unavailable as a metaphysical basis for contemporary theology.

At this point, the gap between the perspectives of theology and an ontology of radical secularity becomes especially apparent and unbridgeable. The theologian is compelled to charge Bloch with having a truncated view of reality or, more specifically, with having failed to deal with the final threat of nothingness. For Bloch, on the other hand, the theologian's charge is not so much false as the ideological expression of an alienated relationship to the contingency of being: "The fact remains that emptiness is only the first definition of the space from which the certainty of being has been cleared out; its second, instantly following definition is *fermentation, an open effective sphere* for the human subject, as well as for a far from finished subject of the natural environment."[25] Rejecting both the theologian's need to hypostasize the open future as the being of God and the nihilistic alternative of grounding ontology in man's subjective projections into the void, Bloch draws instead, as did Marx, on the tradition of left-wing Aristotelianism, which guards the ontological integrity of this "fermentation" by positing it as an intrinsic characteristic of "the world-substance, mundane matter itself."[26] If in this context Bloch still considers his ontology of not-yet-being to be a materialism, it is because, as a radically secular ontology, it must be understood, like traditional materialism and in conscious opposition to every theological perspective, as expressing "the world's explanation of itself."[27]

Milan Prucha, a young Czech philosopher, is another contemporary Marxist who uses the doctrine of the contingency of being to provide the metaphysical foundations for a new Marxist humanism and to reject any kind of theistic alternative. An expert on contemporary phenomenology and existentialism as well as an early pioneer in the European dialogue between Marxists and Christians, Prucha goes even further and is more explicit than Bloch in spelling out the implications of the ontology of finitude for theological thinking. In his article "Marxism as a Philosophy of Human Existence,"[28] Prucha draws on a neo-Heideggerian or ek-sistential analysis of finitude to formulate a nontheological and distinctively Marxist reading of the phenomenon of contingency.

Prucha begins his argument by rejecting, like Bloch, the orthodox Marxist approach to metaphysical materialism. He points out, perhaps more devastatingly than any theistic critic could, that the same arguments which can be brought to bear against the ontotheologic of theism (God as "the principle of all principles") count against the logic of traditional materialism as well. A finitist ontology, Prucha observes, undermines not only the logic of theism but also the speculative ontology of matter: "Seen in this light the style of philosophy possessed in common by materialists and theologians—that is to say the subordination of social life, historicity and the entire immanent sphere to the presuppositions of a cognizable essence of the absolute—is *more important* than the difference between God and matter."[29]

The new-style ontology of radical secularity cuts across this traditional distinction of theism and materialism (or atheism) and, in its place, substitutes a finitist approach to being. Prucha goes on to argue, however, that while this inversion of the traditional logic of being (whether theistic or materialist) is fatal to every theological perspective on being, it is not necessarily fatal to the prospects of a Marxist metaphysics. In fact, it enables Marxist philosophers for the first time to spell out the truly radical implications of Marx's original philosophical ideas.

The issue for theology is as follows: To the extent that a radical theology attempts to assimilate a radically secular doctrine of real, this-worldly transcendence, as opposed to an illusory, precritical notion of transcendence, to the extent that it draws upon an ek-sistential analysis of being as an alternative to the traditional derivation of existence from the highest being, does it not immediately place itself in an untenable position? "If modern philosophy with its new conception of existence is to be accepted by theology, *in what terms will theology then speak of God, how can it still remain theology?*"[30]

The problem for the theologian is that, as Prucha points out (and as we have already learned from Merleau-Ponty), it is a cardinal insight of this contemporary philosophy of existence that "at the frontier of all knowledge no concept exists which, as in a vise, holds the world together in a total unity as one universal order; there is no all-inclusive meaning to be found there in which all knowledge could rest."[31] This does not mean that existence is therefore to be understood, as in Sartre, as based in an empty negativity, a kind of "negative ontological dialectic of the transitory." Nothing would suit the theist better! Rather, for contemporary ontology, existence is a positive space or openness in which is contained the presence and possibilities of things at any given time or place. Contrary to the claims of the theologian, this openness or contingency of being is not a negative or truncated phenomenon; it is, rather, "a far too 'capacious' space for the being issuing from it to be able clearly to unveil its countenance, to betray its true character."[32] In Bloch's terms, it is a reality which is never fully determined, which is permanently not-yet-being.

In other words, it is precisely at this juncture that the cautionary note against the traditional theistic leap must be sounded. What a contemporary ontology of the radical contingency of being is trying to say is not what the theist would like to pretend it is saying. It is completely wrongheaded, says Prucha, to see here simply another effort by metaphysicians to express that which is infinite in the language of that which is finite. The contemporary concept of *Existenz*, or of being as radically finite, does not leave metaphyiscal room for completion from the side of faith. The attempt of contemporary theology to begin speaking of God at this point once again betrays its basic inability to appreciate the radical implications of a finitist approach to being. For contemporary metaphysics, the contingency of being, the irreducibility of finitude, "possesses a considerably deeper meaning" than the traditional theological reference to the incomprehensibility of God.[33]

The question which an ontology of radical finitude poses for theology, is therefore "the primitive but fundamental question: *then why go on using the word 'God'?"*

Because faith demands it? But then theology cannot use this word *beyond* the boundaries of philosophy . . . but exclusively in opposition to philosophy. For if philosophy considers it necessary now to point to existence and now to preserve silence on the subject, it is not abstaining from using the word "God" because it does not know, or know for certain, whether that which it does not know might become an object of belief. On the contrary, philosophy's silence is a *necessity,* and theology's talk of God takes no account of this philosophical necessity.[34]

For the Marxist, on the other hand, the finitist perspective of contemporary ontology is a confirmation of his own position: "Finiteness is the only sphere in which transcendence is present."[35]

For Prucha, it follows that it is the paradoxical task of the Marxist philosopher to bear witness to the insufficiency of the traditional theological notion of transcendence. It is precisely their interpretation of transcendence as infinite, absolute being that hampers the theologians in their pursuit of a radically secular appreciation of transcendence as the open-ended contingency of being. The Marxist's task, ironically, is "to spur them on to greater radicalism in this pursuit."[36] To speak of the transcendence of being is not to speak of something other or higher than the realm of finite being. It is a way of accentuating the irreducibility and positive significance of finitude itself.

There is a general consensus among the Marxist humanists about this fundamental difference between their finitist perspective in ontology and the perspective of every theology. Thus Roger Garaudy too agrees with Bloch and Prucha that "for the Marxist, the infinite is absence and exigency, while for the Christian, it is promise and presence":[37]

This future, open on the infinite, is the only transcendence which is known to us as atheists. . . . The reason is that we, from our experience, similar to the Christian's, of the inadequacy of all relative and partial being, do not conclude to a presence, that of the "one necessary," which answers to our anguish and impatience. If we reject the very name of God, it is because the name implies a presence, a reality, whereas it is only an exigency which we live. . . . We can live this exigency, and we can act it out, but we cannot conceive it, name it or expect it. Even less can we hypostasize it under the name of transcendence. Regarding this totality, this absolute, I can say everything except: It is. For what it is is always deferred, and always growing, like man himself. If we want to give it a name, the name will not be that of God. . . . The most beautiful and exalted name which can be given to this exigency is the name of man. . . . This exigency in man is, I think, the flesh of your God.

In other words, what Marxist atheism (better, humanism) points to in its dialogue with theology is not the transcendence of God but the transcendence of man, a doctrine of horizontal rather than vertical transcendence, an "eschatological humanism without God."

The Marxist humanist cannot in the last analysis separate his criticism of theology from his affirmation of man. The traditional concepts of theology receive what suggestiveness they have from their capacity to reflect indirectly the exigency and mystery of man. For Bloch, for example, the idea of *Deus absconditus* serves to illuminate "the *problem* of the legitimate mystery called *homo absconditus*." The religious notion of that which is ineffable or incomprehensible serves to guarantee that the fundamental mystery of being, which includes the being of man, is not buried or forgotten. "Numen, *numinosum,* mystery, even a No to the existing world: none of these is ever anything but the *secret human element* itself."[38]

Theology affirms only in an indirect manner what an ontology of radical finitude asserts directly. The Marxist humanist's critique of traditional ontotheology is based on his prior commitment to a finitist ontology that secularizes and yet preserves that sense of the enduring mystery of being which humanizes man. It is in the contemporary doctrine of the finitude of being that Marxist philosophers like Bloch, Prucha, and Garaudy find a philosophical basis for that positive-humanist alternative to a merely negative, antitheistic metaphysics which Marx called for a century ago.

The Phenomenon of Man:
Existence as Praxis

Ernst Bloch argues that periods of cultural upheaval and transition *(Zeitwende)* like our own, a time when all of our basic
assumptions about man are being called into question and when
new possibilities are emerging whose significance we can
scarcely discern, are paradoxically those moments in history
when the sort of being man is is suddenly and dramatically
revealed. He is a being who hopes, who lives by the forward-
driving logic of promise and expectation. This fact about man is
not just an accidental feature of human nature in our time. It
points to an existential-ontological structure constitutive of the
way we are in the world. "Man is  . . .  that creature who hopes,
who phantasizes, who dreams about the future and strives to
attain it."[39] Man as such exists as a being who is open to the
future. To be a human being, says Bloch, is to be *unterwegs,* to
be on the way toward something else, something new.[40]
Philosophically speaking, therefore, man's being may be described as a capacity for self-transcendence.

There is of course nothing distinctively Marxist about this
concept of man. It is a concept which Bloch shares with the
existentialists and the radical theologians. But a difference arises
between Bloch and the theologian when it becomes necessary to
provide this concept of man with a grounding in ontology. Bloch
agrees that a Marxist philosophy of man cannot be narrowly
anthropological, but must be rooted in the prior question of the
nature of being. Unlike the theologians, however, and like the
secular existentialists, Bloch views this as a matter of showing
that his concept of man exemplifies the general categories of an
ontology of finitude rather than as a demand to ground man's
being in an alien reality that transcends the structures of finite
being. In fact, Marxism's claim to radicality as a doctrine of
human being is unintelligible apart from this prior grounding in a
finitist doctrine of being itself.[41]

Marxism's distinctiveness as a radical anthropology emerges
more clearly when we pass from these ontological generalities to
the phenomenological specifics which flesh them out. To under-

stand man's capacity for self-transcendence, says Garaudy, we do not need to posit its origins in some higher being essentially alien to man. It is enough simply to observe that this possibility is what distinguishes the human species from the other species of natural beings. The Marxist concept of transcendence rests in man's experience that, though he is in one sense a part of nature, he is also profoundly different from the rest of nature because of his ability by means of practical, self-conscious activity to transcend his immediate natural state and create his own human nature. For the Marxist humanists, as for Marx, man's capacity for self-transcendence is in the first instance identical with this material or practical ability to re-create his own being, to bring into existence and to universalize a human world that transcends the necessities of physical or biological nature. It is not an alienated gift of the gods but that mythical first act of history whereby man leaves behind the closed world of nature and inaugurates the story of human freedom.[42]

For Marxist humanism, man's capacity for self-transcendence is therefore not only an existential-ontological structure of man's being. It is also, more concretely, the practico-historical initiative that launches the movement of history and with it the struggle for what Marx termed universal human emancipation. Not only in the cultural upheavals of our time but already in mankind's first historical act, man is a being who possesses the revolutionary capacity, ontological and historical, to transform himself and the world and in so doing to create a way of being that is qualitatively new.

This linkage of a contemporary ek-sistential ontology of man with the traditional Marxist phenomenology of praxis is the central philosophical achievement of Marxist humanism. It constitutes a radically secular alternative to the traditional Christian understanding of transcendence, and at the same time furnishes conceptual resources for overcoming some of the traditional dilemmas of Marxist anthropology, in particular those associated with a narrowly mechanical or deterministic view of man. On the other hand, it also provides the philosophical basis for Marxist humanism's assertion that it preserves in a higher synthesis the insights of Christian theology into the subjective and transcen-

dental needs of men as well as classical Marxism's stress on the
material and necessitarian aspects of human life. In the remainder of this section, we shall look at how Marxist humanists like
Garaudy, Prucha, and Petrovic employ their new understanding
of praxis to reinterpret such related issues as freedom versus
necessity, or existential subjectivity versus the objectification of
man's being in material activity. It is here that we may see most
clearly the distinctive nature of the metaphysics of Marxist
humanism.

According to Garaudy, the major problem facing contemporary Marxist philosophy is the task of reconciling the two major
strands in the Western humanist tradition: our emphasis upon
man's capacity for rational (especially technical) mastery of the
world, inherited from Greek humanism; and our commitment to
the value of human, historical initiative and responsibility, with
its emphasis upon the phenomena of choice and decision, inherited from the Judeo-Christian tradition. Though these elements
are historically distinct in their origins, Marxism views both as
indispensable ingredients of a radically secular humanism.
Philosophically, however, their juxtaposition has not always
been a comfortable one. By the time Marx was reaching intellectual maturity in the mid-nineteenth century, for example, these
elements had become embodied in the extreme antitheses of
Hegel and Kierkegaard: the former with his stress upon the
intrinsic necessity of the development of reason in the objective
manifestations of nature and history; the latter with his stress
upon the irreducible uniqueness and primacy of man's subjective
or lived existence. Marx's early philosophical writings were, in
part, an attempt to reunite these separate emphases in a single,
unified concept of man. Marx's concept of praxis was consciously
intended to be the key to a higher synthesis in philosophical
anthropology which brought together the Hegelian appreciation
(in mystified form) of the objective necessities that motivated
human history and the Kierkegaardian (or, in Marx's case, the
Feuerbachian) emphasis upon concrete "sensuous human activity."[43]

By the latter part of the nineteenth century, however, under
the influence of Engel's elaboration of Marx's practical

materialism in terms of the quasi-Hegelian formula of "necessity become self-conscious," classical Marxism came to be identified with an unbalanced emphasis upon the more deterministic or necessitarian elements in Western humanism. The presupposition of Engel's neo-Hegelian interpretation of materialism was that man may be conceived metaphysically as a particular (though highly complex) instance of the type of being which characterizes the movement of matter or nature in general. Marx himself had argued that man was a part of nature. But, as we have seen, for Marx, the important thing about praxis as the distinctively human form of species activity was that it represented at the same time a radical break from all previous types of natural being and the emergence of a qualitatively new level of being. It is this original Marxist insight into the qualitative novelty of human existence which, according to contemporary Marxists like Garaudy, was obscured in subsequent Marxism by a reductionistic theory of dialectical materialism and which, accordingly, was left to secular existentialism to articulate in our own day.[44]

When we turn to consider the possibilities for metaphysical agreement between Marxist humanism and existentialism, we find, however, that not all is sweetness and light. First of all, it must be remembered that existentialism, especially Sartre's early existentialism (since his, rather than Heidegger's, was the chief variety of existentialism represented in the initial dialogue with Marxism) also arose partially as a reaction to the excessive claims of rationalism, objectivism, and necessitarianism in the various branches of European philosophy, ranging all the way from the ambitious systems of idealism to the narrow factuality of positivism. It thus included an attack upon the scholastic rigidities of Marxist orthodoxy.[45] However, as if by some internal dialectical necessity, Sartre's own humanism appeared to be characterized by an equal but opposite unbalance. In its violent polemic against a priori rationalism, deterministic materialism, and the transcendental dogmas of Christian theology, Sartre's existentialist humanism took the form of a Kierkegaardian exaltation of the absolute freedom and ontological irreducibility of subjective consciousness and choice.[46]

For the Marxist humanists, Sartre's existentialism therefore

does not represent a significant advance beyond the philosophical problematic already contained in Engels' dialectical
materialism. It is the same situation—only this time seen from
the other side. From whichever side it is approached, this hostile
dialectic of Sartrean existentialism and orthodox Marxist
materialism confronts us with an ontological divorce between
subjective choice and the material conditions which make choice
possible. In the case of Marxist orthodoxy, it has meant the
abandonment of human subjectivity in favor of a one-sided stress
on quasi-natural necessity. In Sartre's case, it results in the at-
tribution of an absolute but abstract and empty freedom to an
equally absolute but empty and abstract, neo-Cartesian ego
whose ultimate concern is with his own bare existence (and his
own death) and whose ultimate insight, accordingly, is an
abstractly despairing (but concretely self-alienated) conviction
of the meaninglessness or futility of life.[47]
   Whatever one may think of the accuracy of the neo-Marxist's
presentation of Sartre's existentialism, it does draw attention, as
did Heidegger, to a curious dialectical interdependency (rather
than contradiction, as Sartre dualistically maintains), and hence a
common basis on ontological agreement, between the metaphysically abstract subject-ism of early existentialism and the equally
speculative and abstract objectivism or determinism of orthodox
Marxist materialism. As Prucha points out:

Mechanical materialism conceived man as a thing among things, as a
machine, but it was not capable of erecting a spiritual dam against
idealism. As a philosophy for which reality exists only in the form
of an object, it unconsciously placed the philosophizing ego before
the reality from which the ego observed and judged it. Thus it
transformed the real ego into a de-realized and unreal ego, into
pure self-consciousness. Reality degenerated into dead matter
incompatible with any kind of subjectivity.[48]

While orthodox Marxism repudiates the label of mechanical
materialism, it is plain that, for the Marxist humanists, orthodox
Marxism's gloss of Marx's historical materialism has, in ontological as well as political fact, resulted in little more than a new
version of the old ontological mystification of man's being in
terms of the being of things (nature).
   Here we have the key to the otherwise puzzling claim that

there is a hidden agreement between Sartrean existentialism and Marxist materialism. In both philosophies, man's being is determined, either positively or negatively, by the categories used to describe the being of (natural) things. Positively, in the case of Marxist materialism, insofar as it sees man's being as a complex instance of the being of nature. Negatively, in Sartre's case, insofar as the categories of man's being are defined as the negation of the categories that determine the world's being—hence their one-sided abstractness or emptiness as positive categories of man's being. In both philosophies, in other words, the description of the being of man rests on what Gilbert Ryle calls a category mistake, a fundamental error in ontological description wherein the phenomena of one logical type or category of being are presented in terms derived from another type of category. On the dualist (Sartrean) hypothesis, for example, because the actions of persons cannot be described in terms of the movements of bodies, it is therefore thought that they must be described in counterpart idioms, that is, "mere negatives of the specific descriptions given to bodies." Consciousness is not being; therefore, it is a kind of nonbeing or nothingness, an absolute freedom from the deterministic categories of being. For Ryle as for Prucha, the antithesis between idealism (or Sartre) and materialism thus proves to be a secondary one. "The belief that there is a polar opposition between Mind and Matter is the belief that they are terms of the same logical type." That is, the differences between consciousness and material existence are agreed on both sides to be differences within a common ontological framework provided by the general notion of a being-a-thing. Between materialism and idealism, consequently, there is no real choice.[49]

For the Marxist humanists, neither classical Marxist materialism nor Sartrean existentialism offers the ontological resources needed to overcome the dualism in Western thinking about man. They agree with Heidegger that a radical philosophy of man requires a new set of categories, one that puts into a different perspective the alleged opposition of subject and object, consciousness and thing, or freedom and necessity, one that is derived from a positive concept of the distinctively human way of being rather than from an ancient ontology based on the being of nonhuman things. If such a philosophy is to bring together both sides of the "weakened tradition" of Western humanism, it must proceed from a "completely new theoretical base."[50] What is required is a logically primitive, or distinct and irreducible, category for man's way of being which nonetheless possesses an internal structure that joins these elements in a logically unified way. It must be a dialectical rather than a dualistic or one-sidedly reductionistic view of man's being as, in Heidegger's term, being-in-the-world.[51] For the Marxist humanists, the category which best expresses this qualitatively novel phenomenon of human being-in-the-world is the concept of praxis. As we have seen, in Marx, this notion stood for a unique and indissoluble synthesis of the subjective-activist and the objective-materialist strands of the Western humanist tradition. Praxis was Marx's demythologized version of Hegel's concrete universal—that is, a metaphysically primitive category of being "whose integrity does not exclude internal differentiation."[52] It is in Marx's concept of praxis as interpreted via Heidegger that the Marxist humanists find the ontological basis for a radical philosophy of man as being-in-the-world.

This dialectical approach to the phenomenon of practical activity enables the Marxist humanists to resist the twin dangers of a subjectivist distortion and an objectivist reduction of man's being. On the one hand, there is the charge that the concept of praxis simply reflects modern man's achievement of technological mastery over nature by means of practical projects which are barely concealed expressions of human will or subjectivity.[53] Bloch tries to counter this subjectivist reading of praxis by reminding us that, for Marxism, man as practical agent must act in concert with the objective movement of historical reality. In other words, he does not view his own ontology of not-yet-being as just another modernist attempt to reduce the openness of man's being to an expression of mere subjectivity. He wants to balance the modern stress on the world's receptivity to the projects of man with its necessary dialectical counterpart, man's responsiveness to the initiatives of the world. For Bloch, the concept of praxis, or human activity, is not simply or even primarily an expression of man's subjective life—that is, his self-reflective consciousness or will. It is a shorthand expression for the total, dialectical situation of man's being-in-the-world: human activity is as much determined by the world's demands upon us, as natural beings, as it is by our designs upon the world as beings who transcend the more immediate or objective relation to nature of other beings.[54]

The other danger to a proper understanding of Marx's concept of praxis comes of course from those critics or apologists who interpret materialism in a quasi-mechanistic or narrowly positivist sense. Marx himself was, however, the first to point out that the chief defect in mechanistic materialism was that it attempted to reduce man to nature, whereas his own concern in developing a practical interpretation of materialism was to relate man to nature.[55] As Marx's First Thesis on Feuerbach makes abundantly clear, this dialectical approach to praxis was meant to ward off both idealist and positivist distortions of the phenomenon of human activity. Praxis (human sensuous activity) represented for Marx the original dialectical matrix, the concrete, living, practical unity, of the active side (consciousness, will, human subjectivity) and the sensuous or objective side (things, reality, man's bodily nature) of man's being-in-the-world. For this reason, it is reappropriated by contemporary Marxist philosophers as the key to a philosophy of man which is capable of serving as a legitimate and philosophically original alternative to the one-sided doctrines of abstract, empty subjectivistic freedom or mechanical, collectivistic determinism that have replaced the antitheses of Kierkegaard and Hegel as the dominant and mutually exclusive anthropologies of our day.

Given their alternative ontological assumptions and starting point in the phenomenon of praxis, how, more specifically, do the Marxist humanists go about resolving the conceptual dichotomies associated with traditional Western thinking about man? Marx himself was convinced that this new category of praxis provided in principle the key to resolving these ancient and hoary dilemmas:

> It is the true resolution of the conflict between existence and essence, objectification and self-affirmation, freedom and necessity, individual and species.
> It is apparent how subjectivism and objectivism, spiritualism and

materialism, activity and passivity lose their opposition and thus
their existence as antitheses. . . .[56]

Unfortunately, Marx never really followed up these suggestive
remarks with a systematic exploration of their further implications. The Marxist humanist is faced once again with the double
task of providing a faithful interpretation of what Marx must
have originally intended but left unsaid together with developing
those insights further in a way that can stand as a contribution in
its own right to the problems of contemporary philosophical
anthropology.

Let us turn first to the traditional dichotomy between freedom
and necessity. The Marxist criticism of secular existentialism
offers as good an entry as any. In their polemic with Sartre, the
Marxist humanists repeatedly stress that the natural structure of
man's finite being is a dialectical openness of man to the world
and of the world to man. Man's chief existential concern, accordingly, will not be with the abstract negativity of his own personal
death but with the ensemble of his practical relationships to the
world of nature and other men.[57] The subjective motor of man's
being-in-the-world, according to Marx, is the passionate urge
toward involvement in the world, or what Marx calls subjective
need. "The sway of the objective entity within me, the sensuous
outbreak of my life-activity, is the passion that here becomes the
*activity* of my being."[58] Praxis, man's productive activity, is the
corresponding objectification of this need and is indispensable
to man's attainment of reality and effectuality in the world. It is
man's self-objectification of himself in the world as a being of
subjective need. What is remarkable about Marx's formulation is
that it understands man's objective reality as simultaneously a
free act wherein he transcends the immediate necessities of
nature and yet an inner, existential necessity of his being. Praxis,
or human activity, is the realization in the world of an ongoing
synthesis or dialectic within man's own being between freedom
(practical activity) and necessity (sensuous need). In fact, for
Marx, it is just this conjunction of opposites that sets man apart
from all other beings. Only of man can it be said that "[his] own
self-realization exists as an inner necessity, a need."[59]

Marx's insistence upon the distinctively practical nature of the

necessity which determines human activity inevitably gives rise
to the question, how does this concept of necessity relate to the
traditional, quasi-mechanistic concept of necessity (as, for example, the laws of natural necessity)? According to Garaudy, this
question is profoundly misleading. For Marx, the only kind of
necessity relevant to a discussion of human activity is that necessity which is an expression of man's subjective needs and the
objective conditions of their satisfaction. Further distinctions
arise only within the framework of this kind of necessity. In
other words, Marx distinguishes between "external and accidental necessity" and "internal and determined necessity."[60] In the
former instance, my activity is a "forced activity, imposed upon
me"; my relations to nature and other men take on a reified
appearance, they appear to me as if they were relations between
things. I begin to think that my practical activity is not the free
expression of my own subjective needs but is indeed only a
manifestion of the laws of natural necessity that apply to the
behavior of nonhuman things. I become, says Marx, externalized
or alienated from my own distinctive possibilities as a human
being. When, on the other hand, my activity is an expression of
internal and determined necessity, it is because I have begun to
achieve a subjective awareness of this alienation and am thus in a
position to initiate a self-determined struggle to overcome it.
Activity which is the result of an internal and determined necessity is thus, for Marx, identical with that free, creative activity
which is the essence of man's distinctive species being.

In the world era of capitalism, according to Marx, it is the
former type of necessity that predominates, for in this system
human relationships are interpreted as economic relationships
between things. Witness the ideological tendency of contemporary philosophers to analyze human action either as an exemplifi-
cation of the categories of natural science or as the abstract,
empty opposite of the categories that apply to things. Positivists
and existentialists alike understand the concept of necessity in
strictly mechanistic, nonpurposive terms. The alienated necessity of human praxis is thus uncritically accepted as an instance of
the natural necessity that characterizes the movement of things.
But the necessity that brings about the transition to a socialist

humanism is, for Marx, a necessity of another sort: "It is no longer a matter of the *external* necessity of the development of a system where man, treated as a mere thing, is not present, but an *inner* necessity in which man is part and parcel of the problem itself."[61] The inner or practical necessity that provides the motive force behind the movement of history is not so much the opposite of mechanical necessity as it is another kind of phenomenon altogether. It is the need and capacity of men to determine for themselves the nature of their activity as opposed to having that activity determined for them under the guise of the impersonal necessity of things. "The chief defect of all previous materialism (including Feuerbach's) is that the object, actuality, sensuousness is conceived only in the form of the *object* . . . but not as *sensuous human activity, praxis,* not subjectively."[62] For Marx, the kind of necessity that matters is not the necessity of "the object" but the necessity peculiar to "human activity, praxis." And here the relevant distinction is between alienated and free activity. "The one takes place without me, the other requires my participation. The one teaches passivity and resignation, while the other is the master of energy and historical initiative."[63] Marx is talking about the needs of persons, not the necessities of things. Above all, he is talking about the need fundamental to human beings—the need of free creative activity.

## 7

The Metaphysics
of Marxist Humanism:
Man and the World

The Phenomen of Man:
Praxis and Subjectivity

The Marxist humanist's task of reconciling the various elements
of the Western tradition cannot be considered complete until he
has shown that the concept of praxis can speak positively to the
subjective dimension of human existence. Specifically, he must
show that Marxism can address itself to the religious or existential needs of man in the boundary situations of life. He must
show also that Marxism is capable of appreciating the independent integrity and practical significance of basic epistemological
notions, including the activity of philosophy itself. Only then can
he presume to offer his philosophy of man as a total humanism.

These are not assignments from which the Marxist humanists
shrink. Roger Garaudy, for example, is willing to admit, in
conscious opposition to the antireligious propaganda of more
orthodox Marxists, that science, including the science of history
or society, does not and cannot answer all the questions which a
man must face. "Science does not give answers to the question
raised by our deepest preoccupations: the meaning of life, for
example—the confrontation with death."[1] It is precisely these
questions, however, which religion traditionally and today existentialism have been concerned to answer. It is therefore not
enough to base a Marxist philosophy of man on economic or
social considerations alone. A living Marxism must exhibit equal

sensitivity to those uniquely human and humanizing questions which disclose the ultimate dimensions of human life.[2]

To be sure, for Garaudy, as for Feuerbach and Marx, the answers given to these questions by religion belong to the realm of myth and therefore constitute unreal or alienated answers. But, as Marx also pointed out, they are answers, however illusory, to genuine human questions. Thus for Garaudy, "the human experience which underlines these questions cannot be ignored by any doctrine, including Marxism."[3] For contemporary Marxists, as for Marx himself, even the death of religion would not signify that these questions had died out. What have traditionally been termed religious questions are, in fact, "deeply human problems, one could say anthropological question."[4] A Marxist philosophy of man therefore has a responsibility to provide positive, secular answers to these questions. Indeed, Marxist humanism can only be enriched by this "need to answer the objections of faith."[5]

As already suggested, Garaudy finds the key to man's quest for ultimate meaning in Marx's definition of man in terms of praxis. As in every philosophical anthropology, the decision as to what constitutes the essence of man's being also governs our understanding of the essential needs of man. Abstractly regarded, the essential need of man is to realize to the fullest possible extent the distinctive capacities or possibilities that make him the sort of being he is. The meaning of human life, accordingly, will lie in man's struggle and success in satisfying this need. For Marx, the essence of man's being is work or labor—that is, a qualitative break with the necessities of nature and a leap forward into the realm of free, conscious, creative activity. It follows that man's essential need is to repeat and extend in each of his acts this original movement of transcendence or history-making freedom. Man's deepest need, the inner or existential necessity which belongs to the very essence of his being and governs the contingencies of his life in history, lies on the far side of the satisfaction of economic interest or biological need. It manifests itself rather as a "transcendent" and "irrepressible need to create."[6] The hidden secret of the material necessity that moves man and history is that it is a need for freedom, for the exercise

and satisfaction of those creative and self-creative capacities that
distinguish man's being from the being of all other things.

Since human activity is subject to the categories of a finitist
ontology, however, man's need and capacity for self-transcendence, along with the search for meaning that these imply,
do not permit us to look for the source or final resolution of
meaning beyond the limits of man's finite being-in-the-world.
Rather, Marx's concept of praxis implies that man can satisfy his
need for ultimate meaning in a real, authentic (as opposed to
illusory) way only through participation in the original and continuing activity of establishing the concrete historical freedom of
men and humanizing the world. Thus Marx and the Marxist
humanists answer the existential question of the ultimate meaning of human life by appealing to a "high doctrine of human work
and of our historic future."[7] Marx's philosophy of praxis is not a
limited, earthbound theory of economic man; it is a vision of
"work in its highest form, creation; unlimited creative work in
the field of scientific research, of literature and the arts, and in
the infinite knowledge of man that is love."[8] To define the
meaning of man's life in terms of his work in the world is not to
demean the demands of the human spirit. It is, rather, to ensure
that his hopes and aspirations will be understood and addressed
in a real rather than an illusory way as a legitimate demand for the
qualitative transformation of his life in this world rather than as
an alienated quest for an ultimate meaning that life in this world,
in the final analysis, is unable to satisfy.

In fact, Garaudy wishes to urge that this is the hidden message of the Judeo-Christian tradition itself. The biblical doctrine
of Creation, over against Greek emanationist theories, views the
existence of the world as the expression not of inevitable necessity but of a free gift of love—in other words, as the expression of
free creative activity. It follows that the nature of human activity
in such a world will be understood not in the terms of Greek
metaphysics as an awareness of necessity but in Judeo-Christian
terms as participation in the creative act of world- and history-
making freedom.[9] For the Marxist humanists, Marx's interpretation of man's being under the category of material praxis is in an
important way a demythologized version of these deepest in-

sights of the biblical tradition. If this is so, then, like that tradition, it is capable of speaking to man's deepest need—the need of sharing in the work of incarnate love, which is the work of world, historical, and human creation. The ultimate meaning of man's life, and of his death, is bodied forth in these works of love.

For the Marxist humanist, Marx's philosophy of praxis represents "the indivisible synthesis of dream and struggle," a practical union of vision and activity designed to inaugurate "a specifically human epoch of history that will no longer be governed by need or the strife of the jungle but by the new dialectics of a creativity of infinite opportunity."[10] It sees man not as a product of the necessities of nature or his historical past but as a being of imaginative vision and practical hope who is capable of transforming the conditions of his present existence and shaping a more human future. The man thus envisioned is a being forever incomplete, never content, "a being for whom self-realization is an unending process, a being who constantly transcends himself and continuously creates his own new and as yet unfulfilled possibilities."[11] In one sense, his quest for ultimate meaning can never be satisfied as long as he remains a man. And yet, in a deeper sense, this is the ultimate, positive significance of what it means to be a man. The concept of praxis is the key to a truly radical humanism which shares with the Judeo-Christian tradition a common desire and commitment "to make a man of every man, to make him a creative being."[12]

This linkage of contemporary ontology to Marx's notion of praxis provides Marxist humanism with philosophical possibilities not available to Marx himself. But it also makes possible an insight into the larger, practical nature of ontology itself. Contemporary ontology must itself be viewed as a species of praxis, albeit praxis on the level of philosophical theory rather than direct political action. For if the Marxist humanist's ontology of praxis enables Marxists to assimilate the insights of Greek and Judeo-Christian humanism, it also enables them to draw ontology itself more directly into the service of actual revolutionary praxis. In this we recognize the typically Marxian stress on the necessary unity between theory and practice. Marxist humanism, like the original philosophy of Marx himself, is not content with being simply a humanism on the level of theory. Its practical approach to humanism means that, even on the level of theory, the demands of practice are already present and making their influence felt. Before concluding our discussion of the contemporary Marxist approach to man, we therefore need to indicate more specifically than we have done so far the distinctively practical implications of the Marxist humanist ontology of praxis.

The Marxist humanist insight into the practical implications of ontology is part of the more general Marxist position on the practical setting of such epistemological phenomena as thinking, knowing, truth, ideology, and philosophy itself. The analysis of such epistemological or theoretical phenomena, for the Marxist humanist, as for Marx, is not separable from prior considerations of an anthropological or practical sort. Thinking and knowing and the like are each expressions of man's specific way of being. It is therefore essential to take that mode of being into account in trying to clarify the nature of these theoretical activities. Further, as we have seen, the question about man's specific way of being cannot be answered apart from an ontological account of the nature of being in general. This chain of conceptual dependencies means that for the Marxist humanist the specific theoretical phenomena in which epistemology is interested must be set within the larger framework of an ontology and anthropology of praxis. Thinking, knowing, the meaning of truth, and the activity of philosophical reflection itself will therefore be conceived as eminently practical in nature.[13]

For the Marxist humanists, as for Marx, the road to knowing starts from man as a practical agent in the world. We begin not from the abstract, ideologically conceived phenomenon of passive sense perception (see Marx's First Thesis on Feuerbach) but from that mode of being which is fullest and most complex— namely, man's being-in-the-world conceived as sensuous-practical activity.[14] And this in two respects. To begin with, the objects of man's reflective concern are practical in nature. The world that man encounters and knows does not exist in itself independently of man's relation to and activity upon it. The objects of man's world, from the sensuously most immediate to the conceptually most abstract, are all manifestations of man's prior sensuous-practical needs and efforts to create and re-create his natural and social environment. The world is accessible to man only in a practical humanized form. The very notion of an external world makes sense only within the dialectical setting of praxis or work, that is, within the original matrix or dialogue between man's subjective needs and the world around him.[15] It is only within this pregiven practical matrix that such derivative epistemological activities as thinking and knowing are able to make contact with the world and achieve their distinctive significance for human life.

But, perhaps more important to stress, the subjective locus or origin of man's reflective activity is also understood by the Marxist humanists, following Marx, as primarily practical in nature. Consciousness, for the Marxist epistemologist, is nothing other than sensuous human activity itself, or perhaps better, it is simply an aspect or moment of praxis itself. As Dupré points out, already for Marx, over against Hegel, the activity of thinking was reinterpreted as the ideal aspect of praxis. It is the reflective expression of that prereflective involvement or activity in the world which forms the matrix of man's dialectical relation to the world and to himself. Praxis, as the dialectical or lived unity of consciousness and nature, once again serves as the ontologically primary and mediating concept which holds the key to understanding the possibility and significance of man's cognitive relationship to the world.[16]

The role played by praxis in contemporary Marxist theory of knowledge has obvious implications for the traditional metaphysical problem of the relation between thought and reality. One of its consequences is the challenge it poses to the Marxist tradition itself. If man is really a free, creative practical-active being, how can his cognitive activity, as the reflective expression of praxis, be construed, as traditional Marxism views it, in a quasi-physicalistic sense as simply a reflection of external reality? As Petrovic observes, the term "reflection" derives originally from the sphere of physics; it means the "throwing back by a surface of sound, light, heat." The problem with this metaphor, for the Marxist humanist, is that "there is nothing creative about it."[17] On the other hand, if thinking be viewed as one of the forms of man's practical being-in-the-world, then it cannot be interpreted as merely a subjective or ideological reflection of an objective, material reality. Our reflective activity must itself be viewed as one of the forms of human life—that is, as one way of creating and changing the world.

For Marxist humanists like Petrovic, one of the clearest illustrations of this point is provided by the example of philosophy itself. Appearances to the contrary (including Marx's famous Eleventh Thesis on Feuerbach), philosophical reflection is in fact one of the ways men have of changing, and not merely interpreting, the world. Now in saying this, contemporary Marxists like Petrovic do not mean to deny the truth of Marx's or Heidegger's contention that in the modern era we have witnessed a one-sided or subjectivistic reduction of metaphysics to a matter of competing world views or ideologies—that is, to philosophies which provide one-sided interpretations of the human world in terms either of consciousness (idealism) or nature (materialism, positivism) alone.[18] But Petrovic, for one, wishes to argue that, in accord with a concept of man's being as praxis, even metaphysics, even philosophical interpretations of the world are at the same time theoretical expressions of practical activity aimed at changing the world. To assume, as does the modern equation of metaphysics with a view of the world, that it is possible to interpret the world without changing it is, in the opinion of Petrovic, contrary to the sense of Marx's own philosophy. To be sure, according to Marx's Eleventh Thesis on Feuerbach, "The philosophers have only interpreted the world in various ways; the point is, to change it." This statement refers not to philosophy as such, however, but to that one-sided and ideological concept of philosophy which characterized German idealist metaphysics. Marx intends by his abolition of philosophy to eliminate only that kind of reflective activity which, in non-dialectical or a priori fashion, attempts to explain the world apart from an awareness of, and positive relationship to, its own setting in man's prior, practical involvement in the world. Marx does not intend to eliminate philosophy, in other words, but to remind philosophers that the truth of their interpretations of the world can be established only by reference to the capacity of such theories to assist men in their practical efforts to change the world.

How, specifically, does philosophy go about this practical task? In part, just by being philosphy itself. For as Petrovic argues:

> An interpretation of the world that does not change the world is both logically and empirically impossible. When man interprets the world, by this very fact he changes at least his conception of the world. In changing his conception of the world he cannot help changing his relationship to the world as well. And in changing his conception and his behavior, he influences the conceptions and actions of other people with whom he is in different relationships.[19]

For example, even on the most abstract and general level of the question of the meaning of being, the practical implications of philosophical inquiry are already to be found. As both Feuerbach and Heidegger have pointed out, the question of the meaning of being is a question in which the meaning of our own being is simultaneously involved.[20] But more to the point for the Marxist, when the philosopher raises the question of the meaning of freedom, or of the being of man, the very activity of that questioning itself constitutes a participation in the realization of that which is asked about. In other words, for the Marxist humanist, the very activity of thinking or philosophizing is itself, at least potentially, an activity through which man frees or humanizes himself.[21]

For Petrovic, therefore, as for Garaudy, the realization of freedom, of man's ability to realize his essential capacities, is to be found in an awareness and projection of the possibilities of concrete human action. Every new philosophical interpretation of the world, depending on its relationship to the praxis in which it originates and which, in turn, it shapes, presents us with a new set of possibilities for changing the world. In the case of Marx's interpretation of man's being as praxis, we are confronted by a philosophy which explicitly draws our attention to these facts and which, in particular, entails the practical conclusion that man is truly himself only when, in realizing his historically given possibilities, he is simultaneously engaged in the permanent and never-ending activity of creating new and higher ones. In fact, in the case of Marx's philosophy, we are confronted by a unique example of the practical nature of philosophy, for the Marxist concept of praxis entails that action is not added to theory from without but, rather, follows from the essence of theory insofar as theory itself is in every case (whether it is aware of it or not) the reflection of a prior matrix of praxis.[22] Marx's philosophy, above all, is an illustration of the practical nature of theory, because its conceptual nucleus is precisely a practical concept of man as a mode of being whose very essence is to be directed outward in concrete world- and self-transforming activity, a practical essence which extends to all his theoretical activities as well.

Marxist humanism is an ontology of praxis. Like original Marxism, it is a philosophy of man which is radical in the twofold theoretical and practical sense. It is a radically finitist metaphysics of man which issues simultaneously in "a demand for a revolutionary change of the world and an act of such a change."[23] For the Marxist humanist, as for Marx and the later Sartre, philosphical theory has both of these functions, which, in the last analysis, are dialectically one: it is an attempt to work out a comprehensive theory of human reality; but it is also an attempt to actualize that theory in the reality to which, as theory, it refers.[24] The theoretical expression of a radical humanism must, of logical necessity, also be a practical imperative for revolutionary action. A radical perspective on man will, of logical necessity, require a dialectical movement between the theoretical abstractions of ontology and the practical imperative of historical change—and back again. In this sense, Marxist humanism, like original Marxism, is a philosophy which not only interprets but changes the world. The point is that for any theory that claims to have a radical perspective on man, this is how it has to be.

## The Openness of the World

With this interest in changing the world, it becomes important for a Marxist philosophy of man to know whether the process of world history is such as to justify a revolutionary rather than, say, an evolutionary or a conservative posture toward it. The question which arises at this point is whether Marxism as a humanism is capable of providing a cosmological basis for its doctrine of revolutionary action. As Ernst Bloch argues, "There can be no new Marxist anthropology without a new Marxist cosmology."[25] In this section, we must therefore look at the general features and implications of the new cosmology which has emerged as a metaphysical setting for the Marxist humanist view of man. As we did in an earlier chapter, we shall consider under the rubric of cosmology the Marxist humanist approach to such topics as the concept of the world, the movement of history, and man's vision of the future.

## The World

The revolutionary thrust of Marx's approach to reality places his view of the world, and of philosophy's task vis-à-vis the world, in obvious contrast to the conservative implications of Hegel's philosophy of world history and his doctrine of anamnesis. As Bloch points out, "With grays in gray the figure cannot be rejuvenated, but merely known." Despite its dialectical nature, the movement of the Hegelian Idea in world history is, Bloch argues, basically nonrevolutionary: "Only that is called forth which was already there anyway. No surprise is possible, no genuine future."[26] It is against this background, with both God and the Hegelian Absolute removed from the picture, that we are to understand what Bloch regards as the crucial question: "what holds history open for man and man open for history?"[27] What sort of cosmology, what view of the being of the world, must be presupposed if, over against Hegel, history is to be interpreted as open to man's revolutionary attempts to construct an order of human emancipation, on the one hand, while, on the other hand, such efforts to change the world, to bring into existence that which is unexpected and new, are to be seen as in fundamental accord with the laws of being of the world itself? What sort of world must it be in order for a philosophy of revolutionary praxis to invoke, metaphysically, "a positively-possible, possibly-positive meaning" on behalf of its stance toward history?

For Bloch, the answer to the question, "What holds the world open for man, and vice versa?" is derived from his interpretation of the nature of being in general. The power which holds man and history open for one another is, in Bloch's terms, the power of that which is not-yet. In other words, the openness of the world to the possibilities of human action is simply an aspect of the general contingency of all being. It is the radical contingency or finitude of being that Bloch has in mind when he says, "But something other than this [i.e., pure, noncontingent Being] —something implied precisely in the material unity of the world —is to keep this vacuum [i.e., the threat of nonbeing] open for a possible, still undecided reality of the future."[28] This "something other" is simply the contingent being of the world itself: "The world-substance, mundane matter itself, is not yet finished and complete, but persists in a utopian-open state. . . . It is wholly incomplete precisely in its essential being."[29] Or again: "I presuppose that the world is open, that objectively real possibility exists in it and not merely determined necessity, not merely mechanical determinism."[30] In other words, for Bloch the being of the world is characterized by the same features of temporality, contingency, and possibility which characterize the meaning of being in general.

What is interesting is that, in working out this distinctively neo-Marxist cosmology, Bloch has acknowledged his debt to the eschatological imagery of the biblical tradition, in particular the notion of the *saeculum* as a temporally conceived world age which is determined in part not by the past but by a future toward which it is moving, "a future which it never attains but which continually prevents it from accepting itself as finished and final."[31] It is this view of the contingency of the world-historical process—namely, the contingency of the present world order in view of the possibility of a freer and more open future—which permits the Marxist humanist to pronounce his radical "no" to the existing state of affairs while continuing, as a secular thinker, to say a hopeful "yes" to the world of man as a whole. Paradoxically, it is because of his ability to work out a secular interpretation of the meaning of transcendence—namely, in terms of an ontology of the radical contingency of being—that a Marxist humanist like Bloch is able, when the traditional symbol of the Kindgom of God is no longer functioning, to view himself as the legitimate heir of biblical man's capacity to affirm the goodness of the created world order while saying "no" to this particular world age. Bloch's neo-Marxist view of the openness of "the world-substance, mundane matter itself" allows him, in an entirely consistent and thoroughly secular way, to be "unremittingly concerned with the secular without sacrificing the transcendent."[32] In Bloch's cosmology, in other words, the power of critical or revolutionary transcendence is understood in a way that both preserves and overcomes the eschatological view of the Bible by grounding its critique and affirmation of the world in a view of the being of the world as irreducibly finite yet open to the future.

Garaudy too, though drawing on the biblical doctrine of creation rather than the motifs of eschatology, arrives at a similar ontological view of the openness of the world. The cosmology which originated in Greek metaphysics, and which was subsequently reflected in the works of such thinkers as Spinoza and Hegel, depicted the world process as a totality that was sufficient unto itself. It was a noncreated world in which nothing new could really occur, a world in which movement and change were a mere reorganization of something that already existed. In the biblical view, by contrast, the world was not something that existed in and of itself; rather, it owed its existence to an outside, transcendent source. In demythologized terms, it represented the possibility of genuine creation, of the coming into being of that which is radically new, of that which leads to a future that is different and better. Although the mythological language of the Bible expressed this radical contingency of the world in naïve or inverted form as an ontological dependence upon a superior Being, nevertheless it captured the essential insight of contemporary cosmology that this creative process "either occurs continuously or it never occurs at all." From a secular viewpoint, that is, "Creation, far from being a unique miracle, is the most constant experience: it is the continuous emergence of something new."[33]

Thus for Garaudy, as for Bloch, revolutionary praxis is possible only in the setting of, and as an integral part of, a world process that is viewed not as the manifestation of inevitable necessity, as in Greek metaphysics, but, as in the biblical myth, as the gratuitous gift of creative love, or, in modern terms, as the continuing ungrounded miracle of contingent being. If the laws of being of the world in which we live are the laws of mechanical necessity or the product of the requirements of reason, "then we are a fragment of an element, necessary and rational, of the closed totality of the universe."[34] But if, as according to the biblical myth and the Marxist humanist, the world is the outcome of free, creative activity, then we, in turn, are free to transform and humanize the world in the direction of a more liberated future. In so doing, we are simply extending and making more real that fundamental goodness or openness of the world to man, and of man to the world, which, for the Bible and Marxism alike, is the basis and goal of creative activity.

*History*

It is on the basis of this general view of the world that the Marxist humanist conception of history rests. The first thing that follows from a view of the world as open is that a deterministic reading of man's historical existence must be judged alien to the new Marxist outlook. In fact, Machovec goes so far as to state that "so-called historical determinism, when it is interpreted as a sure guarantee of the future . . . or as meaning that we can lay down a complete blueprint for the man of the future, seems to me to be something repulsive and I have never found anything of this sort in Karl Marx."[35] This antimechanistic understanding of historical determinism is a widespread phenomenon among contemporary Marxist philosophers. They regard the hard or neopositivist determinism of Marxist orthodoxy as a fetishism of law which subsumes human initiative, à la Hegel, under the mystified notion of a world process dragging us along with it willy-nilly.

For the Marxist humanist, however, historical determinism has another, almost opposite meaning. For these new Marxists, as for Marx himself, history is not viewed as an autonomous reality that contains in itself the conditions for its own inevitable development independent of the activity of men. Though Marx does say, "The problem itself arises only when the material conditions necessary for its solution already exist or are at least in process of formation," he also insists that

It is not "history" but *man,* real, living man who does everything, who owns everything, and who is the cause of all struggles. "History" does not utilize man as a means for the attainment of *its* own ends—as if history were some type of distinct person. History is nothing other than the activity of man aspiring toward his aims.[36]

Given Marx's own balanced, dialectical approach to man's action in history, the Marxist humanists feel justified in concluding that, while the appropriate material conditions must be present for historical change to occur, man is not simply the product of these conditions. He is also the agent who has brought about these prior conditions and who has given them such distinctively human significance as they have. Thus, for the Marxist humanist the determinism of history is both "a fact, a reality that man encounters," and also "a set of problems to be unravelled, a field of man's activity, of human praxis."[37] The truth of historical determinism lies not in a one-sided interpretation of history as the inevitable outcome of the economic necessities of the past but in a dialectical view of history as the field of man's practical responsibility for shaping his own future.

For the new Marxists, history is therefore not the inevitable outcome of the past but the continual transformation of the past and the creation of that which is qualitatively new. Just as the being of the world is to be pictured as radically contingent and open-ended, so too the being of history is to be understood in creationist and futural, not deterministic or past-oriented terms. The essence of history may be seen wherever men are at work creating new possibilities of existence for their collective future.

But this means that even the determinism of the past must be reinterpreted in futural terms. For, as Bloch points out:

To grasp what has been means to grasp something now as that which it was, not as having-come-into-being *(das Gewordensein),* but as coming-into-being *(Werden),* a thing which has not yet played out its hand, but which seeks what belongs to it and which above all needs man in order to realize the potential pending in the world-process—the transition out of the realm of necessity into the realm of freedom.[38]

It is the theologian of hope Moltmann who perhaps best describes the implications of Bloch's radically futural interpretation of the nature of history and the influence of the past. Historically significant or determining events (circumstances, conditions) of the past

> do not then have only the accidental, individual and relative
> character which we normally ascribe to historic events but then
> they have always at the same time also an unfinished and
> provisional character that points forward. . . . The events
> themselves . . . bear the mark of something that is still
> outstanding, not yet finished, not yet realized. . . . The facts of
> history can never be regarded as processes complete in themselves
> which have had their day and can manifest their own truth by
> themselves. They must be understood as stages on a road that goes
> further and elements in a process that continues. . . . Hence the
> history that is thus experienced and transmitted forces every new
> present to analysis and interpretation. Events that have been
> experienced in this way "must" be passed on, because in them
> something is seen which is determinative also for future
> generations. They cast their shadow, or shed their light, on the way
> ahead.[39]

The past, in other words, is not to be regarded as simply the previously existing condition or given of our present situation. It must be seen as having itself once been "the present and the front-line towards the future." In this radically humanist reading of history, it is the concept of man's openness to the future that provides, as it were, the common front between the past and his present situation. "The dialectic of past happening and present understanding is always motivated by anticipation of the future and by the question of what makes the future possible."[40] Indeed, man's past can weigh upon his present like the dead hand of necessity only because it was itself at one time a practical ensemble alive with the possibilities of the future.

For the Marxist humanist, this dialectical reading of history (the dialectic of determining conditions and free activity, of a living past and the promise of the future) is intended, over against both positivist and existentialist approaches to history, to remind us "how closely fact and possibility are interwoven in history, how much new possibilities of existence depend upon

historic events and how full historic events are of possibilities."[41]
This dialectic is, however, not an abstract one. For the Marxist
humanists interpret this dialectic in historically specific terms, as
did Marx before them. For them, as for Marx, the important
point to be stressed in a materialist reading of history is that man
has in fact moved increasingly from the old era of material
necessity and economic determinism toward a new era of social
and human liberation, and that, as he has done so, he can begin to
be understood less and less in terms of the givens of the past and
more and more as a being of free, creative activity, a being whose
essential nature increasingly coincides not with what he has been
but with what he may yet be, a being whose wildest hopes for the
future may yet prove to be the most practical, realistic proposals
of all.

## The Future

For the Marxist humanists, the concept of utopia therefore plays
an important part in thinking about the future. And interestingly
enough, it functions for them not simply as a vehicle for testing
alternative visions of the future but also and at least as important
as a critical weapon against both liberal and Marxist orthodox
approaches to history. As we have already seen, Marxist
humanism is clearly an effort to respond to the charge of secular
and religious critics that Marxism must inevitably reduce the
actualities of our historical past to aspects of an economic determinism. But it has also arisen as a reply to the charge that Marxism entails an equally dogmatic and deterministic utopianism
concerning man's future. The Marxist humanist proposes,
rather, a concept of utopia that is at once more self-critical and
more hopeful than the corresponding stances toward the future
of either its liberal or Marxist orthodox critics.

  The dilemma of the liberal critic of traditional Marxist dogmatism about the future is that his own alternative is largely
conditioned by the dogmatism he is concerned to combat.
The liberal ideologist threatens to leave us with no larger
sociopolitical vision of morality or of the humanizing possibilities of man's collective future. As Iris Murdoch notes:

It may be well to say: believe in a *living* future, a future that
belongs to existing human beings, and not in a rational ideal of a
politically deduced future time. Do not sacrifice a known present
for a problematic unknown future. But does this leave one with only
a personal morality, and with no political morality or only a
negative one?[42]

The problem is that liberalism's humanistic values seem incapable of being embodied in the reality of our social order. Though
they provide the substance of our official political ideology, they
present themselves as something transcendent or applicable to
individuals rather than to the social order as a whole. Hence the
dilemma of a liberal today when confronted by the critique of a
sociopolitical radical: "We want to think morally about politics
but our moral categories are confused and our political
categories are empty."[43] The gap between our humanistic aspirations and our official theory of society inevitably means that the
most humane and visionary politicians such a system can
produce—the Eugene McCarthys and George McGoverns, for
example—must appear, and in fact are, hopelessly utopian (in
the accustomed negative sense).

On the other hand, the alternative to the intellectual and moral
bankruptcy of liberal social philosophy appears to be the scholastic rigidity of orthodox Marxist social philosophy. The dogmatism of Marxist orthodoxy has meant, in the realm of social-
humanistic aspiration, the suppression of all genuinely empirical
criticism of the historical process and, as a necessary corollary,
the suppression of "all dreaming, all anticipation, all hope, the
pioneer existence which we as humans lead on the foremost
frontier of the world-process."[44] Both social science and social
vision have been casualties of this hardening of the Marxist
tradition. The result has been a field day for the antiutopian and
allegedly nonideological realists (the technicians, the bureau-
crats, the official ideologues) of liberal pragmatism. Marxist
humanism, with its vision of "socialism with a human face," thus
has the task of articulating a different, more realistic, yet unre-
lenting concept of the utopian demand, one that will enable it to
transcend the current impasse between liberal and orthodox
Marxist speculation and enter into the increasingly urgent busi-

ness of transforming our humanistic visions of tomorrow into the
social realities of today.

The key to this revisionary task is, as we have indicated, the
attempt by the new Marxists to provide a genuinely humanistic
interpretation of Marxism's dialectical approach to history. For
Bloch, a truly dialectical understanding of the movement of
history entails, in contrast to Engels's Hegelian distortion of
Marx, an understanding of historical reality as "reality criticizing itself":

> The dialectic has to be set up as a critical method, as a bitingly
> critical method of upheaval: first, so that *something* happens, so that
> something is going on not merely in the head under the sleeping cap;
> second, so that one knows *what sort* of contradictions are taking
> place, so that the Utopia-making, the chasing after things in advance
> which have never existed, has a foot to stand on, so that it becomes
> concrete and mediates with the world.[45]

A dialectical understanding of history must, in the first place, be
a truly critical approach to existing empirical, social reality—and
that means that it must also be self-critical of its own pretensions
to knowledge and objectivity. Only in this way, says Bloch, can
such a method stand in service of man's "openness toward the
future, a genuine future which amounts to more than simply
being before us."[46]

But this critical-scientific rather than ideological understanding of the dialectic of history must be balanced by a renewed
appreciation of the historical function of utopia; or, rather, any
truly critical theory of society can be scientific only if it provides
a realistic basis for man's necessary activity of utopia-making,
just as, conversely, our activity of utopia-making becomes dangerous and ideological if it is not grounded in a prior, scientific reading of the movement and objective possibilities of our
history. Here Bloch calls our attention to a distinction between
utopias of an abstract sort and what he calls concrete utopias.
What makes a utopian dream abstract or "merely utopian" is its
failure to allow itself to be "mediated with the existing social
tendency and possibility." Such visions are perhaps socially premature and hence have to be abstract. On the other hand, we
must distinguish between even an abstract utopia and an ideol-

ogy. For Bloch, at least, an ideology is, as it was for Marx, a vehicle for expressing and reinforcing the interests of the ruling classes in a given society, whereas a utopia reflects the aspirations of a new class for a future dwelling place that transcends the alienation of the present world order. Utopian thinking of this sort, says Bloch, "is *rectified*—but never *refuted* by the mere power of that which, at any particular time, *is*."[47] The task of a truly scientific theory of society is therefore not complete until or unless it locates for us those "utopian margins which surround actuality with *real and objective* possibility."[48] Part of what is involved in a Marxist humanist interpretation of the dialectic of history, therefore, is this living and creative balance between man's humanistic aspirations for the future and a scientific, sociocritical awareness of that which currently is.

When it comes to the search for specific imaginative resources for utopian speculation, the Marxist humanists, unlike their orthodox counterparts, are not at all averse to exploring the untried or controversial possibilities of the past as well as to challenging those elements in their own heritage which have become sacrosanct or dead. This has taken a number of different forms. It has meant, in some cases, reviving the (properly understood) utopian visions of an earlier day, visions which may have now become more realistic as conditions have changed. It has also, and perhaps even more important, meant the imaginative construction of new, more realistic visions of our possible common future.[49] Freed from the pieties and dogmatisms of their Christian and Marxist pasts, and supported by the new ontology of radical secularity that has replaced the metaphysical assumptions on which both traditions earlier relied, the new Marxists have found themselves free, both philosophically and practically, to attempt to construct new social and moral visions of man's historical future. Guarding against unwarranted projections of human hope, they have nevertheless attempted to formulate a new basis for that hope in a vision of the future that stands in both a humane and scientific relation to the actual possibilities and limitations of the present. It is a vision of a future state of affairs for which, in fact, there is no last dialectical step or final stage, not because the union of human freedom and historical necessity is an impossible ideal but because that ideal itself stands for the possibility of a future in which man's material needs have been definitively transcended and the way opened for the potentially infinite activity of continuous creation.[50]

I think it is easy to see why this utopian ideology of the new Marxist humanism is regarded by its proponents to be a critical yet creative appropriation, a secular, humanistic transformation, of the best elements of the Western humanist tradition: its Greek and Judeo-Christian strands, its post-Kantian as well as post-Marxian understanding of the task of criticism, its moral or existential depths as well as its sociopolitical or historical sense. Brought together under the rubric of an ontology of praxis and historical initiative, these elements conjoin to fashion a utopian dream of a future world community of social freedom and free, creative human activity.

The new Marxist humanism is, like every other large-scale philosophy of man, an expression of faith. But it is not a faith in a narrowly religious sense. It represents an attitude of trust and openness to our finite existence in history, together with a militant, practical commitment to the this-worldly liberation of men from every form of individual and collective unfreedom.

## Some Provisional Concluding Remarks

In his prefatory essay to the *Critique of Dialectical Reason,* Jean-Paul Sartre advances the controversial claim that Marxism is "the philosophy of our time."[51] It is, he says, the totalization of contemporary knowledge which does for our time what Descartes and Locke, Kant, and Hegel did for their times. It provides "a method, a regulative idea, an offensive weapon, and a community of language"—in short, a vision of the world for an entire age, including the critics of that age. Thus, Sartre quotes with approval Garaudy's assertion that "Marxism forms today the system of coordinates which alone makes it possible to situate and to define a thought in any domain whatsoever—from political economy to physics, from history to ethics."[52]

It is not only Marxists or would-be Marxists who place this

high estimate on the theoretical significance of this philosophy. Surprisingly, Heidegger too states that the Marxist philosophy of history is superior to any other in our time, and that, specifically, neither Husserl's phenomenology nor Sartre's existentialism is adequate to engaging it in a productive dialogue on the critical issues of our age.[53] To cite just one example: Heidegger argues that Sartre's negative and abstract doctrine of the metaphysical freedom of the individual, an ontological commitment which Sartre never really abandons in his later, Marxist period, is, unlike Marx's own philosophy, incapable of providing a theoretical basis for a positive and concrete doctrine of the social freedom of man.[54]

From the side of contemporary theology too, it has been admitted, even by nonradical theologians, that "while we are living in a post-Christian world, we are not living in a post-Marxian one."[55] Because of its determination to confront and work out new answers to the standing problem of reconciling science and utopia, because of its militant commitment to realizing specific sociopolitical visions and objectives in revolutionary praxis, Marxist humanism demonstrates its active superiority to Christian realism and eschatology with their reactionary or individualistic tendencies. Marxism, rather than Christianity or political liberalism, is the vehicle of the revolutionary spirit in our time, because, as Lehmann points out, "The Marxist-Leninist account of the impact of power upon social change and of social change upon power is still the point from which to take our bearings in the revolutionary situation in which we live."[56]

Whether one's concern is with ontology, philosophy of history, or specific social and political analyses, contemporary Marxists like Bloch, Garaudy, and Marcuse contend that in our time only Marxism is capable of providing a systematic framework that can assimilate and make overall sense of the best insights from the more partial world views of such contemporary philosophies as existentialism, pragmatism, liberalism, or a narrowly empirical concept of social science, as well as from the great humanistic affirmations of the classical and biblical traditions. Furthermore, only Marxism provides these elements with an historical vehicle and dynamic for effecting their full realization. Only Marxism therefore satisfies the two criteria of a radical philosophy of man—namely, "to develop a comprehensive metaphysics of human reality" and "to actualize such a metaphysics in history."[57]

It can, and has, been argued of course that Marxism has seen its day, that it is philosophically and scientifically (if not yet historically) outmoded, and that serious metaphysicians and social theorists have long since gone beyond the original, admittedly seminal insights of Marx's own thought. Obviously these are complex issues and cannot easily or quickly be resolved, but for the present it is enough to indicate the general character of a Marxist humanist response. In the first place, the critics of Marxism, whether secular or religious, would do well to remind themselves, even as Marxists have reminded the defenders of the Christian tradition, that this new perspective in philosophy is "still very young, almost in its infancy" so far as its historical tradition and possibilities for future development are concerned.[58] As the considerations of this chapter have shown, the capacity for contemporary Marxism to revitalize itself by drawing on the best of current non-Marxist philosophy without sacrificing its own distinctive emphases indicates that Marxism is at the very least *a,* if not *the,* living philosophy in our time. It would be premature to conclude that its essential philosophical possibilities were definitively presented or exhausted by the classical formulations of Engels or Lenin or their subsequent developments in Stalin or Mao. The work of such thinkers as Lukacs, Gramsci, Bloch, or Marcuse is sufficient testimony to that fact.

But, second, there is good reason to pause and take seriously an equally controversial corollary of Sartre's claim. Any effort to go beyond Marxism must ask itself whether it is not in fact simply another attempt to go behind or in some other way to circumvent the specifically Marxist formulation of a positive humanism in our time. It is Sartre's contention that, as in the case of Cartesianism and the other great philosophies that put their stamp on specific historical eras, "there is no going beyond them so long as man has not gone beyond the historical movement they express." As Sartre goes on to explain: "an 'anti-Marxist' argument is only the apparent rejuvenation of a pre-Marxist idea. A so-

called going beyond Marxism will be at worst only a return to
pre-Marxism, at best, only the rediscovery of a thought already
contained in the philosophy which one believes he has gone beyond."[59] Sartre's argument follows of course from the Marxist
insight into the functional dependence of every major ideology
on that particular stage of historical or socioeconomic development whose structures, assumptions, and inner dynamic it is its
task to reflect.

On the basis of this Marxist understanding of Marxism itself, it
follows that until the advent of a new era of human, historical
praxis—one which, for Sartre and the new Marxists, will be
defined by the completion of the transition from the capitalist
world of economic (material) necessity to the social-humanist
realm of total human emancipation—the major efforts of thinkers in our present circumstances will (if they are to be more than
simply efforts to refurbish the philosophies of an earlier day)
best be understood as attempts, vis-à-vis the original insights of
Marx, "to set the systems in order or to use the new methods to
conquer territory not yet fully explored" or, again, "to provide
practical applications for the theory and employ it as a tool to
destroy and to construct."[60]

This proposition can be negatively formulated so as to appear
to constitute a devastating criticism. The Marxists could be
viewed as arbitrarily ruling out (as utopian in the bad sense)
every effort to go beyond Marxism to construct a positive philosophy of freedom on the far side of the Marxists' work of negative or destructive criticism. If so, this would appear to be giving
the Marxists carte blanche. In fact, the situation is less one-sided
and more complicated, more dialectical, than this. What the new
Marxists are calling for is something more like the projection of a
future alternative which nevertheless "cannot yet be known
except by way of negation of the present because it goes beyond
what is possible within the existing world."[61] Positively expressed, Marxism still serves as the original philosophy of our time,
because it has given birth to the current ideological epoch not as
a completed, systematic whole but as a reservoir of imaginative
and infinitely suggestive starting points for whole new areas of
theoretical inquiry—possibilities for thought, both critical and

constructive, which have still not been completely understood or
acted upon, let alone exhausted or gone beyond.

Marx himself declared that on the far side of the struggle for
total human emancipation that marks the present era there lies
what he envisaged as a new historical era of human freedom, of
liberated activity (labor, work, praxis) whose nearest paradigm
would be the creative work of the artist, activity carried out
"according to the laws of beauty," activity which produces or
reflects "man in this entire wealth of his being, produces the *rich*,
deep, and *entirely sensitive* man."[62] The Marxist humanists are
therefore not averse to following out the more radical implications of Sartre's observation that "as soon as there will exist for
*everyone* a margin of *real* freedom beyond the production of life,
Marxism will have lived out its span; a philosophy of freedom
will take its place."[63] Today, as neo-Marxists like Marcuse point
out, this historical possibility is, for larger numbers of people,
closer to fulfillment than it was in the nineteenth century. To that
extent, it is necessary to make at least preliminary or provisional
attempts to prepare the way for a new philosophy, a post-Marxist
philosophy in which utopia has become nearly synonymous with
the imperatives of realism itself.[64] Marxist humanism is therefore not simply an extension of the possibilities contained in
previous Marxism. It is also an effort within Marxism to begin to
explore, in proleptic or utopian fashion, the possible outlines of
that future philosophy of freedom. Here especially, the positive
values for Marxism of the emerging dialogue with the great
religious conceptions of human emancipation become particularly evident and promising.

However, until the actual practical and historical conditions
have been laid down for the emergence of that new, post-
historical or eschatological epoch, creative thinking in our time
must, according to the neo-Marxists, continue to direct itself to
the as yet unexplored possibilities opened up by the present
philosophy of radical secularity, particularly in its Marxist
humanist form. The final shape and content of the new man and
the new world must remain, for the present, beyond the reach of
our practical abilities or specific social vision. Even Sartre admits
that "We have no means, no intellectual instrument, no concrete

experience which allows us to conceive of this freedom or this philosophy."[65] For, as Marx put it at the beginning of our epoch, "This reign of freedom does not begin until the time when the work imposed by necessity and external finality shall cease; it is found, therefore, beyond the sphere of material production proper."[66]

As these two chapters have attempted to show, the phenomenon of Marxist humanism represents an attempt to bring together in an innovative and constructive way the insights of the young Marx, who first issued the call and suggested the outlines for a radical metaphysics, and the subsequent development of an ontology of radical secularity by the secular existentialists. In so doing, it has provided us with a radically humanistic and non-theistic alternative to the way of thinking that has characterized the efforts of even the radical theologians while retaining the distinctively Marxist conception of a metaphysics that is genuinely radical in both a philosophical and a political sense. It is on grounds such as these that the Marxist humanists are able to argue, as their orthodox counterparts cannot, that in the dialogue with radical religion, it is Marxism that continues to be the philosophy of our time, that it is the new Marxist humanism that presents the best means for understanding in theory and bringing about in practice the implications of the new ontology of radical secularity. To make this claim is not, as should by now be evident, to maintain that Marxism somehow contains the eternal truth of things. It is simply to state that for us, in our time, it is truer than any of the available options, and that, in particular, it is more truly related to the general movement of history and human praxis from which it arose, which it in turn reflects, and whose inner necessities or objective possibilities it projects in the form of sketches of our hoped-for-future.

# 8

## Radical Christian Thinking: Limits and Transcendence

Given our earlier criticisms of secular theology and our sketch of an alternative metaphysics, it might seem that the major issues in the Marxist-Christian dialogue have been resolved in favor of the Marxist side. But such a conclusion would be premature. The radical metaphysics of Marx and secular existentialism is more than just a secular counterpart to theism. It is also a philosophical framework for rethinking the concept of radical religion. This means that our previous criticisms may not have exhausted the possibilities for a kind of thinking that is both radical and Christian. If so, there is still room for conversation between Marxists and Christians in a post-theistic age.

In this chapter and the one that follows, we shall begin by restating the issues involved in this dialogue. The philosophical problems which confront Marxists and Christians can no longer be posed in the traditional way (as they were, for example, in our opening chapter). The reason for this change is the presence of a third partner in the dialogue. Secular existentialism represents a revolution that has inverted all of our previous ontological assumptions and priorities. The pressure of this philosophical third force has brought about equally radical changes in Marxist and Christian understanding of both their own positions and their criticisms of one another.

Once we have restated the issues, we shall use the new ontology as a lever for pressing the traditional Christian answers to the breaking point, hoping that if we can crack them open something new might emerge. We have already described how contemporary Marxists have used this new philosophical perspective to rework the basic concepts of their own tradition. In the process, Marxism has opened itself to some of the most valuable insights of the Christian tradition. We must now see whether the radical Christian can use this same ontology to rethink the assumptions of his tradition. If he can, he will have put the Marxist-Christian dialogue on an entirely new philosophical footing.[1]

This argument assumes that it is possible for Marxists and Christians to reach agreement on their general concepts of being, man, and the world. If they can, their dialogue will increasingly concern itself with differences in historical perspective rather than in metaphysical belief. After we look at how the radical Christian rethinks some of his basic philosophical concepts, we shall therefore look, in the next chapter, at what his new concepts mean for his approach to history and to the Christian tradition in particular. We shall then be close to completing the task we undertook at the outset of this study—namely, to explore the ways in which Marxists and Christians can move once the conventional rules of their dialogue have been either changed or suspended altogether.

The Problematic of
God and Man

Christian thinkers who are theists make two assumptions in responding to their secular critics. They assume that talk about God, even if only in demythologized form, is necessary for any thinking that wishes to call itself Christian. Their point is not simply a semantic one. Theism is held to be necessary on grounds that are ontological and existential. God is the theologian's answer to the metaphysical question, Why is there something rather than nothing? It is also his answer to the very human question, What is the ultimate meaning of life? From a theistic perspective, an ontology of finitude is unable to provide satisfactory answers to either of these essential questions of Christian faith.

A second and related assumption is that any thinking which proposes to call itself Christian must affirm the existence of a transcendent dimension in man's being. Without an opening

onto transcendence, the metaphysical and existential assurances
of faith would not only be false; they would make no sense. To
eliminate this dimension from man's being is to undermine his
higher needs and aspirations and to cripple his capacity to deal
with the limit situations of life (guilt, death, the threat of
meaninglessness). It is to cut him off from the one source capable
of offering him the support and consolation he seeks. Once
again, from a theistic perspective it would appear that a finitist
ontology represents a shallow and incomplete understanding of
the man spoken to by Christian faith.

The radical Christian thinker, however, must reject both of
these assumptions from the start. We have already argued that
both traditional and contemporary doctrines of God fail to meet
the logical and existential criticisms brought against them by
secular thought. We have also argued that Christian thinking has
no independent future metaphysically apart from an ontology of
radical secularity. The radical Christian must therefore begin his
own theoretical effort by abandoning at the outset not only talk
about God but also any metaphysics of transcendent being that
could serve as a philosophical basis or substitute for such talk.
Radical Christian thinking begins from the alternative premise
that theological thinking, or talk about God, no longer makes
any theoretical sense.

This does not mean that there are no positive features in
traditional or contemporary talk about God worth preserving if
proper means can be found. For the radical Christian, there is
still a need to find other ways of saying some of the things
formerly said by talk about God. For example, there needs to be
a way in which we can express the mystery that there is something rather than nothing without making a covert appeal to
theism, on the one hand, or reducing this mystery to a logical
confusion or a temporarily unsolved problem of technical
reason, on the other. Or again, insofar as we distinguish the
general concept of being from the notion of human existence, we
need to find a way to reinterpret the traditional predicates of
divine being (infinity, the absolute, eternity) as predicates of
finite being without divinizing man.

The point is that the radical Christian thinker does not regard

his hermeneutical effort as another in the series of attempts by
theologians to radically reconstruct the doctrine of God. He is
convinced, even if the theologian is not, that this strategy is no
longer sound. His approach is therefore to be distinguished from
those which feature a novel philosophical approach to God (e.g.,
via process metaphysics) or a revolutionary reinterpretation of
traditional biblical motifs (e.g., political eschatology). It is also to
be distinguished from those which involve a retreat to conceptual substitutes for talking about God but which still share the
assumptions of more openly theistic ways of thinking (e.g.,
Tillich's "ground of being"). It has to be clear from the outset, in
other words, that radical Christian thinking is not a species of
theological thinking in any sense whatsoever.

The radical Christian does not begin from the premise that talk
about God has to be reconstructed. He starts from the position
that it is just this assumption which has to be rejected. What is
called for is a different kind of thinking and therefore a different
starting point as well. The radical Christian proposes that we
look to an ontology of finitude for the resources we need to
resolve the problematic of God and man. By offering a finitist
interpretation of being and the limit concepts that cluster around
it, he offers to free us from the assumption imposed upon us by
theologians that, unless theism can be radically reconstructed,
Christian thinking will have to be abandoned altogether.

The radical Christian also rejects the second assumption made
by theists—namely, that to qualify for the title "Christian," a
doctrine of man must leave room for a dimension of transcendence. The issues here are more complex because of the notori-
ous ambiguity of the term "transcendence." It is clear, however,
that in its traditional usage as well as in the example of the secular
theologians, it functions to support a number of related claims
concerning the limits of man's capacities and his need for help
from a higher source. As Marxist critics have pointed out, it also
plays a key role in Christianity's tendency toward a spiritualistic
metaphysics of man and its general reluctance to accept this
world as the ultimate horizon of man's destiny. From a radically
secular perspective, however, there appears to be a contradiction
in this use of the term. It is used to emphasize man's distinctive

autonomy and responsibility for shaping the world, but it also
serves as a vehicle for expressing reservations about the extent of
man's capacities to do just that. Even the contemporary theological affirmation of radically secular man turns out to be another
device for reaffirming the traditional theistic view of man rather
than an occasion for rethinking the nature of man in a way that is
Christian and radical as well.

Once again, this does not mean that there is nothing to be said
for traditional Christian thinking about man. As we have seen,
even its Marxist critics acknowledge the value of Christianity's
insights into the subjective and transcendental dimensions of
man. For the radical Christian, too, there is still a need to say in
other ways some of the things formerly said about man from a
theistic point of view. One is the need to express man's higher
needs and aspirations without resorting to the dualist or idealist
assumptions of theism, on the one hand, or reducing them to
epiphenomena of narrowly psychological or socioeconomic
needs, on the other. Another is the need to preserve Christianity's realistic sense of the limits placed upon human intellect,
character, and destiny while avoiding an alienated, theistic interpretation of them, on the one hand, or a refusal to take them
seriously because of the fervor of one's commitment to some
utopian future, on the other. As these examples suggest, traditional Christian insights into man's capacity for self-criticism and
self-transcendence are reflections of an underlying humanistic
concern that men not view themselves solely in the terms imposed upon them by their present situation in a "fallen" world.
Marx's critique of secular alienation and his appreciation of the
radical (humanistic) elements in religion is a more direct expression of the same concern.

It is important to repeat that in looking for ways to restate
traditional Christian insights, the radical Christian is not attempting to reconstruct a theistic view of man. Because he starts from a
different set of assumptions, he understands his task in quite
another way. He is trying to construct a doctrine of man on the
foundations laid by a finitist ontology. His aim is therefore to
show that the phenomenon of transcendence can be understood
as a way of talking about man's being in this world rather than

about an opening to some other world beyond. His argument is that an ontology of finitude provides all the concepts he needs for making sense of the dimension of transcendence and the limit situations of life, and that it frees us from the ancient theological (i.e., alienated) claim that, apart from an appeal to a higher dimension of reality, secular philosophy cannot speak of these phenomena in a way that satisfies the whole man, the man of faith.

## The Problematic of Faith

Awareness of a dimension of transcendence and of the existential significance of boundary situations is an essential part of what Christians mean when they talk about faith. The primary task of Christian thinking is to clarify and defend the integrity of faith, both as a theoretical concept and as a stance toward life. This is the task of the radical Christian thinker too, and in this respect he does not differ from his theistic colleagues. The issue between them is whether it is necessary to talk about God (or its conceptual equivalent) in order to express on the level of theory what Christians understand by faith on the level of everyday life. The argument proceeds on both levels: it is a dispute in metaphysics, but it is also a disagreement over the proper description of faith as a phenomenon of life. The radical Christian's criticism of theism likewise occurs on both levels: theism is not only theoretically untenable, it distorts the very life-phenomenon it was meant to clarify.

It is probably safe to say that metaphysical arguments take second place to arguments from experience in most Christian thinking about faith. The basic motive behind traditional Christian affirmations of the transcendental nature and destiny of man is not commitment to some particular metaphysical doctrine but a more immediate awareness of the boundary situations that are permanent and inescapable features of the human condition. Whatever their theoretical persuasions, all men sooner or later encounter the threat of nonbeing in their lives. All men find themselves in such limit situations as the awareness of death, the experience of sin and guilt, or despair over the meaning of life.

Since these limit phenomena appear to be universal givens of
human experience, Christian thinkers have felt it necessary to
construct a view of man which not only makes sense of them but
which offers men spiritual resources for meeting their needs
when they find themselves in such situations. Conversely, they
have felt obliged to challenge those doctrines of man which
either fail to acknowledge these situations or treat them with less
than the ultimate seriousness they deserve. Christian concern for
the whole man is not allayed but heightened and confirmed when
Marxists, by their own admission, come to the dialogue with
empty hands regarding experiences such as these.

For the radical Christian, however, there are several problems
with the traditional Christian response to these boundary situations. To begin with, it appears difficult for theologians to separate the task of accurately describing men's limit experiences
from the further job of interpreting their theological significance. At a very early stage, the theologian's general description
shades over into a subtle or not so subtle appeal to the natural
anxiety of men who find themselves at the limits of their
strength. As we have seen, even the secular theologians do not
seem to appreciate the difference between these two tasks.

Having blurred these different tasks, the theologian can then
claim that the problems men face in limit situations can be
resolved only by an appeal to resources that lie beyond the limits
of man's finite capacities. The argument is as follows. A careful
description of man's boundary experiences shows that men have
a need for reassurance and certitude precisely at those points in
life where their own strength runs out. Men experience these
situations as threatening to their being. The only response
adequate to the needs experienced by finite beings at the limits
of their resources is one that is itself not subject to these limitations, one that is more than finite or absolute in nature. But such
assurance can be provided only if it is grounded in a source of
being that is itself infinite or absolute. By this criterion, an
ontology of finitude remains truncated or incomplete. It is
incapable of speaking to the whole man, to man as a being with
higher needs. Hence, only an anthropology that allows room in
its view of man and its concept of being for a dimension of

transcendence can adequately speak to the existential or religious needs of men.

At each stage in this argument, the radical Christian takes a different stand. To begin with, he proceeds from a viewpoint that is radically secular. This does not mean that he does not take these situations seriously or find them as significant as does the theologian. Theologians often fail to give credit to secular thinkers at this point—sometimes, one thinks, willfully. Where the radical Christian parts company with the theologian is in the latter's assumption that these limit experiences constitute evidence for a dimension of meaning or reality that transcends the limits of finite being. The radical Christian accepts these boundary situations for what they are: instances of human experience having arrived at limits beyond which it cannot go, limits on the far side of which there is nothing further to be said. He recognizes and accepts these limits, but he does so in a way that avoids the further, alienated assumptions of the theologian.

What this disagreement indicates is that radical Christian thinking is in part an effort to respond in a more satisfactory way on the level of theory to a profound shift that has taken place in contemporary man's attitude toward the world. This shift in contemporary experience is the result of the revolutionary transformation of modern existence in every sphere of human activity: economic, technological, social, political, and cultural. One of its expressions has been a sea change in our attitude toward the boundary situations of life. The pressure for nontheistic ways of interpreting these limit experiences does not come in the first instance from the arguments of the metaphysicians. It is a reflection on the level of theory of a shift that has already occurred on the level of our prereflective, lived experience of the world.

The radical Christian sees this shift as involving a move away from the existential assumptions underlying the theistic view of man. Modern man no longer experiences his relationship to the world in terms of a feeling of absolute dependence. He no longer credits the ancient assertion that where man's finite resources come to an end, there a basic and enduring religious need arises, a need which can be satisfied only by assurances that are equally religious or absolute. To be sure, the modern era has also been characterized as an age of anxiety, testimony to an underlying uncertainty that the death of God might spell the death of man as well. In general, however, modern man has increasingly come to feel no need for the absolute reassurances of traditional belief. At this point, we begin to see how closely the existential and the metaphysical dimensions of Christian thinking are linked to one another. How we experience and make sense of the limit situations of life cannot, in the last analysis, be understood apart from the framework of interpretation we use to describe them. To understand the radical Christian position in particular, we must therefore take a closer look at how the modern shift from a religious to a secular attitude toward life is reflected in a similar shift in our philosophical interpretation of the limits and transcendence of finite being. First, we shall look at how such key limit concepts as self and world are understood within the framework of a finitist ontology. Then we shall consider how the basic concepts of a finitist ontology might be used by the radical Christian to reinterpret some of the traditional doctrines of faith associated with the phenomenon of transcendence.

## The Logic of Limits

To understand how the limit concepts of a finitist ontology might be used to support a radical Christian interpretation of the metaphysical and existential elements of faith, we must first consider the nature and function of limit concepts themselves. We may take as our example Heidegger's ontological formula for man, "being-in-the world." This formula serves as a limiting concept in several ways. First, it delimits the sort of being man is in such a way as to distinguish him from all other entities or types of being. Being-in-the-world is a basic and irreducible category of metaphysical analysis. Human existence cannot be analysed in terms of a lower level or logically more primitive set of categories such as might apply, for example, to biological or physical entities. Being-in-the-world is what Heidegger calls an ontologically primordial category.[2]

Being-in-the-world is a limiting concept in a second sense. Together with the co-primordial concepts associated with it, it articulates the logical space or conceptual framework within which all inquiries about man are to be carried on. There is no higher or other dimension of intelligibility beyond the logical (or ontological) limits set for us by this formula.

Negatively viewed, the concept of being-in-the-world appears to place limits on our inquiry into man's nature and destiny, limits beyond which we cannot and ought not go. Viewed positively, however, it may be seen as opening up or making possible (in a Kantian sense) the ontologically distinctive space or world within which man is freed to be. On the other hand, therefore, Heidegger's formula "being-in-the-world" is the key to a metaphysics that is radically secular and finitist, a philosophy which rejects any interpretation of man grounded in a mode of being that transcends man's being in the world. But it is also the key to a metaphysics that is radically humanistic in that it opposes any naturalistic reduction of human existence to a lower level of being (physical or biological) and affirms, instead, its unique conceptual character.

The radical Christian's problem is whether this humanistic and finitist perspective has not in effect ruled itself out when it comes to limit situations where men experience a need to understand the meaning of their lives as a whole. The advantage of the traditional religious or theological perspective is that it addresses itself to the human condition precisely at that point where finitude itself has been called into question. How can an ontology of finitude pretend to be of any help when it itself has been called into question? In such a situation, the only satisfactory answer presumably is one that can appeal to a reality that transcends the limitations of the merely finite.

To see how the radical Christian might approach this problem, let us look at how two secular philosophers, Heidegger and Wittgenstein, understand the relationship between a finitist perspective in metaphysics and questions about the existential (Heidegger) or ethical (Wittgenstein) significance of life. For both philosophers, the concepts of self (*Dasein,* the I) and world are limit concepts. (For Heidegger, they are also co-primordial elements of the logically prior complex, being-in-the-world.) Our language about these phenomena illustrates both their

peculiar logical status and their central importance for an understanding of what it means to be a finite being. Our utterances
about them do not exhibit the grammar of ordinary assertions
about entities within the world. Nor do they point to any further
entities beyond the limits of what can be said about the self or the
world as wholes in themselves. Statements about limit phenomena are ways of expressing certain primordial facts not capable
of further analysis—for example, that we are, that the world is, or
(combining the two) that we are able (through reflection, say) to
exist at the limits of our being-in-the-world.

Some sample limit statements by Wittgenstein and Heidegger
will illustrate this point. First, Wittgenstein commenting on the
self and its relation to the world:

> *Where in* the world is a metaphysical subject to be noted?
> The subject does not belong to the world but it is a limit of the
> world.
> There is therefore really a sense in which in philosophy we can
> talk of a non-psychological I.
> The I occurs in philosophy through the fact that the "world is my
> world."
> The philosophical I is not the man, not the human body or the
> human soul of which psychology treats, but the metaphysical
> subject, the limit—not a part of the world.
> The world and life are one.
> I am my world (The microcosm.)[3]

Again, Wittgenstein on the world:

> Not *how* the world is, is the metaphysical, but *that* it is.
> The contemplation of the world sub specie aeterni is its
> contemplation as a—limited—whole.
> The feeling of the world as a limited whole is the mystical
> feeling.[4]

Heidegger on the world and its relation to *Dasein:*

> The world itself is not an entity within-the-world; and yet it is so
> determinative for such entities that only in so far as "there is" a
> world can they be encountered and show themselves, in their
> Being, as entities which have been discovered. But in what way "is
> there" a world?
> The world *is* not, but *worlds.*
> Dasein *is* its world existingly.
> If no *Dasein* exists, no world is "there" either.
> *That* it is factically, may be obscure and hidden as regards the
> *"why"* of it; but the *"that-it-is"* *itself* has been disclosed to Dasein.

(*Dass* es faktisch ist, mag hinsichtlich des *Warum* verborgen sein, das
"*Dass*" *selbst* jedoch ist dem Dasein erschlossen.)

The disclosure of the "there" discloses co-primordially the whole
of Being-in-the-world—that is, the world, the being-in, and the self
which, as an "I am," this entity is.[5]

In making statements of this sort, both Wittgenstein and
Heidegger mean for us to see, first of all, that the sorts of limit
phenomena with which religion and theology have traditionally
dealt can in fact be meaningfully talked about in finitist terms
without assuming that such utterances are either mistaken ways
of talking about entities within the world, on the one hand, as a
narrowly positivist viewpoint might insist, or signs of a need to
refer to another realm of being beyond the limits of the self and
the world, as the theist might suppose.

Heidegger and Wittgenstein also see these assertations as having another, more existential function in addition to the transcendental or logical ones we have been considering. For both
philosophers, utterances about limit phenomena can be occa-
sions for insight into the meaning of life as a (limited) whole.
They can be seen as disclosures and affirmations of meaning that
have a distinctively wholistic and unifying function, but which
cannot be reduced to psychological or sociological facts about
man's existence within the world, on the one hand, or interpreted as evidence of the possibility of a higher meaning that
transcends the limits of the finite self and a limited world.

To understand this latter point, let us look more closely at the
examples from Heidegger, since he, more than Wittgenstein, has
developed the implications of a finitist perspective for an understanding of man's basic metaphysical experiences.

Following Jaspers, Heidegger views man's anxiety (*Angst*) in
the face of death as a primordial limit situation. Through an
analysis of this phenomenon, Heidegger attempts to disclose
what he calls the "primordial totality of Dasein's structural
whole." In man's anxiety before death, Heidegger sees the possibility for an act of existential resolve which is capable of em-
bracing and giving meaning to man's finite being as a whole.[6] The
mood of anxiety, in other words, seems particularly well suited
for giving us insight into the relationship between our funda-

mental awareness of our finitude and our subsequent affirmations about the meaning of life.

Basic moods, such as anxiety, says Heidegger, are not simply one-sided disclosures of our subjective states. They are ontologically relational phenomena which disclose to us the whole of the situation in which we find ourselves. If nothing else, a mood discloses to us the fact that we find ourselves given over to a particular situation, "thrown" into it, for no immediately apparent rhyme or reason. It discloses in the most immediate and elementary way the bare fact that we are here—in this given situation or, more broadly, in the world.

Among our various moods, anxiety stands out in particular: "Dasein's mood brings it face to face with the thrownness of its 'that it is there.' *But the state-of-mind which can hold open the utter and constant threat to itself arising from Dasein's ownmost individualized Being, is anxiety.*"[7] Why? Because this mood discloses two limit facts about the human situation. First, it discloses the totality of our being-in-the-world as such (what, for reasons we shall see, Heidegger also calls "the Nothingness" of our being); and second, it discloses my being-toward-death, the "nothing" of the possible impossibility of my own individual existence.

On the one hand, the mood of anxiety (which, again, is not simply a subjective feeling but an objective disclosure of what it means to be a human being) discloses the fundamental fact of my being-in-the-world as such. This is not an ordinary, empirical fact about some entity within the world. It is an extra-ordinary or limit fact that calls attention to the nature of my situation as a whole. As the mood that accompanies this disclosure attests, the fact that I find myself in the world is not simply a straightforward, unproblematic matter. It is an issue of concern, a fact that brings with it a fundamental unease. What is peculiar about this concern is that it is not focused on some subject or fact about my situation within the world. It is in this sense about nothing at all—except the most important fact ("the most primordial 'something' "), my being-in-the-world itself. Anxiety in the face of this limit fact means that one has suddenly been confronted with the contingency of one's existence—the fact that one's existence seems to have no prior or ultimate reason. One is simply confronted by the naked fact that one is. "The pure 'that it is' shows itself, but the 'whence' and the 'whither' remain in darkness."[8] Anxiety discloses the nullity, the "Nothing," which underlies one's being-in-the-world. "As the most elemental way in which thrown Dasein is disclosed, it puts Dasein's Being-in-the-world face to face with the 'nothing' of the world; in the face of this 'nothing,' Dasein is anxious about its ownmost potentiality-for-Being."[9]

   This brings us to the second limit fact disclosed by anxiety. "The 'nothing' with which anxiety brings us face to face unveils the nullity by which Dasein, in its very *basis,* is defined; and this basis itself is as thrownness into death."[10] Not only does anxiety disclose the "nothing" of our contingency as beings who find themselves in the world without an ultimate whence or whither; it also makes us painfully aware that the one possibility about which we can have some certainty is the eventual cessation of our being-in-the-world, the time when there will be no world for us.[11] Anxiety therefore confronts us with both the "nothing" (contingency) of our being-in-the-world and the "nothing" (finitude) of our being-toward-death.

   For Heidegger, this double disclosure of the "nothing" which underlies our finite being, or which, more precisely, spells out the intrinsic logical meaning of our finitude, is one of the irreducible and defining aspects (limit features) of a distinctively human mode of being. The important hermeneutical question which arises at this point is, What further significance are we to attribute to our finitude? As viewed by theologians, this is the occasion and indeed the justification for positing a transcendent ground of being which is capable of making a higher sense out of, and therefore of overcoming, the nullity of finite being. For Heidegger, however, as a radically secular thinker, the significance of this phenomenon is quite different, and leads to a radically different conclusion. Anxiety does not lead us beyond the realm of finitude. It points us back to, and repeatedly circles around, the primordial fact of our being-in-the world as such. It redirects us to the world and to ourselves in such a way that we are not simply reabsorbed into our everyday concerns but are

aware simultaneously of our existence within the world and at its
borders. We are conscious of the ultimate gratuitousness of our
existence and yet of our total responsibility for it as well. We are
aware of the fundamental mystery of being—that there is something rather than nothing, that we find ourselves here, "thrown"
into the world. But we are aware of its joy and wonder too—that
in the midst of this contingency, we have been set free to live. For
Heidegger, in other words, the anxious experience of the "nothing" at the heart of existence can be viewed as the prelude to a
liberating experience of the fact and freedom of our being. The
two experiences are opposite sides of the same disclosure. The
miracle of meaning takes place in the passage, or conversion,
from one to the other. It is as though we now lived in another
world—and of course, in a most important sense, we do.¹²

In a later work, Heidegger says: "Das Nichts . . . ist der
Schleier des Seins"¹³—loosely translated, "The experience of
nothingness . . . is the veil which conceals the disclosure of the
mystery of being." There is an obvious similarity, as we have
already noted, between this finitist dialectic of nothingness and
being and the traditional theistic dialectic of God and the original
*nihil* out of which God brought beings into being. In both cases,
an initial apprehension of the nothingness at the heart of existence is transformed into an awareness and affirmation of the
positive mystery of being. But here the similarity ends. For
Heidegger, given his finitist perspective, the outcome of this
dialectic is not an affirmation of a transcendent ground of being
but a reaffirmation of the intrinsic mystery and value of finitude
itself. On the far side of the anxiety which discloses the nothingness of our being, we do not find God; we find a transformed and
renewed capacity to say yes to finite being. *Angst,* Heidegger
tells us, is not an excuse to escape from our situation, whether by
withdrawing from the world or by making demands upon it
which it cannot possibly fulfill. Nor is anxiety an excuse for
nihilism or pessimism or unremitting despair. Along with "the
sober anxiety" which discloses our contingency and mortality
there arises the possibility of a new and liberating attitude, "an
unshakable joy" in the gift of one's being, a belief that the world,

however mysterious or uncanny *(unheimlich)*, is indeed our home, a place within which and at whose edges the miracle of meaning can occur.[14]

## The Logic of Transcendence

Philosophers like Wittgenstein and Heidegger follow Kant in arguing that limit concepts such as self and world do not refer to quasi-empirical entities which are themselves, in turn, grounded on an entity that transcends the world. Rather they are logical or ontological terms, Ideas of Pure Reason, whose function is to describe in a very general way the sort of entity we are and to indicate the outer limits of intelligibility for any inquiry into the nature of that entity. They are the fundamental categories of an ontology of finitude.

An acceptance of this approach to the self and the world poses obvious problems for the radical Christian. Traditionally, an awareness of the limits of finite being has always been accompanied by a belief in the possibility of transcending those limits. The radical Christian has ruled this possibility out. How then does he hope to salvage anything from the traditional doctrines of God and man, which clearly presuppose a reality that transcends both self and world? How, in particular, does he propose to make sense of such examples of transcendence as the traditional predicates of divine being, the eschatological function of God, man's experience of grace, or our need for a higher perspective from which to judge the limitations of our present life? These notions appear to be called into question by a perspective whose own highest categories are those of self and world, and whose basic categories are those of contingency or finitude.

For the radical Christian, however, the situation is not quite as it appears. The predicates of finite being (contingency, possibility, temporality) can in fact be used to reinterpret some of the traditional predicates of transcendent being (infinity, unconditionality, eternity). We have argued in an earlier chapter that what sets the new ontology apart from the traditional metaphysics of transcendence is that it involves a fundamental shift

or inversion of categorial priorities. The previously derivative
or inferior categories of becoming (contingency, temporality,
possibility) have ousted the hitherto dominant categories of
classical metaphysics (absolute, unchanging, perfect being) from
their position of primacy in the hierarchy of being. The understanding of being, and hence the highest values, of the new
ontology are radically finitist in nature.

But what exactly does this mean for the traditional categories
of divine being? Contrary to the assumption of theologians, this
death of God does not lead inexorably to the abyss of relativism
or nihilism. It makes possible a retrieval and reaffirmation of
many of the insights into transcendence furnished by the old
predicates of being, but this time in a new and unalienated way.
The radical Christian reinterprets the former categories of transcendence, but no longer on the basis of the old assumptions. He
sees them, instead, as predicates or qualifiers of the new categories of finite being.

How so? The concepts of contingency, temporality, and possibility are the basic ingredients of a new concept of being as
irreducibly open to that which is new or that which is not yet.
These concepts, in turn, make possible a new reading of such
traditional concepts as infinity, the absolute, the unconditioned,
the eternal—and thus of the central concept of transcendence as
well. The traditional predicates of divine being therefore no
longer need to be viewed as ways of describing a realm of being
that transcends the realm of finitude. Instead, they may be seen
as our strongest possible terms for emphasizing in an absolute
and unqualified way the irreducible openness of finite being,
above all in its aspect as openness toward the future. The infinity
or eternality of finite being lies in its preeminent openness to the
future.

Put in another way, the traditional categories of transcendence
can be understood as ways of saying that, despite all those things
that have determined us in the past or that condition us in the
present, man exists in such a way that there are always future
possibilities which are still outstanding, possibilities for going
beyond that which is toward that which might yet be. The dimension of the future stands for that which is not yet finished, not

completely determined, that which is open to the possibility of
something new. It is our opening onto the eternal, in the sense
that it represents the ever-present possibility of going beyond
the givens of the present (thought not beyond our temporal
being as a whole).

Now as we have seen, some of the secular theologians have
claimed that an ontology which stresses the temporal openness
of being is not necessarily incompatible with a theistic perspective. To the contrary, they argue, it provides the metaphysical
key for disclosing the heretofore hidden essence of the biblical
view of God—a dynamic view of God quite different from the
Parmenidean view of God inherited from the Greeks. For these
theologians, the irreducible openness of being, or the power of
the open future, is nothing other than the being of God himself.
Even if we grant the radical Christian his nontheistic appropriation of an ontology of finitude, we have therefore still not made
our case. For now the question arises, What is to distinguish his
position from the use to which this ontology is put by the secular
theologian? Are there in fact any significant differences between
their views of the ontological status of the future? How does one
justify the decision to use, or not to use, the term "God" to
interpret the temporal openness of being?

One obvious difference between the two positions is that for
the radical Christian, to say that being is radically contingent or
temporally open is not to imply that being is ultimately favorable
to man. It is not a promise, for example, that our specific hopes
for the future will, if we have faith, find ultimate satisfaction. Nor
is it necessarily to say, in a more modest, Jamesian sense, that the
universe at least allows for the possibility that our eschatological
beliefs may prove true. Not all the evidence is in, and it is
conceivable that it will never be. In any case, this reduced scale of
expectation would rule out some of the more ambitious claims of
traditional Christian belief. If one reinterprets these hopes along
consistently finitist lines, as the radical Christian proposes to do,
it becomes questionable whether one can legitimately claim to
be delivering the essence of traditional faith. To the radical
Christian's credit, he makes no such claim. On the other hand, he
is no more convinced than are orthodox believers that halfway

houses of the sort constructed by the secular theologians (and in
an earlier day, by liberal theology) can succeed in preserving the
elusive essence of Christianity.

The fact that theists who affirm an open future really believe
that they can affirm a radically temporal concept of being, on the
one hand, and yet preserve some version of the traditional
eschatological assurances of Christian faith, on the other, is a
sure sign that, outward affirmations to the contrary, they are still
committed to an underlying belief that fatally compromises their
adherence to the new secular perspective. The belief that eschatological fulfillment lies somewhere ahead in the open future,
the hope that someday the promises of God will be fulfilled,
necessarily commits the theologian to one of two alternatives:
either he must guarantee this possibility in advance by postulat-
ing a transcendent being or he must posit within the temporal
process itself a necessary movement toward this goal. Either of
these beliefs, as we have already seen, is incomptabile with the
fundamental categories of a finitist ontology.

If we eliminate the concept of a transcendent being or the
similarly inspired notion of a predetermined course of being,
there is no sense left to the assertion that the power of the open
future is identical with the being of God. Implicit in the theologian's view that the being of God is preeminently futural is the
eschatological hope that one day the open future will be converted into an absolute future, a state of affairs in which there is a
final resolution of the contradictions of finite being. But it is
precisely this "over-belief," a belief which exceeds the boundaries of a finitist understanding of the openness of the future,
which the radical Christian, along with post-theistic thinkers
generally, must unequivocally reject. To do less is to confuse the
sense in which the future always transcends the present (a logical
sense, quite compatible with—in fact, essential to—an ontology
of finitude) with the traditional ontotheological belief in an
order of being which transcends the temporal order as a whole. It
is this confusion, finally, which lies behind the equivocal treatment the concept of the open future receives at the hands of the
secularizing theologians (seen most clearly, for example, in
Rahner's theologically motivated substitution of the phrase "the

absolute future" for the descriptively more accurate and less
prejudicial term "the open future").

The secular theologian may, however, reply that, apart from a
prior divine guarantee, there is no assurance that the future will
remain open. On what ontological grounds can a philosopher of
finitude justify his own belief in the openness of the future?
What ontological guarantee does he have that man will continue
to be able to open himself to that future? Again, how can one
make sense of the power of the future to disrupt the givens of the
past and present unless one presupposes some transcendent
basis for that power?

Here again, the radical Christian's strategy is to remind the
theologian of Kant's arguments against transforming the limit
concepts and regulative ideals of a descriptive metaphysics of
temporal experience into the quasi-referential terms of a
speculative metaphysics of transcendent being. When we resort
to such metaphors as the "power" or "openness" of the future,
we are speaking in a compressed and abstract manner about the
most general features of our way of comprehending and ordering
the phenomena of temporal experience. We are saying, for
example, that phenomena never present themselves to us as
simply what they are at an abstract instant in time. We see them
in that same moment in terms of what they will be, can be, might
yet be, or ought to be. What really is always includes something
more than what *currently* is. Our perception of every actual entity
or state of affairs always includes a com-prehension of its further
possibilities. In that sense, we might be led to say, as does
Heidegger, that possibility is higher than actuality or that the
future transcends the present. All of these metaphysical assertions are abstract or metaphorical ways of calling attention to the
most general features of finite, temporal experience. To hypostasize these metaphors for the logical features of finitude, and
then to ask in quasi-empirical fashion what grounds or guarantees them, is to misconceive both the phenomenon of finitude
and the sort of limit analysis in which the descriptive metaphysician is engaged.

The only other reply the radical Christian can make to mis-

guided questions about man's capacity for transcendence, apart
from brushing them aside, is simply to say the same thing over
again, perhaps in an even more compressed way, until his hearer
"just sees." That is, he may speak of such limit concepts as the
openness of the future, or the fact that the world is, by using
tautologies (from the Greek, *tautos-logos,* same-saying), perhaps
repeating the subject term in the predicate *(etymologica figura),*
employing neologisms if necessary. Thus Heidegger: "Die Zeit
sich zeitigt"; die Welt *ist* nicht, sondern *weltet*"; "die Zukunft
kunft uns zu." Such statements are the metaphysician's equivalent of the Zen master's whack on the head or Wittgenstein's
bump that suddenly produces a new way of seeing.

If the theologian or, at the other end of the spectrum, the
linguistic positivist persists in finding such utterances unaccept-
able, either because they do not follow the rules of the theist's
transcendental logic or because they do not adhere to the rules of
language used to talk about entities within the world, then the
rest is probably silence. Language is of course capable of saying a
great deal about those limit phenomena about which nothing
further can be "said," and of doing so in logically proper ways.
There are recognized and well-defined rules for the appropriate
uses of language at the limits of language—for example, the rules
of platitude and paradox, tautology and metaphor. In such con-
texts, silence too is a legitimate linguistic move. It, along with the
others, is one way we have as finite beings to express our awareness of the fundamental mystery or contingency of our being-in-
the-world.

The difference between a radical Christian and a theological
concept of the open future is also reflected in another issue
associated with the phenomenon of transcendence. As we have
noted, the secular theologians were not entirely able to avoid the
contradictions contained in the traditional dialectic linking the
independent power of the future (grace) to man's responsibility
for shaping the future (freedom). Despite their appreciation of
the open future as an important category for humanizing the
concept of God, they seemed reluctant to join with their Marxist
counterparts in affirming that man has the final responsibility for

determining the shape of that future, that man is capable of carving his own destiny out of the "nothingness" (not-yet-being) of the future.

The radical Christian, on the other hand, has to reject the theist's solution to this apparent dilemma. The theist interprets the openness of the future not as an exigency at the heart of man's being but as a plenitude of being and power that under-girds man's own finite efforts. The radical Christian wishes to affirm a new and different paradox: man's nature is sufficient or complete unto itself just because he exists in a fundamentally incomplete or open-ended way. The theistic paradox of human freedom and divine grace translates into a radically secular affir-mation of the identity of freedom and finitude. An ontology of finitude leads necessarily to a paradoxical or dialectical concept of man's being as finite freedom: man is totally responsible for his own "thrown" being-in-the-world.[15]

But just how does this resolutely finitist approach go about reconciling these two apparently contradictory aspects of man's being: his sense of complete responsibility for his own existence, on the one hand, and his sense of the giftlike character of his being, on the other? Here again the radical Christian's initial move is to point to the confusion that follows from the assump-tion that when we are talking about the openness of the future (a logical feature of finite, temporal being), we are talking about a hypostasized realm of being somewhere out there ahead (like an object on the road ahead of us). References to the independent power of the future are not references to an external force but to the a priori or transcendental status of this phenomenon as a general feature of man's mode of being. On the one hand, the future is open quite apart from any particular thing I may happen to do. It is simply a necessary feature of my existence, a truth about the way I have (logically) to exist. On the other hand, it is man's own being which is the locus or place where this power of the open future is realized (*Da-sein* as the *Da* of *Sein* in its futural aspect). It is not a phenomenon which can be separated from, or talked about independently of, man's distinctive way of being.[16] It cannot therefore be made the object of a seemingly insoluble

theological conundrum about the relation between God and
man. It is a descriptive feature of man's existence, not a pointer
to a source of being that lies beyond.[17]

The traditional Christian insight into the tension between
immanence and transcendence, man's freedom (or misuse of his
freedom) and God's grace, does not simply disappear with the
introduction of a finitist perspective on man. It reappears in a
new form as the dialectic between a future conceived as the
predetermined extension of the givens of the past and present
and a future which, though situated in a past and present,
nevertheless comes toward us *(die Zukunft kommt uns zu)* with
surprises and possibilities of its own. In the latter instance, the
future sets us free to undertake new initiatives beyond those
which are determined solely by our past or present circumstances. Thus, while the radical Christian retains his sense
for the mysterious, giftlike character of our being, including the
possibilities for renewal that arise when we discover the limits of
our current ways of being, he does so in a way that frees us from a
mystified or alienated understanding of these phenomena and
that frees us for the task of shaping our own destinies. As finite
beings, we are both "thrown" and free.

For the radical Christian, there is no inconsistency in asserting
that men are responsible for their own destinies while at the
same time agreeing that the future constantly surprises and
upends our plans. For if the latter were not so, the former would
not be possible either. It is this dialectical insight, and not the
positing of some transcendent power, which points to the true
paradox of human freedom. If the future did not break up the
accomplishments and certitudes of the past, we, in turn, would
neither need nor be able to engage in those higher, imaginative
acts of criticism and fresh creation which are essential to the
exercise of responsibility for one's future. To be open to the fact
that the future will inevitably bring with it possibilities that
transcend one's past or present circumstances is to be willing to
adopt a critical attitude toward one's present reality and to be
ready to undertake the necessary activity of transforming it. If
there were no such possibility that something new could come

into being, something which we initially could not foresee or control, then we would be unable to assume responsibility even for that which we already are.

This brings us to one last difference between a radical Christian and a theological view of transcendence. The theist claims that a finitist (or immanentalist) interpretation of transcendence necessarily involves the sacrifice of a critical perspective on man. By ruling out the possibility of a higher court of appeal, it renders itself vulnerable to man's demonic tendency to absolutize himself. For the radical Christian, on the other hand, a radical temporalization of transcendence need not lend itself to a justification of what is. It functions as does the traditional notion—though no longer in a mystifying or alienating way—to remind us of the penultimacy of all our works. The openness of the future is not only a source of promise and of hope. It is also our hedge against the uncritical elevation of every existing state of affairs. As finite beings, we can never regard our past or present achievements as final or unqualifiedly good; nor can we view our claims or potentials for the future as absolutely sure or right. They are always subject to the judgment and correction of what is yet to come.

To summarize, for the radical Christian, a positive understanding of transcendence is quite compatible with a finitist perspective on being. There need not be any reference to a reality that transcends the limits of finite being for such a concept to make sense. To some of course, any attempt to define transcendence in terms of the categories of finitude must already be a parody of the traditional concept and will be a less than satisfactory way of helping men come to terms with the limits of their being. But this need not be so. Our understanding of the meaning of transcendence is shaped by our understanding of what it means to be a finite, limited being. If we are preoccupied with limits in the sense of that which renders powerless or confines, then the theistic position will continue to have appeal. But if we understand limits in the sense of that which makes possible, that which lets a being be, then the theistic answer is not the only one to which we can turn. By interpreting the limit concepts of finitude (contingency, possibility, temporality) as symbols for the intrinsic openness of being, for the mystery of being that lets beings be, the radical Christian invites us to share in the ever-fresh and recurring miracle of be-ing itself. He presents us with a new possibility, a new attitude of openness and gratitude for the gift of our finite being. For the radical Christian at least, a finitist interpretation of being need not condemn us to a life of "sober anxiety." It can do much more. It can also disclose to us an unexpected path by which we are set free for "an unshakable joy."

# 9

## Radical Christian Thinking: The Working of History

In the previous chapter, we looked at a radical Christian approach to rethinking the problematic of God and man by interpreting the phenomena of limits and transcendence in terms of an ontology of finitude. In the present chapter, we shall look at how the radical Christian can use this same ontology to rethink the concepts of history and the world and, in so doing, come to a new appreciation of the relationship between his own thinking and the Christian tradition. A description of the radical Christian's perspective on the working of history in his own tradition will lead us to consider, in a final chapter, why the future of the Marxist-Christian dialogue may depend less upon questions of metaphysical belief and more upon differences in the historical resources each brings to the task of setting men free.

## The Human World

Our existence as historical beings can be understood only in the context of our existence in the world. The drama of history, which includes the problematic of our relationship to the past as well as our practical hopes for the future, takes place against a cosmological backdrop. Our first task is therefore to determine what would be a radical Christian way of thinking about the world. The task is a twofold one. A radical Christian concept of the world must be compatible with the general categories of a finitist ontology. It must be able to take its place alongside the

concepts of being and man presented in the preceding chapter.
This is required by the general ontological schema we have been
presupposing throughout this study. But a radical Christian concept of the world must also be able to meet the more specific
criticisms which Marxists have lodged against the traditional
cosmological doctrines of Christianity. The radical Christian
must therefore find a way of thinking about the world that both
affirms this world as the only world there is and yet sets itself
in principle against the present world order in the name of a
more human world of the future. In traditional terms, he must
work out a doctrine of Creation and a doctrine of eschatology,
but within the setting of a radically secular ontology.

A radically secular view of the world provides the radical
Christian, in the first place, with the opportunity for a new
doctrine of Creation. It is this world, and not some other world,
that the radical Christian affirms to be good. It is this world which
is a desirable and proper place in which to live and work, in which
to shape a meaningful human life. It is good in all the ordinary
ways we recognize as ways of existing and acting in the world.
Philosophically and practically, the radical Christian agrees with
the secular thinker that this is the only world there is and that it is
a world for us, a human world, a proper place for human beings
to live and be.

This notion of the human world is not to be confused with the
traditional metaphysical concept of the world as the totality of all
that is (the physical universe and all its contents). It refers rather
to the totality of the practical relations within which human
beings exist. For the radical Christian especially, the world is not
a totality of things; it is the totality of our ways of being in the
world. The proper categories for describing the world in this
sense will therefore not be the categories which fit the world
conceived simply as the totality of the objects of empirical
knowledge. They will be categories derived from the logically
(or ontologically) prior concept of finite being-in-the-world. In
other words, the proper ontological categories for describing the
human world will be the categories of contingency, possibility,
and temporality. As in the case of the phenomenon of human

existence, the being of the world will be described as a process of continual self-transcendence. The world of man is a practical-relational totality of finite but open-ended change.

In accepting this finitist concept of the world as the practical environment of human activity, the radical Christian is willing to agree that all that he knows about the world is, and must be obtained from, our various types of practical involvement in the world. This includes our scientific investigation and technological manipulation of the world, as well as those economic, social, and cultural activities by which we shape our larger, human environment. Beyond this knowledge of the world, there is nothing further to be known about the world. Thus the radical Christian rejects from the outset any claim to furnish knowledge about the world that differs from or is superior to that which the world is capable of obtaining for itself. In particular, he rejects the possibility of any knowledge about another world which is accessible only through nonsecular channels such as revelation.

If the radical Christian rejects the traditional ontology of two worlds, he is still concerned to find a way of preserving the insight of biblical faith that man is in some sense an inhabitant of two different worlds. As we have noted, faith represents, in the first instance, not a quantitative increment in our knowledge but a qualitative change in our perspective on the one and only world we know. It points to the fact that we are capable of being in the world in two fundamentally different ways. Given our definition of the (human) world as the practical totality of our relationships to the world, insofar as we see and live in the world in two different ways, we in fact inhabit two different worlds.[1] From the perspective of faith, the radical Christian sees an important experiential difference between a religious view of the world which sees this world (not another) as holy and good, which sees this world *sub specie aeternitatis* as a limited whole, and that sort of secular view which fails to perceive or perhaps deliberately excludes any sense of the ultimate mystery or wonder of the world. In this lived rather than metaphysical sense of two worlds, the radical Christian affirms (as the Marxist humanist does in his way) the significance of his historical perspective for the attempt to work out a radically secular concept of the world that both accepts this world as good and holds before it a higher vision of a more human world of the future.

As this last comment indicates, the radical Christian is concerned not only to rethink his concept of the secular world as a whole (a doctrine of Creation). He is also concerned to rethink his understanding of the relationship between the present world order and its future possibilities (a doctrine of eschatology). Once again, he finds in a radically secular or finitist concept of the world the conceptual resources he needs. In addition to being seen in practical rather than physicalistic terms, the world is viewed in specifically futural terms. As the relational totality of human activity, the world of man is interpreted in terms of the priority of the future. Logically (or ontologically), it is this dimension of temporality which makes possible or intelligible the concept of action in general. The future opens up the logical space needed for men to distance themselves from their past or present situation and project ahead of themselves higher or as yet unrealized possibilities of a more human world. The cosmology of a radically finitist ontology is thus a doctrine of *secularia semper reformanda,* of a world which is always open to the future and thus open to criticism, transformation, and continuous self-transcendence. An ontology of finitude provides the basis for an affirmation of the world as the proper setting for human existence, but it does so in a way that ensures a permanently critical or revolutionary attitude toward the existing structures of the world in the name of a more human world of the future.

When the radical Christian speaks of a world that transcends this world, he is therefore not speaking in metaphysically dualistic terms. He is speaking experientially and historically of a way of being in the world that is qualitatively different from, and transcendent to, the way of being that characterizes the present world order of alienation. He is speaking, in other words, just as the Marxist or any other secular critic of the existing world must speak. He is speaking about a way of life that goes beyond the way of life we currently know. He is not speaking of a world that transcends the secular order as a whole.

The eschatological vision, the promises and hopes of biblical faith, which theists take as pointers to a different order of reality

situated on the far side of secular history, are taken by the radical
Christian as a permanent blend of realistic expectation and utopian imagination which bears on the never-ending task of making
this world a more human place in which to be. This blend is
structured, logically, to fit the perpetual paradox which the
future represents. The future is, on the one hand, the determinate outgrowth of our past traditions and present plans—our
realistic projects for changing the world and shaping a more
human future. But the future is also the ever-outstanding dimension of the not-yet-realized, that which eludes our past and
present calculations, the realm of the surprising and the new—of
utopian dreams and aspirations which lead us forward, which can
never be completely realized, but which give us the strength to
hold the future open for that which is yet to come.

One criterion for judging between two different views of the
world is the extent to which each enables us to affirm this world
as a human world, the proper place for man to be. On this score,
the radical Christian perspective seems at least as adequate as a
Marxist humanist one. But a second criterion is the ability of a
particular world view to provide a practical impetus and methods
for transforming the present world in the direction of a more
human world of the future. For the radical Christian, the question inevitably arises: is this cosmology any better able than the
traditional one to commit itself to specific programs of analysis
and practical action, or does it too remain at the level of
eschatological-utopian generalities?

Here, I think, the radical Christian's position is bound to be
somewhat more complex. Even in its radical form, the Christian
perspective, as a religious perspective, is not designed primarily
to provide, from out of its own resources, either a scientific
analysis of society or a specific set of guidelines for a program of
revolutionary activity. Though its eschatological perspective
may be reinterpreted as supporting particular critical-revolu-
tionary projects, as a distinctly Christian or broadly religious
perspective it cannot really go much farther than to provide
the agents of such activity with an overall historical perspective
within which to view their specific revolutionary praxis, a vision
based on certain events and symbols central to that tradition. The

important point, however, is that the radical Christian need not
regret this fact. For it does not necessarily follow that a *radical*
Christian view of the world is therefore finally religious or unreal
in Marx's sense—that is, that it is incapable of giving specific
guidance to the work of real, this-worldly transformation.
Another interpretation is possible.

When it comes to changing the world, the radical Christian is,
in the first instance, in the same situation as every other man. He,
like others, must look to the sciences and institutions of secular
society for guidance as to the best ways of bringing about such
change. As a Christian, however, he brings with him certain
additional imaginative resources (images of man, paradigms of
self and society) which give much more specific shape to his own
activities and hopes for the future of man. Moreover, this imaginative vision serves as a resource upon which even the Marxist
himself may feel compelled to draw as the program of world
transformation moves closer toward historical realization. Programs of revolutionary change require more than scientific
analyses of society and specific methods of implementation.
They also presuppose an imaginative vision of man and society,
as well as a larger historical and interpretive tradition within
which this vision is embodied and which, in turn, it extends.
Without this larger imaginative setting, programs of revolutionary activity can lead to consequences which are the tragic
opposite of those which were originally intended. In certain
circumstances, the biblical vision of man, which was earlier
judged by its secular critics to be utopian, could therefore conceivably come to express the realistic requirement of a new
historical era.[2] In this respect, as some of the Marxist participants
in this dialogue have already admitted, it may well be the Christian who turns out to be the creative rather than dependent
partner in the contemporary effort to liberate man.

To summarize, the radical Christian approach to the traditional two worlds cosmology is one that is entirely compatible
with a radically secular, finitist ontology. It is equally important
to note, however, that apart from such an ontology, the radical
Christian distinction between the present world and the world to
come would be in danger of losing its meaning. It would tend to

be understood, as was traditional Christian cosmology, in dualistic, metaphysical terms that would rob of its ultimate seriousness the radical Christian's hope for the future of this world, the only world in which it is given men to live. Radical Christian thinking needs an ontology of secularity not simply to gain a hearing from the contemporary world but because it needs to know for itself which insights of its own tradition are still living ones for Christians today.

## A Hermeneutical Shift

This brings us to the central issue of this chapter. If, as I have been arguing, the theoretical world views and practical hopes of Marxist humanism and radical Christian thinking can be shown to be compatible (at least in principle), then the decisive factor in any attempt to choose between them is the historical or hermeneutical one.[3] What do we see when we look at their respective histories—the stories, events, traditions, symbols, and perspectives within which their general theories of being, man, and the world have been embodied? What do these tell us about the fidelity and efficacy of each tradition's attempt to set men free? This criterion is doubly pertinent in the case of two traditions whose view of the world is historical in nature. Christianity distinguishes itself from the Eastern religions as an historical religion. Marxism distinguishes itself from its French positivist predecessors as an historical materialism. By their own standards, the world views and praxis of these two traditions must be judged against the broader background of their historical truth.

The question of historical truth can be formulated in several ways. Up until now I have been assuming that the basic hermeneutical question was: Which of these historical perspectives does the most justice to the modern story of the struggle for human emancipation? Which provides the best grounds, theoretical and practical, for interpreting and assisting that struggle? It is possible, however, that this way of putting the question is neither the only one nor best. It may commit us to methodological or ontological assumptions that have themselves been called into question by the story we are seeking to tell. It is possible, for example, that, along with the contemporary shift in

ontological assumptions, there has gone a parallel shift in the
methodological assumptions we make when we ask the question
of historical truth. Perhaps along with the shift from an ontotheological to a radically secular way of thinking there has gone
a shift in the way we understand and formulate the question of
the continuing vitality of a particular historical tradition. It will
be our task in the remainder of this chapter to see whether there
is not another and better way to understand the question of
historical truth and, if so, to determine what this means for the
radical Christian's attempt to understand the working of history
in his own tradition.

To do this, we must first review the impasse to which radical
Christian thinking was brought by our initial formulation of the
hermeneutical question. That question asked whether there was
a positive relationship between the Christian historical tradition
and the new view of man and the world represented by a
philosophy of radical secularity. The secular criticism of the
claims made on behalf of the Christian tradition focused on the
question whether the figure of Jesus could legitimately be
viewed as the historical basis and norm for this new attitude toward the world. We argued that such a conclusion required dis-
torting the few facts we have about the historical Jesus and putting on them a weight of interpretation they could not possibly
carry. The facts suggest, rather, that the rise of a secular and revolutionary attitude toward the world took place in the events of
our own modern era. However indebted this modern tradition
may be to the biblical tradition, it is quite another thing to
suggest that it finds its historical origins and continuing validity
only therein. It comes as no surprise, therefore, when the secular
critic concludes that the Christian tradition, whether theologically or radically conceived, is at best an incomplete, mythological,
and alienated story about the liberation of men, a temporary and
culturally provincial halfway house in the larger world-historical
drama.

This argument leaves the Christian defending an uncomfort-
able and even dubious position. If he is a radical Christian, he
must admit that it is he, not the secular thinker, who is in
a position of indebtedness—dependent upon modern, post-

Christian consciousness for the norms of his own radical consciousness and his practical efficacy as an agent of change in the
world. Moreover, he is forced to admit that even the essentials of
his own tradition may be images of man and the world as they
used to be, not images of what they have become or what they
may yet be.[4] To the extent that he wishes to retain his identity as
a Christian, he may therefore be condemning himself to repeat
the past, to retell the old story, rather than to participate in the
active creation of a new one. The radical Christian's hermeneutical task—to link the biblical tradition to his own thinking as a
modern, secular man—would therefore appear to be an all but
impossible one.

Here we return to the very first question we directed against
the theologians of secularity: How, if one is truly a radical
thinker, can one even engage in dialogue with these texts, with
this specific tradition? The assumption that one can appears
to have been taken for granted, even by our radical Christian
thinker. Has not the argument of these chapters been that the
radical Christian can accept a secular interpretation of being,
man, and the world and still define himself in terms of the specific difference of the Christian tradition? And yet, is this not precisely what we said it is no longer possible to do? Was it not just
at this point that secular theology was found to be a hopelessly
self-contradictory enterprise? For beneath this historical-hermeneutical question is an ontotheological one. How can one
eliminate God from one's thinking and still maintain the Christocentric focus necessary for identifying oneself as a Christian?
Does not Christian thinking, however radical, depend upon a
prior doctrine of God to ground its historical or hermeneutical
claims? The Christian's argument from history (that Jesus is the
Christ) depends, logically, upon the concept of God. Once this
link is severed, how can there be any normative basis for a
distinctively Christian perspective?

We appear to be faced with a hermeneutical impasse which
itself is based on a prior theological contradiction: How can one
have a doctrine of Christ (of Jesus as the norm of one's historical
perspective) without a doctrine of God? However, as I should

now like to argue, this doctrinal objection obscures the real
situation in which the radical Christian finds himself. The end
of the metaphysics of transcendent, theistic being means,
methodologically, that we are now free to work out a radically
new ontology of history and thus to formulate the question of the
historical truth of the Christian tradition in quite another way. If
we operate from the presuppositions of an ontology of historical
being rather than an ontology of transcendent being, the question of the truth of the Christian tradition need not be linked to
theological claims, but can be stated in terms that reflect our
understanding of what it means to exist as historical beings. The
question of the normative significance of the Christian tradition
will thus be one of historical not theological interpretation. It
will be concerned with the continuing historical availability of
the events, symbols, and institutions that constitute the historical
(not metaphysical) reality of that particular tradition.

How, then, does the conversion from traditional ontotheology to a metaphysics of radical historicity affect the hermeneutical assumptions of the radical Christian thinker? In general, it
means that the truth of a particular tradition is not to be viewed as
something that is fixed and given for all time, a set of essentials
that never change no matter how much the surface features of
language and thought may vary. Rather, the truth of a tradition is
judged as much by its capacity to change and grow, to be open to
the future and that which is new, as by the size of its contribution
toward making us what we presently are. For the radical Christian, the hermeneutical question about the truth of the Christian
tradition is therefore wrongly formulated if taken as asking
whether secular thinking can assist the Christian to regain the
alleged essentials of his tradition. The radical Christian is concerned to know rather whether he can draw upon the resources
of contemporary secular thought to create new possibilities for
Christian thinking—possibilities which did not exist before. The
radical Christian does not contend that these new possibilities
were somehow implicitly contained in the Christian tradition all
along. He is quite clear that they constitute borrowings, addi-
tions, insights originally arrived at and developed in the setting

of another, subsequent tradition (the modern, secular story). What he does claim, as a Christian thinker, is that they can become possibilities for the Christian tradition too—and that sometimes this makes all the difference. The hermeneutical question for the radical Christian is therefore not whether the new can be grounded in the old, but whether the old is open to the new and thereby capable of continuing to live.

The radical Christian, unlike the secular theologian, has no difficulty accepting the argument that the Christian tradition is not the spiritual ancestor of the modern world view. He agrees with the secular critic of theology that the quest for the essentials of the Christian tradition is misguided from the start. Indeed, one of the first essentials to go is the doctrine of God itself. Unlike both the secular thinker and the theologian, however, the radical Christian contends that the Christian tradition is in fact open to the new secular view of the world and that, for historical (not essentialist) reasons, an ontology of radical secularity can be viewed as one of the future possibilities for Christianity as well. The new story of radical secularity is not grounded in the older story of Christianity, but neither does it bring the older story to an end. It is the radical Christian's conviction that the story of secular man gives new life to the Christian story and thereby makes possible a new historical perspective that avoids the criticisms directed against the secular theologians, on the one hand, while presenting a clear alternative to the Marxist historical perspective, on the other. The radical Christian does not see himself as retelling an old story. He is telling a new story, though it is a Christian one still.

Obviously, the radical Christian's position is not a simple one. It rests, as I have indicated, on two rather unusual and debatable claims. First, it assumes that the new ontology of finitude makes possible a radically different understanding of the hermeneutical question. Second, it argues that this novel approach to ontology and the hermeneutical question stands in significant historical continuity (and discontinuity) with the historical tradition of Christianity itself. In the remaining two sections of this chapter, we shall examine each of these propositions in turn.

The Working of History

The radical Christian bases his interpretation of the Christian tradition on a way of thinking about history that is grounded in an ontology of finitude. The basic categories of this ontology are those of contingency, possibility, and temporality. As we have seen in the cases of Marx and Heidegger, these categories spell the end of a Parmenidean or ontotheological concept of absolute, unchanging, transtemporal being. They lead, instead, to a concept of being as historical in nature. As Heidegger points out, this new ontology is particularly well suited for a dialogue with Marxism, because "it recognizes the essential way in which the historical belongs to being itself."[5] From a finitist perspective on being, Heidegger says, the essence *(Wesen)* of being is the happening *(Geschehen)* of being.

What does this mean? The concept of being is defined by the categories of finitude. The categories of finitude describe the nature of things in terms of contingency, temporality, change. It is essential to our understanding of finite things, in other words, that we not interpret them simply in terms of what they are at any moment. We must also see them in terms of what they have been or what they yet may be. Finite things have no unchanging essence which stays the same throughout all the events that happen to them on the surface of their being. The essence of anything finite consists, rather, in the working out of a temporal dialectic of continuity and discontinuity, sameness and change, in which the forces of the past, the circumstances of the present, and the possibilities of the future are all effectively present. This dialectic at work in the being of every finite thing is essential not only for our understanding of what that thing is but also for that entity's continued ability to be. A finite thing cannot continue to be by simply continuing to be what it already or currently is. If it is unable to change so as to meet the changes in the world around (or within) it, it inevitably ceases to be. For an ontology of finitude, the eventlike happening of being is therefore a necessary (not accidental) feature both of our concept of being and of the essence of being itself.

208 Post-Theistic Thinking

To say that history is of the essence of being is to say that being is of the essence of history. History, which we normally think of as a mode of being distinctive of man, must, like the being of man himself, first be understood in ontological terms. Philosophers like Heidegger and Marx have taught us to interpret man not in one-sided, subjective terms as an isolated subject or activity of reflective self-consciousness but in relational and dialectical terms as a being-in-the-world. Similarly, history is not to be interpreted in narrowly subjective or existential terms, but should be seen as a matrix of happening that precedes the analysis of man's being-in-the-world into the derivative categories of subjective and objective being. The reality of history is first of all the "working" or operation *(Wirkung)* of a complex dialectic of subject and object, past and present, continuity and change, old and new, reality and possibility, that makes up an indissoluble web, the ontological substance of our being-in-the-world. Only secondarily, if even then, can this prior reality be reduced to our contemporary "view" of things. When Heidegger proposes that we begin by interpreting history ontologically, he is therefore not falling back into a Hegelian or quasi-theological way of thinking. He is simply reminding us at the outset of our reflections that this working of history *(Wirkungsgeschichte)* is something more than a projection of the sensibilities of the contemporary interpreter of history. It addresses us with an independent and prior ontological integrity of its own.[6]

This finitist approach to historical reality as the working of history makes possible a new understanding of the activity of historical interpretation and a new formulation of the hermeneutical principles which guide this activity. We shall consider each of these developments in turn.

If history, in its primary sense as the historical reality of human existence *(Geschichte),* is to be understood in ontological terms, then so must history in its related sense as the human activity of interpreting the past *(Historie).* As one of the ways in which human beings can be, the specific activity of historical interpretation shares the ontological features that characterize human existence as a whole.[7] Since man is to be understood in the first

instance as a being-in-the-world, rather than a thinking subject
or being-as-self-consciousness, every act of human understanding, including our interpretation of the past, must initially be
viewed in ontological rather than one-sided, subjectivistic
terms.[8] Historical interpretation is therefore not an expression
of the subjectivity of the interpreter. It is an activity that shares in
the movement of history itself.

It follows from this general fact that the particular story we tell
is an inseparable and constitutive part of the particular history we
live.[9] Our interpretation of history is not simply a subjective
view of the past but an event in its own right that participates in
the working of the very reality it describes. Our histories, our
stories about the world we have inherited, are contributions we
ourselves make to the ongoing reality whose story they narrate.
We write history, we tell our story, not as disinterested observers
but as participants, agents responsible for the further development of the story we tell. By telling the particular story we do, we
are shaping a specific future for ourselves as well. In our interpretation of the past, we therefore cannot entirely distinguish
between the act of understanding and the being of what is
understood. As historical beings, we are both the subjects and
the objects of the stories we tell.[10] This does not mean, however,
a vicious subjectivizing of our interpretations of the past. Our
understanding of history is itself a part of the operative reality,
the being, of what is understood.[11]

To refute the charge of a subjectivizing view of history, we
need to stress a side of the concept of history as *Wirkungsgeschichte* that has not yet been made clear. According to this view,
the past is not a pile of dead facts which can be manipulated to
suit the needs of contemporary self-consciousness. It is something which is a happening in its own right. In saying this, we are
not confining its ontological reality to the historical past. We
mean to say that through the working of history the past gives
substance and direction to our experiential present as well. What
Gadamer means by a *wirkungsgeschichtliche Bewüsstsein* is a "consciousness in which history is an operative, present reality."
When we interpret our history, this act of interpretation is itself
an event, a happening taking place now. But it is not an event for

which we alone are responsible, a deed that we alone do. It is an
event in which something happens to us. In our interpretation of
the past, the past itself addresses and interprets us. Quite literally, it speaks to us "like a Thou."[12]

When we tell the story of our past, our past comes to life again.
It enters into an effective or operative *(wirklich)* relationship
with us in the same way in which the voice of a contemporary of
ours, when listened and responded to, effects our present situation. The voices of the past are not dead objects which have
finished speaking and are now permanently fixed in the amber of
time. They are living voices, as alive and forceful in their capacity to elicit fresh understanding and new possibilities of
existence—to effect a new historical reality—as are the persons
we meet or the words we read today. In the telling and retelling
of their story, they are freed to live and speak again—and they do
so indeed. The past is not a realm of dead, objectified being that
once was and is no more. It is a realm of still-living events which
are as much a part of our present lives, which are still as much at
work, as those happenings which in the normal course of our
thinking we assign to the present.

In our interpretation of history, the past therefore discloses
itself as a working reality in the present. History *(Historie)* is seen
not as an activity of the subject—that is, the contemporary
interpreter—but as part of the movement of the subject matter
*(Geschichte)* itself. It should be clear by now that this working of
history, the effective presence of the past in the present, is not an
example of the chain of cause and effect that links the events of
the natural sciences. It is an illustration of the dialectical logic of
human address and response. Our acts of historical interpretation are not the objectifying acts of a scientific consciousness that
stands over against the lived, nonobjectifiable reality of its own
historical life. They are living responses to the voices of the past
which called our historical world into being—responses by
which that historical reality is further extended and transformed.
When we interpret historical reality *(Geschichte)* ontologically in
terms of the concept of the working of history *(Wirkungsgeschichte)*, we are therefore not subscribing to a deterministic
reading of the past. We are simply acknowledging that in shaping

our future, we do so in working continuity with what men have previously done and made it possible for us to do.

The concept of history as *Wirkungsgeschichte* thus provides a new understanding of the activity of historical interpretation. But it also makes possible a new formulation of the hermeneutical principles by which this activity proceeds. Negatively stated, the concept of history as *Wirkungsgeschichte* entails the following hermeneutical principle: The key to the understanding of history is the unequivocal rejection of the kernel-husk method of interpreting the past.

The kernel-husk method of interpretation assumes that the essential content of an historical event or historical tradition can be distinguished and separated from the outward forms of its appearance. One version of this assumption is held by existentialist theologians. According to Bultmann, there is a difference between the essential possibilities of human existence realized in the past (for example, the possibility of faith as contained in the message of Jesus) and the language or thought forms in which these existential possibilities were expressed (the eschatological world view of first-century Christianity). In fact, there is an unbridgeable gap, both then and now, between the lived reality of history (existence in faith, say) and the objectifying language by which it is understood (initially the language of Jewish eschatology, later the categories of Greek metaphysics, today the terminology of existentialist philosophy).

It follows from this initial assumption that it is possible in theory (though admittedly difficult in practice) for the interpreter of history to tell the story of the past in such a way that its essential nature or truth stands before us unchanged. The historian, that is, can repeat or re-present in the language and thought forms of a later generation (for example, in a way that conforms to the secular world view of the modern age) the very same truths (e.g., existential possibilities) that were present and embodied in the events, the language, and the thought forms of an earlier time.

This hermeneutical principle requires as its necessary presupposition a general ontology of human existence that affirms an unchanging essence of man—for example, a set of fundamental

existential possibilities that is, in principle, experientially available to all men at all times and places (albeit under changing
forms and circumstances). The essence of a past event or tradition, in other words, is not necessarily something that is proposi-
tional in nature—something that can be summed up in a particular doctrine or philosophical truth. It can also be, according to
the existentialist theologians, a particular possibility of human
existence—in this instance, the possibility of a life of faith.

From the point of view of a concept of historical reality as the
working of history, however, the kernel-husk method of interpretation, along with its necessary philosophical presuppositions, simply will no longer do. From a finitist perspective on
human history, the quest for fundamental, unchanging truths
about man (including basic, unchanging existential possibilities)
is a misguided hermeneutical effort. It presupposes, first of all,
that there is some place outside history, some vantage point of
eternity, where the historian can stand while interpreting what
goes on within history. It presupposes that it is possible for
the interpreter to attain to an absolute knowledge, either philosophical or existential, about man's historical reality while
remaining untouched by the historical reality of his own situation. But second, and more important, it presupposes that time
and history, language and tradition, are not really of the essence
of being.

For the radical Christian, as distinguished from the existentialist theologian, the search for the essential content (existential
possibilities) lying beneath the temporal-historical surface of
man's being must be replaced by a sense of fidelity to the concrete historical reality of human existence. This means that the
radical Christian will take seriously, for example, the essential
and not merely accidental status of language in the ontological
makeup of man's historical being. Language is not the outer,
objectifying expression of an inner, existential reality. It is a
constitutive element, part of the substance, of the historical
realities it expresses (better: effects, realizes). Language is part of
the ontological kernel, not the removable husk, of our being in
the world. It is, as Heidegger puts it, co-primordial with our
understanding and interpretation of being. Language, like his-

tory, is the essence of our being. It follows that changes in the
linguistic expression of our being are not simply invaluable clues
to underlying changes in the reality of our lives. They effect and
are co-primordial with the changes in that underlying reality
itself. When we adopt a new way of talking about the past, when
we use a new language for responding to the events or traditions
which address us from out of our past, it is imperative that we
recognize that we are not merely changing the accidental forms
in which the essence of those events or traditions are expressed.
We are changing the very substance of that reality itself.[13]

We see here how the radical Christian's commitment to the
essential historicality of our being follows from the general
requirements of an ontology of radical secularity. In requiring
men to take full responsibility for making their own history, a
radical ontology also requires that we acknowledge the element
of unavoidable novelty this involves. Things simply cannot stay
the same. This means that the interpreter must take responsibility for the fact that in retelling the story of the past he is no longer
telling the same story. Since the language we use to retell the
story is no longer that used by the men who lived and created that
story, we change the story in the very retelling of it. The interpreter must acknowledge that he himself is an agent in the
substantial change and transformation of that story. More, he
must be prepared to admit that he may have created a new and
different story altogether. Here the secular theologians, rather
than the existentialists, are a case in point. Under the guise of
retelling the old story in modern, secular terms, they are in fact
engaged, whether consciously or not, in the fashioning of a new
story—a story that had not, and could not have, been told before.

In retelling the old story, we are no longer telling the same
story; we are necessarily telling a new one. So far we have only
stated the ontological reasons why. We now need to ask what it is
about the hermeneutical situation itself that requires that this be
so. The reasons are to be found in the peculiar sort of epistemological (and real) dialectic such a situation involves. We
have already discussed one such dialectical fact. As interpreters
of history, we are at the same time participants in the history we
are talking about. There is an otherness and yet sameness, a

so-called hermeneutical circle, which we cannot methodologically avoid. But the dialectic involved in interpreting the past is
more rigorous and many-sided than this. It is not just confined to
the side of the interpreter, viewed now as subject, now as object
of his own investigation. Before that, the interpretation of the
past is a two-way dialogue between the interpreter and another
reality that is in many ways, in essential ways, radically different.
Quite clearly, what is happening is something dialectical indeed.
In the act of historical interpretation, the interpreter's voice is
not the only one that is being heard. In a retelling of the past, the
past itself, as we have said, comes to life again and addresses us in
turn.

Not only philosophically but existentially, this is how it has to
be. As Emilio Betti has rightly insisted, in arguing against hermeneutical theories which would reduce the past to an epi-
phenomenon of the present: If the past is not in some sense
different from, and other than, the interpreter's present, if it
does not in its own right speak to us in return, then why should
we, or do we, bother to listen in the first place?[14] We are
interested in telling the story of the past precisely because we
know that it does have something to say, perhaps something that
we need to hear again—in any case, something which we cannot
entirely anticipate or reduce to an echo of our own voices. We
have therefore to approach the past in a way that allows what has
already been said to speak again, to interrogate us in turn,
perhaps to call our own interpretive horizon into question and to
work a fundamental change in our own historical reality as well.[15]

The real hermeneutical situation, in other words, is not one in
which the past is reduced to the object of a contemporary, disinterested or narrowly self-interested consciousness. Rather,
it is a situation in which the past itself is present in a living way,
making its own reality felt in and through our responses to what
it has to say. This hermeneutical situation may be characterized
as a situation of mutual dialogue, but not a dialogue from which
all struggle has been excluded. Between the world of the past and
our present horizon, there exists a state of creative tension. The
interpreter, insofar as he is able, sets them in conscious, calculated juxtaposition to one another. But he also finds himself in a

novel position halfway between strangeness and familiarity, between a world that he knows to be other yet somehow important
and a world he knows all too well but does not fully understand.
*"In this 'between' is the true place of hermeneutics."*[16]
    What happens in this "between" is that, out of the mutual
interrogation and listening of past and present, something new
emerges, something that did not exist before. What Gadmer calls
a "fusion of horizons" takes place. Elements of our own experience are negated by the disclosures of the past, while others are
reaffirmed. Elements of the past give way under the interrogation of the present, while others are strengthened and confirmed. What comes out of this encounter is something that is
identical with neither the past nor the present, something with a
new historical identity of its own. In this sense, every act of
historical interpretation, every genuine hermeneutical encounter, represents a new creation, a new disclosure of being. The
story that emerges from the dialectic of past and present is a new
story, a story that could not have been told before. Yet it is a
story which, for all its novelty, stands in a firm, working relationship with the past. It could not have been told *before.* But it could
not have been told *at all* if it was not, in its essence, a story about
our past.[17]
    Contrary to the assumptions of the kernel-husk method of
reading history, the alternative principle of hermeneutical juxtaposition accepts the fact that the world of the past is in many
ways essentially different from, and discontinuous with, the
world of the present. It is not absolutely discontinuous. Insofar
as we can listen and respond to the voices of the past, insofar as
we can bring to it our own concerns and find help therein,
insofar as we find that in this dialogue our own experience is
enlarged or transformed, insofar as together with the human
voices of the past we can come to share in the creation of a new
story—a story that is neither ours nor the past's alone, but one we
create together—then, without in any way obscuring the distance or the otherness that remains and will always remain
between the Thous of past and present, we can still affirm that
meaning can be found, that historical understanding can take
place, and that in those happenings of meaning the working of

history—the miraculous creation of new being—will continue to occur.

This sense of meaning, despite discontinuity, frees and encourages us, second, to accept and even stress the positive value of historical differences not only between traditions but within the continuity of one's own tradition as well. In view of the emotional content and the normative issues at stake in the dialogue between Marxists and Christians, a hermeneutical principle which stresses historical difference and discontinuity is of more than merely theoretical interest. It frees us from the existential (and hence ideological) necessity of having to find the eternal, unchanging essence of either tradition, thus clearing the way for a more balanced and believable assessment of such historical continuities as actually exist. It also encourages us to be open to, and, indeed, to share in the creation of, new possibilities within and between these traditions that go beyond the givens or assumed essence of their respective pasts.

The acceptance of the radically historical nature of his existence is one of the profoundest expressions of a more basic acceptance by man of the finitude of his being. All of human experience, including our experience of the past, is an experience of finitude. Part of what it has meant for modern, secular man to come of age is that he has had to recognize and accept his essential finitude. This hard-won maturity, so far as it concerns our existence as historical beings, consists in having achieved a proper sense of openness to our past in all its contingency as well as to the future with its power to transform what were previously regarded as unchanging truths. That openness—to essential discontinuity as well as continuity—is incompatible, finally, with any and every theory of being, man, or history for which all that is essential has already been said or realized. The maturity that comes with the acceptance of man's essential finitude is, on the other hand, of the essence of man's "consciousness of history as a present, working reality."[18]

This concept of our historical being as a process of *Wirkungsgeschichte* serves to remind us that the presence of meaning in history is more ambiguous and open-ended and yet, paradoxically, more real and accessible than either the advocates of

eternal truth or the philosophers of an absurd universe would
have us believe. The task of discovering this meaning and telling
the story is of course a never-ending one. The story itself is
about mankind's inability completely to see. But in a strange
way, would we really wish it to be any different? Though the
working of history is a process of simultaneous disclosure and
concealment, yet it tells a story of being in all of its mystery and
inexhaustible richness. The working of history, like the being of
man, is grounded in mysterious negativity or, better, an ungrounded creativity. It expresses the finite happening of being.
Only a being who is finite is capable of being, in the sense we
have been discussing, an historical being. One who has come
to accept the historical nature of his being is one who is ready to
accept a larger, deeper truth—that happening, finiteness, is the
essence of being itself.

## A Question of
## Historical Truth

In addition to arguing that an ontology of finitude makes possible a new way of thinking about history, the radical Christian
also argues that this concept of history, despite its novelty, stands
in significant continuity with the Christian tradition. Some version of this argument from history is necessary for any thinker
who regards himself as a Christian, since his is an historical
religion. For the radical Christian, however, there is an added
necessity. To defend the potential significance of the Christian
tradition for a radically secular way of thinking, he cannot
simply argue that the new ontology of history provides a useful
framework for interpreting that tradition. He must also argue
that it does so because it stands in effective continuity with the
perspective on history found in that tradition in particular. As a
Christian thinker, he must defend a Christian perspective. As a
radical thinker, he must defend a finitist ontology of history. And
as a thinker who is both a radical and a Christian, he must
maintain that this concept of history stands in some sort of
working relationship, historically and ideologically, to the Chris-

tian perspective. Not to argue this way would be to surrender his claim to be a thinker who is at once both radical and Christian.

The radical Christian views his version of this argument from history as significantly different from, and immune to the criticisms brought against, the argument of the secular theologians presented in an earlier chapter. He bases this claim on the fact that his own argument is grounded in, and consistent with, the new concept of history itself. According to the concept of *Wirkungsgeschichte* and the corollary notion of hermeneutical juxtaposition, one need not prove an essential identity but only a working continuity between the past and the present. Such an argument leaves ample room for discontinuity and novelty as well.

To establish the effective continuity of the Christian tradition with the new concept of history, it is, however, not sufficient simply to retell the earlier Christian story. Rather, the radical Christian must attempt a creative fusion of horizons between the Christian story and the new story of radical secularity. The radical Christian's interest in his own tradition, after all, is that of a radically secular thinker—one whose primary interest is to help create a new future, not repeat the past. His argument from history will therefore differ from that of his theological counterpart. His argument is not that the future can be based on the past but that the past can be brought into creative juxtaposition with a new future. This hermeneutical approach necessarily results in a new story that is discontinuous in essential ways with the earlier story. But this is not necessarily a bad thing. For as one contemporary writer observes: "Conscious discontinuity with the tradition does not mean one either betrays or abandons it. Rather we use the tradition as the assumption from which a new departure is orbited. Calculated discontinuity exploits the friction between the past and the present to generate new possibilities for the future."[19]

There are two parts to the radical Christian's argument. The first is that there exists real, historical continuity between the events that originated the Christian tradition and the events of our own time. The second is that the concept of history as *Wirkungsgeschichte* can be used to tell the Christian story in a new

way in our time. In examining this twofold argument more
closely, we shall limit ourselves to the historical reality of Jesus
rather than trying to include the larger history of early Christianity or its Judaic background. Since Jesus stands in significant
continuity with both of these traditions, and since for Christians
he plays the central role in establishing their own historical
identity, it may be held that the reflections which follow have a
broader range of application.

The radical Christian's approach to the continuity of the past
and the present differs from that of the secular theologian or his
Marxist critic. The secular theologian argued, it will be recalled,
that the historical Jesus was a revolutionary figure whose aim was
the transformation of the secular, political world. Or, if the facts
about Jesus are too sketchy to support this view, that the stories
that sprang up around him served, and continue to serve, as
powerful symbols for a revolutionary stance in an alienated
world. From a radical Christian perspective, this line of argument
distorts the facts and asks the symbols to do a job they were
never intended to do. Behind the secular theologian's argument
is the kernel-husk method of interpreting history. The linguistic
forms and world view in which Jesus understood his own life
and preaching are reduced, in this argument, to the outer and
easily rearrangeable clothing of an existential or revolutionary
stance whose unchanging message transcends all differences of
time and place.

The Marxist humanist, on the other hand, quite readily
acknowledges his deep indebtedness to his Judeo-Christian
heritage—but not without substantial qualification. He grants
that these religious traditions are significant realities of our
cultural past. They are mythological, prescientific, but dramatically effective way stations on the historical road to a world of
radical secularity. However, though these biblical voices were
once living ones, they no longer speak effectively to us today.
Though they once held out the vision of a more human, emancipated world—and in a way that made possible the subsequent,
though different, vision that ushered in our modern world—
we no longer turn to them today for our images of man or a
more human society. The Marxist's position, while it is the

opposite of the secular theologian's view, makes a curiously similar assumption about the relation of the past to the present. The past, in its historical particulars, is over and done with. It can safely be reduced to a possession of the contemporary inheritor of all this cultural wealth. But it has lost its independent integrity, its power to address us as a reality that is different from, and in some ways opposed to, our contemporary world, a reality that has the power to throw the horizon of the interpreter himself into sudden and radical doubt.

The question which each of these positions raises is the same. If the message of the past is existentially identical with, or even inferior to, the one we already know, why—whether as a secularizing theologian or a sympathetic Marxist critic—bother to listen? For one who, like the radical Christian, operates from a principle of deliberate juxtaposition, of calculated discontinuity, there is every reason to listen. The biblical images of man and the world may, in their linguistic and historical particulars, be images of man and the world as they used to be, not what they have become. But they still stand in a continuing, effective relationship with our present reality. And through a new fusion of horizons, they could conceivably play a deciding role in determining what may yet become. If they do, it will, however, not be because they stand in any simple continuity with the present. If they do speak to us "like a Thou," it will be because of their radical otherness, because of the essential difference and discontinuity between then and now. And that, for the radical Christian, literally makes all the difference in the world.

The radical Christian's paradoxical hermeneutic of continuity-through-discontinuity leads to a view of the contemporary significance of the Christian tradition which is both more qualified than that of the theologian but more affirmative than that of the secular critic. It is more complex and qualified than that of the theologian, because it contends that the biblical events and stories are fatally misunderstood if taken as symbolic vehicles for unchanging existential truths about man or history. The events and stories which make up the Christian tradition point to concrete, history-making realities, not just symbols of existential possibilities. They are events which actually effected a

particular historical destiny that continues to make its presence
effectively known today wherever the Christian story is told and
lived. The events of the Christian story are not the accidental
vehicles of a transhistorical message. They are the originating
and ongoing events, the *wirkungsgeschichtliche* reality, of the contemporary existence of every Christian. In this respect, at least,
the radical Christian and the orthodox Christian agree over
against the liberal or secularizing theologians. One cannot separate the lived, historical reality of Christian faith from its specific
linguistic and historical forms of expression.

Because of the continuing *wirkungsgeschichtliche* reality of the
originating events of the Christian tradition, the radical Christian
views the discontinuities between past and present in a more
dialectical and affirmative way than does the secular critic.
Whereas the Marxist humanist, having generously acknowledged his cultural debts, then dismisses the biblical tradition as
having no further capacity to address or disrupt the world of the
contemporary interpreter, the radical Christian maintains that,
despite its irreducible pastness and otherness, this tradition
speaks to us in words of judgment and promise wherever the
Christian story continues to be told.

What, more specifically, lies behind the difference of the
radical Christian and the Marxist humanist on this particular
point? Before we try to answer this, let us be sure that the
measure of their agreement as radically secular thinkers is fully
understood. Both affirm the profound differences of language,
thought, and praxis that separate the first-century world of
Christianity from the twentieth-century world of secular man.
Both admit that the modern world is, on the other hand, profoundly indebted to that earlier tradition, and that indeed it may
not have been historically or ideologically possible without it.
Both agree, finally, that that earlier world is no longer the world
in which we live or a world in which we can ever live again. In a
situation of such fundamental agreement, how is it, then, that
one party can say: Nevertheless, I am a Marxist, and this view of
the Christian tradition is part of what it means to be a Marxist;
while the other continues to affirm: I am a Christian, and this
view of the Christian tradition is part of what it means to

be a Christian today?[20] The answer is of course that, for all their agreement, the world of the Marxist and the world of the radical Christian are not, in the final analysis, the same historical world at all. What we must do in our remaining remarks is to determine precisely wherein the significant difference resides for the radical Christian. How, despite, and indeed because of, the discontinuity of past and present, does the past continue to speak for the Christian today?

To begin with, it should be noted that the radical Christian does not call himself a Christian because he finds a greater degree of continuity between the Christian tradition and the present than the Marxist does. Degrees of continuity or discontinuity with the past have no obvious significance when the question is where we should go from here. Such a question might easily be imagined as having the opposite effect. Like the Marxist's, the radical Christian's primary concern is not to establish threads of continuity with the past but to discover norms for creating a more human future. Because the radical Christian finds in the working history of the Christian tradition events which functioned to open the future and a story about those events designed to keep that future open, he regards this tradition as one that can speak to our own future as well. Specifically, it is the radical Christian's claim—subject only to the test of (in Schweitzer's words) "radical historical honesty"—that the voices of the Christian tradition have not yet stopped speaking and that their message concerns the very question we ourselves as radically secular men are asking—the question of the future of man. Unlike the Marxist, the radical Christian therefore feels a continuing responsibility for—that is, an obligation to continue actively responding to—the originating events and story of this particular tradition.

The radical Christian's argument proceeds, as we have said, in two stages. The first part rests on what he believes to be the facts about the historical reality of Jesus' ministry in his own time. Those who responded to the words and deeds of Jesus found that their lives and the world in which they lived had in fact been radically transformed. Men were in fact emancipated from their former unfreedom, and were called together to work for a future

which would be, in the terms in which they understood it, totally
different from anything they had ever known before. In Jesus, as
in earlier figures in the history of the biblical tradition, we see a
decisive step forward in the realization—the secularization—of
the Kingdom of God—that is, one more step in a continuing
struggle to demystify and free men from the this-worldly or
other-worldly alienation of their true capacities as human beings.
What distinguishes Jesus from other figures or movements of his
time is not that in his person a metaphysical miracle occurred.
What sets him apart is his eschatological conviction that it is his
task to assist in the next stage of the in-breaking reality of the
Kingdom of God. And indeed it was the conviction of those who
heard and responded to him that in the reality of his person the
inauguration of the new messianic (i.e., emancipated) era had
begun. For the first Christians, a new story, a new history, had
begun.

The radical Christian is of course the first to acknowledge that
the eschatological language and beliefs of Jesus cannot be
brought forward unchanged into our contemporary world. As
Schweitzer already established in his radical critique of liberal
theology, the historical Jesus is fundamentally a stranger to our
time. He inhabits a totally different world from ours. His strange
interim ethic, for example—an ethic which corresponds to his
heightened sense that the eschatological timetable was about to
be fulfilled and with it a radical judgment brought against our
attachment to the present world—no longer speaks directly to
modern, secular man. We no longer think eschatologically as
Jesus did—not, that is, in the mythological terms of first-century
eschatology. If we adopt a revolutionary stance toward the
world, we do so in radically secular terms. To that extent, Jesus
and his world are irretrievably past. In his linguistic strangeness,
we confront his existential and historical strangeness too. For us,
as for Schweitzer, every effort to find a suitably modern translation of what Jesus really means must inevitably fail. It is ontologically and therefore historically and conceptually impossible to
overcome the fundamental differences that separate the historical reality of Jesus from the reality of the world in which we live.
Thus Schweitzer's injunction still stands: whatever else we may

decide about our relationship to the Jesus of history, he must be allowed to remain in his own time as someone who will always be a stranger to us.

But if Jesus must remain a stranger, how can the radical Christian say that he still speaks effectively to us? How does the radical Christian propose to move from the first part of his argument—the facts about the reality of Jesus in his own time—to the second part of his argument—the continuing significance of Jesus for us in our time? Schweitzer himself argued, in the conclusion to his great study *The Quest of the Historical Jesus,* that we must leave Jesus in his time and must turn, instead, to those tasks which our present time assigns to us. Yet even Schweitzer felt that he could provide a secular equivalent for the religious symbol of the Kingdom of God. He felt that there was a spirit of Jesus, distinguishable and separable from the reality of the historical Jesus, which had the power to communicate effectively over the distance of the ages, despite the fact that Jesus himself remained within the confines of his own first-century world. It is difficult to see how Schweitzer could have maintained this distinction between the spirit of Jesus and the historical Jesus without violating his own prohibition against the kernel-husk method of interpretation. It is possible, however, that he was saying something slightly different, perhaps something more like the following.

In the historical Jesus, we see a decisive step forward in the long Western story of the quest for the secular emancipation of man. Jesus' ministry, when viewed in its original historical setting, represents an attempt to free men from their need and longing for another world by making that world a present and living reality. For Christians, the initial and normative steps in this process of secular emancipation were effected in the very language and events of Jesus' own life. Jesus' words and deeds are not only clues or symbols but the constituting events, the very substance, of a new historical reality. To the extent that the language and deeds of our world are not the same as those of the first century, to that extent our human and historical reality are no longer the same. Yet, despite the differences which separate the original Christian story from the story we are living now, we

can still discern lines of effective historical continuity that link
Jesus' time to ours. Because Jesus said and did the things he did,
he speaks to us when we find ourselves engaged in the analogous
struggles for human emancipation that exist for us today.

Let us elaborate this argument a bit further. On the one hand,
because of the differences between then and now, Jesus' significance for us cannot be expressed in the religious titles or eschatological beliefs of an earlier world. We must necessarily find
some other way of expressing what he means for us. Accordingly, we will not speak in terms of the Messiah, the Christ, or the
Kingdom of God. Rather, we will talk about the man for others
or universal human emancipation. Such terms would be false or
misleading if regarded as applicable to the meaning he had for
men in his own time. They are true only if we understand them as
describing the meaning he has for men today. In this sense, an
ethical or radically secular interpretation of the truth of the historical Jesus is not subject to the methodological criticisms
directed against the liberal or secular theologians. The reason is
that for any such interpretation to be valid, it cannot claim to be
identical with, or to capture the essence of, what Jesus meant for
those who first heard him. Such an interpretation is the product
of a complex hermeneutical experience of the discontinuities as
well as continuities that exist between Jesus as he was seen in his
time and Jesus as he presents himself to ours. It is a sense for
those differences, and not just for the similarities, which is
crucial for defining the specific historical situation of the radical
Christian as one who is not simply a Christian but a Christian
who lives in the twentieth-century, not a first-century, world.

On the other hand, because the radical Christian sees a real
historical continuity (not essential identity) between the events
that brought the Christian tradition into existence and the revolutionary events of our own day, he in fact inhabits an historically different world than does his Marxist counterpart. His
language and actions constitute new historical links in a *wirkungsgeschichtliche* reality that extends back to the originating
events of his tradition and forward to a specific historical future
that fulfills the promise of those original events. If the radical
Christian's reading of the facts about the historical Jesus is cor-

rect, it was the aim and effect of Jesus himself to have assisted in bringing about a more human future—in a real, not merely symbolical or otherworldly way. His sayings and doings are the first fruits, the history-making events and grounds, of every subsequent effort of Christians to realize, in the language and setting of their own day, the liberating effects of that which was begun in him.

On the one hand, the historical Jesus belongs to a world that understood itself in religious (specifically, eschatological) terms. To that extent, he remains a stranger to a world which understands itself in secular terms. But the significance of his life, both for him and for those who heard him, was that, through him, a revolutionary new reality had been ushered in. To that extent, we too can approach him for help in the struggles that define our time. The historical fact is that Jesus stands in effective continuity with the present reality of our lives. He himself—not just his spirit, continues to speak to us like a Thou. Through our encounter with him in the tasks he sets for us, we learn for ourselves who he is.

# Conclusion

# 10    The Future of Religion in a Secular World

In Part I of this study, we argued that theism is no longer a valid theoretical option for interpreting the world, and that religion is no longer a valid practical approach to changing the world. In Part II, we argued that an ontology of radical secularity provides a theoretical alternative to theistic and antitheistic metaphysics. In Part III, we described the new Marxist humanism as a response to this ontology which expresses it in a more practical form. We also described the attempt of the radical Christian to use this ontology to rethink his own tradition. Our task now is to determine what, if any, conclusions we can draw about this dialogue, and to indicate, if only by way of speculation, what its significance for the future might be.

To do this I should like to consider the thesis that religion still has an essential role to play in a secular future. Two things need to be said by way of immediate clarification. First, this is not an empirical hypothesis—that is, a prediction of the sort that could be based on the statistical researches of, say, a sociologist of religion. Whatever the outcome of such an investigation, it would be irrelevant to the sort of proposition I want to examine here. The thesis is, rather, a normative or ideological one. Second, there is an element of paradox in this thesis, since I earlier argued against a continuing role for religion. There are, however, at least two ways of interpreting it, each of which is consistent with our earlier criticisms. One can defend it from either a radical Christian or a Marxist humanist point of view. Neither of these approaches entirely eliminates the paradox involved. But a consideration of each should clarify the conclusion that can be drawn.

## The Radical Christian View

The radical Christian view of this thesis holds that religion, specifically the biblical tradition, will continue to have a role to play as long as alienation is a fact of secular life.[1] In an alienated world, religion will continue to stand for a qualitatively different view of man and his this-worldly future.

Radical Christianity can help overcome the alienation of secular life in a number of ways. First, it can furnish a humanizing perspective on the fact of human being itself. Confronted by overwhelming technological and political power in the service of forces of economic and social alienation, religion can invite men to remember and to celebrate the fundamental mystery of their being. It can offer something more than simply an anxious or polemical view of the limits of human life. It can show men how such a perspective can humanize their perception of what they do in their everyday life.

This reminder of mystery is not intended by the radical Christian to be a substitute for social and political concern. The biblical tradition also contains very specific examples of social and political criticism, as well as images of man and human community which stand in the strongest possible contrast to those which currently govern men. For the radical Christian, these specific alternatives are every bit as revolutionary and valid as those derived from the secular movements of our own day.

The radical Christian's alternative begins with the belief of the first Christians that Jesus represented the beginnings of a new humanity, that in Jesus a new order has been established, here and now, in the midst of a passing order of secular alienation. But this primitive Christian belief also found embodiment in the subsequent history of Christianity. From the beginning, there were a variety of radical heretic movements which attempted to work out a Christian perspective on revolutionary change and to embody that perspective in appropriate forms of radical com-

munity.[2] At a later date, it was social and political models drawn
from the Bible which proved decisive in shaping the revolutionary events which ushered in the modern world. The Puritan
movement is only one example in which a new vision of the
world and new forms of life were translated from an initial
religious and ecclesiastical setting into ideological and institu-
tional forms that were their secular analogue.[3]

The radical Christian's argument receives added force when
one observes that often it is only the religious community which
is able to initiate the demand for revolutionary change. There are
times when the alienation of secular society runs so deep that it is
unable, of its own, to seize such an initiative itself. The biblical
tradition, on the other hand, has repeatedly pronounced the
prophetic word not only against the world but against itself. As
long as alienation persists in secular life, and as long as the
religious community has the resources for the necessary sort of
criticism, men will continue to need the help that religion
uniquely brings.

So far, the radical Christian's argument appears to be
straightforward. But we have said that the thesis he is defending
contains an element of paradox. At this point, therefore, certain
qualifying remarks must be made. Although the radical Christian
is quite clearly arguing on behalf of his tradition, unlike most of
the theologians discussed in Part I, he does not see his primary
task as an apologetic one. His concern, that is, is not so much to
defend his own tradition as it is to change the world. Admittedly
his concept of what it means to change the world is derived in
part from his sense of the original Christian mission to the world.
But even for that original mission, it was not so much its own fate
as that of the world in its desperation which was the focal object
of its concern. If the apologetic task is conceived in any other
terms—as holding onto the old story for its own sake, or as
demonstrating that the old story can adapt itself like a chameleon
to whatever contemporary culture dictates—then it cannot be
considered a sufficient end in itself for radical Christian thinking.
This does not rule out the possibility that, as a side benefit, the
Christian may come to see more clearly what the old story was, in

its own way, trying to say or what its secular meaning might yet be. He will not discover this, however, if he makes this the primary object of his concern.

For many Christians, this qualification is not a difficult one to accept. It accords with their own understanding of the message of their tradition. But it leads to a further observation, one that may be harder to accept. Implicit in the premises of the radical Christian's argument are the seeds of its conversion into another and apparently opposite conclusion. The value of the biblical tradition is here being judged not in terms of any independent religious considerations but for its capacity to respond to the needs of men in a world conceived in radically secular terms. But this means that, even for the radical Christian, the place of religion in human life can no longer be considered an ultimate one. Its status has been reduced to a penultimate one.

The task of religion in the secular future, accordingly, is to eliminate the need for itself as religion by overcoming secular, not religious or ecclesiastical, alienation. For the radical Christian, this is the hidden secret of the biblical tradition itself. The ultimate fate of religion, like that of the state for Marxist thinkers, is to disappear as a special realm of life once the secular conditions which gave rise to it have been overcome.[4] For the radical Christian, as for Marx, religion will then wither away of its own accord—not because it has succumbed to a state propaganda campaign but because when men are truly free, the need for it will disappear.

A theist might wish to respond that, since it is utopian to think that alienation can ever be completely overcome, this argument for the penultimacy of religion in fact proves just the opposite— that religion is a permanent necessity of human life. But the argument, unfortunately for the theologian, is not open to this theistic sleight of hand. For the radical Christian, religion is essential because of the questions it raises and because of its protest against the conditions of human alienation. But its answers are not ultimate ones. As Garaudy puts it, "The perversion of religion is to provide answers." What he means is that, though the protests of religion are directed against real problems, its answers, at least when expressed in theistic terms, are unreal ones. The problems posed by the contradictions of secular life demand real—that is, socioeconomic and political—solutions, not simply unreal—that is, purely religious or ideological ones. The answers of religion can become real only if they move beyond the realm of religious or ecclesiastical life and begin to transform the rest of human life as well: education, law, society, work, economics, politics, culture. But that is simply another way of saying that religious answers will not become real answers until they become secular answers—that is, until they are no longer religious answers at all. The ultimacy of the theist's answers is purchased at the cost of a corresponding unreality. It is a good indicator of the distance yet to go in overcoming the real sources of human alienation.

From a radical Christian viewpoint, the answers of the biblical tradition can be realized only if the imaginative and historical resources of that tradition are translated into resources for the secular community as a whole. This will occur only if, as in the case of the Puritan movement, those resources can be grasped not in narrowly religious or ecclesiastical terms but as broadly human, secular possibilities. The object of such a translation is not the creation of a Christian world. It is just the opposite. It is the withering away of a distinctively religious or ecclesiastical sphere as a new world of human freedom comes into being. In such a world, religion as a distinctive sphere of life would become less and less necessary as men succeeded in overcoming the conditions of secular alienation which gave rise to religion in the first place.

For the radical Christian, this is the inner secret of the biblical tradition itself. The truth of religion lies in its capacity to go outside itself to the world, to so give itself that a greater life may come to be. For the radical Christian, this is the paradoxical dilemma but also the revolutionary opportunity of religion in the secular future.

## The Marxist Humanist View

For the Marxist humanist, there is a less paradoxical and more straightforward way of explaining how religion, despite its penultimacy, is still essential to the secular future of man. Just as existentialism was defended by Sartre as a humanistic supplement to Marxism, so religion can be seen as necessary for the development of a more humanistic version of Marxism. On this view, the biblical tradition does not stand outside or above the Marxist tradition. It is an earlier and, in many ways, decisive stage in the development of a radical humanism whose most adequate contemporary expression is a Marxist one.

For Bloch, Garaudy, and others, the new Marxist humanism is a legitimate heir of the best insights of that earlier tradition. These thinkers are very much interested in exploring the images of man and forms of community that are found in the biblical tradition and in the later history of Christianity. (Witness the contemporary Marxist interest in the political-theological visions of Joachim of Fiore, Thomas Münzer, and the various figures and sects of the left-wing Reformation.) They are, however, interested in doing so as Marxists—as thinkers who are committed to a radically secular vision of man and to efforts to realize that vision in a real and not merely utopian way. Here, in less involuted terms than on our first, or radical Christian, reading, we have a genuinely secular appreciation of the biblical tradition—its general resources if not its specific world view.[5]

In arguing for the significance of the biblical tradition, the Marxist humanist is not simply making an historical point. He is not simply saying that because this tradition was important in the past, we should acknowledge our debts to it today. He is making a far stronger claim, one that would probably not be acceptable to a more orthodox Marxist. He is saying that the biblical tradition is still relevant to his own efforts to rethink the present and future possibilities of Marxism. For the Marxist humanist, Marxism is not only indebted to the biblical tradition. It can still be reshaped by it as well.

What distinguishes the Marxist humanist from his orthodox counterpart is his awareness of the need for Marxists to turn their attention to the possibilities for human existence that arise once men's material needs have been satisfied. This was not a top-priority item for Marxism in its initial stages. Contemporary

Marxists are, however, under increasing pressure to give content to their rhetoric about the new order of freedom that is to emerge on the far side of material necessity. Questions about the superstructure are coming to the fore as problems of the material base are being overcome. Marxism has been a technological and political success. People now want to know about its human face.

It is just at this point that the Marxist humanist appeals to the biblical tradition for additional help. It is just here, for example, that the traditional eschatological symbols begin to speak. In Jesus, the Marxist humanist sees a symbolic representation of what it means to be a new man. In the Holy Spirit, he finds dramatic testimony to the liberating power of a future that is open. The Kingdom of God stands as a forceful reminder of the depth of man's commitment to a future in which all men shall be free. For the Marxist humanist, these symbols are not simply cultural artifacts in the background of his tradition. They are much-needed correctives and sources of inspiration for the further development of the humanist tradition today.

For the Marxist humanist, therefore, as for the radical Christian, so long as the conditions of secular life continue to perpetuate the alienation of men, so long will the symbols and imperatives of religion, like those of art and morality, continue to speak. On this point the Marxist humanist can even appeal to the later Marx. As Marx comments in *Capital:* "The religious reflex of the real world can, in any case, only then vanish when the practical relations of everyday life offer to man none but perfectly intelligible and reasonable relations with regard to his fellowmen and to nature."[6] Obviously there is no consolation for the theist in this concession, since what Marx is saying is that religion will continue to speak to men only so long as it assists them in gaining their secular freedom. The problem this causes for religion is obvious. To the extent that it succeeds in this task, its own distinctive function in human life is overcome. But, the Marxist asks, is this not the triumph of religion as well? For religion can be overcome, according to Marx himself, only when in fact there has come into being that new humanity which has always been the goal of religious hope itself.[7]

The Parties of the Future

On both the radical Christian and the Marxist humanist views, the biblical tradition has a contribution to make to man's struggle for a more human future. Where does this leave us with regard to the dialogue between them? Should we now try to decide which of these parties emerges with the better view? Or is a different approach in order? Perhaps it is wrong to assume that Christians and Marxists are competing in the same arena for the same prize, and that, at point after point, one of them is to be judged superior. Perhaps in some areas of mutual concern, they are not competing at all. If so, to approach their dialogue with the idea of establishing which one is the winner is to deny oneself the possibility of understanding another opportunity it presents. In fact, the situation which results from this dialogue is a great deal more interesting and complex.

To begin with, the new story of radical secularity and revolutionary humanism is a relatively unfinished one. In addition, the more constructive phase of the Marxist-Christian dialogue has been of relatively short duration. For both of these reasons, possibilities for new vision and new kinds of action still exist within each of these traditions. It would therefore seem more important and, in any case, more sensible, not to focus our conclusions on what may prove to be a distinction of secondary importance—namely, the distinction between Christians and Marxists. We would do better to focus on a distinction that is of more immediate and perhaps long-run significance, and that is the distinction between those within each tradition who are devoted to overthrowing the present order on behalf of a qualitatively different future and those who are dedicated to defending and perpetuating the existing order of things. More important for our reflections is the fact that within both Marxism and Christianity there exist a party of the future and a party of the present.

It has been remarked that Marxism and Christianity are each the name of an establishment and of a protest against the establishment in the name of man.[8] What this suggests is that the question we should be concerned to ask as a result of this dialogue is not whether one perspective is truer than the other but whether within each tradition it is the party of the future or the party of the present which shall determine the attitude of that tradition toward the great revolutionary tasks of our time. In the final analysis, it will not matter whether Christians or Marxists win but whether men have been set free.

With this alternative question in mind, what is the present situation of the Marxist-Christian dialogue? Philosophically, as we have seen, the rediscovery of the early Marx has made possible a renewed affirmation of radical humanism by Marxists and Christians alike. Thinkers in both traditions have found in the young Marx theoretical weapons for challenging their respective establishments—liberalism and Marxist orthodoxy, the market, the church, and the state. They have found support too for the assertion that Marxism need not be identified with Stalinism, that it has the potential for being what Marx himself proclaimed—the revolutionary embodiment of the most enduring values of the Western humanistic tradition.

By drawing upon the young Marx, Marxist humanists have attempted to resecularize the humanistic possibilities within their own tradition. Christians, similarly, have been freed to reappropriate the radical heretic and other revolutionary elements which for so long lay dormant and found only marginal expression over against the dominant realism of Christendom's many Constantinian establishments. It has become possible, in other words, for Marxists, conscious of the unfinished nature of their revolution, to forge a larger understanding of themselves as both Marxists and humanists. For Christians moving toward an explicit commitment to a revolutionary humanism, it has become possible to arrive at a new understanding of themselves as both radicals and Christians. Within both traditions, parties of the future have come into being.

At this point, one might wish to raise the following objection. By deemphasizing the distinction between Marxists and Christians, does not one run the risk of overlooking the significant differences that remain? How can there be any dialogue between these two parties if, as has been alleged, they are in such fundamental agreement? The distinction between parties of the future and parties of the present, far from helping to clarify things, instead produces such anomalies as Marxists who appear to be more Christian in their appreciation of the Christian tradition than many Christians themselves; or Christians who are more Marxist in their commitment to the young Marx than are most Marxists. How far can one go in stretching the meaning of such labels as "Marxist" and "Christian" and still expect them to have any significant application? Or should one really believe that there are no essential differences between these two traditions, that it is, in fact, quite possible for Christians to be Marxists and for Marxists to be Christians? (Compare: can there be Christian Platonists or Christian Aristotelians?)

Well, one is tempted to reply, why not? If one were to come up with a label that was incompatible with "Marxist," would it not more likely to be one like "liberal" or "capitalist" than one like "Christian"? And if one were to imagine a label that was incompatible with "Christian," would it not more likely be one that named another religious tradition or perhaps some ideology that understood itself primarily in antireligious terms? Of course Marxism and Christianity overlap in a number of ways. Marxism is more than simply a social theory. It is also a humanistic philosophy of man. Christianity has functioned as more than just a religion. It has also provided ideological support for, among others, liberal capitalism. Nevertheless, one wants to say, there is no particular reason why at this stage in the dialogue a Christian cannot also be a Marxist, or vice versa. Then what is the point of the objection?

The point of the objection is that what is true for individuals is not necessarily true for parties, let alone entire traditions. The objection is therefore a good one, and deserves a further reply. The parties to our dialogue are both parties of the future. Each is committed to a radical, antiestablishmentarian humanism. There is a great deal on which they can agree. But neither understands its commitment in philosophically abstract or historically disembodied terms. For one party, it is a commitment to Marxist humanism. For the other, it is a commitment to Christian radicalism. This does not mean that there are different essences after all, certain fundamental incompatibilities such that Chris-

tians in principle can never be Marxists, or vice versa. It does not
mean that we have to go back to looking at them as competitors.
What it does mean is that we are dealing here with two historical
traditions, two significantly different but not necessarily incompatible ways of seeing things.

Our task, therefore, is neither to play down nor to exaggerate
their differences but to see what it is that each of these traditions
can give to the other. Here we can take as our guideline the
observation of one writer that "religion will contribute insights
into man the myth and symbol maker, man the dreamer of
visions, man the promise maker, man the creature who alone
seems able to experience mystery, wonder and phantasy. Marxism will remind us of man the maker, man the irreducibly social
being, man the custodian of change."[9] This will not satisfy those
who insist that there must be clearly specifiable differences
behind the labels we apply, or that, for dialogue to be possible,
each side must have a clear sense of the essentials of its own
tradition. But it does point the way for the parties of the future in
their efforts to build a common future.

The question of Marxist-Christian dialogue does not arise on
the level of theory alone. Inevitably it leads to the realm of praxis
too. Here our original question repeats itself with greater insis-
tency. If the choice between these two traditions remains
clouded on the level of theory, should we not try to determine
which of these offers a more realistic hope on the level of praxis?
The problem is that there is no way in which one can answer such
a question by thought alone. Even for the Marxist, the answer
can be discovered only through praxis. Then what is the alternative? It is not simply to continue a theoretical dialogue, for that
could turn into a comfortable end in itself, a privileged illusion
for intellectuals. Both the radical Christian and the Marxist
humanist agree that the test of praxis should be applied. What
this calls for is, however, not a choice between them but an effort
at practical collaboration—an effort to go beyond the era of
dialogue to a new era of *pro-existence.*[10]

According to a thesis of the young Marx, differences among
competing views of the world, secular or religious, are of little
significance unless they can be shown to reflect differences in

ways of changing the world. This shift from an ideological to a practical criterion changes things considerably. We begin to see that our primary goal should not be ecumenical dialogue between the religions or between religious and secular views of the world. It should be to bring the resources of each of these traditions to bear upon the common struggle "to overthrow all the conditions under which man is an oppressed, enslaved, destitute and degraded being" (Marx). The criterion of praxis evokes the same polar response within every tradition. On the one side, forces arise to press for dramatic change in the name of a more human future. Others rededicate themselves to perpetuating the existing conditions of men. The issue changes from the question of whether a Marxist or a Christian, a secular or a religious, view should prevail. What begins to matter is whether within each tradition, and across the lines of each tradition, it is the parties of the future or the parties of the present who determine the direction we shall take. What comes to matter most is not whether we all see the world in the same way but whether we can work together to change it.

It may be that as a result of such changes, neither Marxism nor Christianity will prove to be the truer story about man. Perhaps, along with the world, each of these traditions will be changed into something that is different and new. If so, we can see why it would be a mistake to try to conclude at this point that one of them is essentially superior. That we no longer need to do so is already evidence of the liberating potential of this dialogue for the future.

## Toward a Common World

The reference to dialogue with other religions and other secular world views suggests that the question about the future of religion in a secular world is not identical with the question about the future of the Marxist-Christian dialogue. It would be provincial, if not presumptuous, to think that it was. And yet it is a fact that both Christianity and Marxism have appeared on the historical scene as movements claiming a universal significance. The task of determining the significance of their dialogue for the global future of religion is therefore not an easy one.

Ideologically, Christianity has always understood itself in universalistic terms. The goal of Christian eschatology is that universal reign of God when Christ shall once more be subordinate to the Father, when all nations shall be reconciled, and when God will be all in all.[11] Historically, it has been Christianity's fate to have helped initiate and, in turn, be surpassed by a worldwide movement toward social and political emancipation. The form taken by that movement has, for the most part, been that of Marxism. As Marx himself made abundantly clear, this revolutionary movement, like the biblical vision, is to be conceived in nothing less than universal terms. Its historical agent, like the Christ, is a universal man (the proletariat is the only universal class). The goal it envisions is, like the Kingdom of God, a universal one (the revolution cannot be won in one country alone; it must be worldwide). For Christianity and Marxism, the issues at stake in this dialogue are, ideologically and historically, universal or global in scope.

Yet for both traditions, these universalistic claims have become increasingly problematical. The reasons are several. We have already described the protest within each tradition against those hardened doctrines or institutions that have compromised the universal outreach of the original vision. Second, Marxists are beginning to discover what Christians have had to puzzle about for several centuries. There is not one Marxism (not even one Marxist humanism). The faces of Marxism are proving to be as varied and essentially different as there are different national and cultural traditions. Since the breakup of the hegemony of the Russian definition of Marxism, it is no longer clear which version of Marxism is the true, universal one. The assertion of the Roman Catholic Church that it is the one, true Church has long since lost its potential global validity.

The challenge to the universalistic claims of these two traditions does not come only from the ranks of these traditions themselves. Even this internal criticism has, to a significant degree, been influenced by criticism from another source. Christianity understands its universalism in a way that is distinctive of the Semitic religions. The universalism of Marxism bears the double stamp of its background in the biblical tradition and of its origins in the secular philosophical culture of the European

West. But what if one comes from a people or a nation or a cultural tradition whose vision of man (whether universalistic or tribal) is formulated in different terms? And what if one's socio-economic or world-historical situation is that of rising or revolutionary expectation? One will see things quite differently. The suspicion will arise that the self-proclaimed universalisms of Christianity and Marxism are in fact vehicles for white, European cultural imperialism—that universal humanity is a code name for the world-historical supremacy of a particular religious or national tradition.

Finally, there is a dialectical-historical reason why both Marxism and Christianity must consider that perhaps neither of them may be the universal ideology of our global future. Both of these world views are linked by an inner bond to a world era that is passing away. In this respect, each of them shares in the historical fate of the other. The triumph of one over the other must inevitably represent the triumph of the other over the first—and the triumph of neither. The withering away of the one (religion, Christianity) is possible only if the other (Marxism) withers away as well. We have already emphasized this point as it applies to Christianity. What has not been so often observed, and what is only hinted at by Marx himself, is that the same sort of consideration applies to Marxism as well. Marxism too is an ideology of alienation. It is itself not entirely free of the contradictions that characterize the alienated world it reflects. Marxism, Marx seems to suggest, is not yet that future philosophy of freedom which will arise in a world no longer governed by the laws of material necessity—that is, by the conditions of alienation.

And so we find ourselves with yet another paradox in our speculations about the significance of this dialogue for the future. It would appear that neither Christianity nor Marxism can confidently look forward to being the universal ideology (or ideologies) of the future. Christianity may have been the predominant form of Western culture until modern times. Marxism may be the leading candidate for the philosophy of our time. But that philosophy of the future whose name Sartre would not hazard to guess will in all likelihood be no more Christian or Marxist than the world itself ever was or is today. The only thing we can say in advance about such a philosophy is that "Its universality must be able to redeem local space, time and identity. The revolt of Black, Brown, Red, and Yellow peoples against that myth of universal humanity which turns out to be the White Christian's tribalism imperialistically imposed on the universe: this is surely a symptom of the demand for a universalism which can redeem the plurality of identities and histories, rather than abolishing all other history before the one history of the Master Race."[12] Such a universalism will rest on a vision of man far richer, more varied, and more genuinely comprehensive of the global aspirations of men, East and West, secular and religious, than any we have hitherto known.

Such speculations take us far beyond the limits of the Marxist-Christian dialogue. But they are not unrelated to our attempt to understand the significance of this dialogue for the future. For it is just here that the Marxist-Christian dialogue offers evidence of the possibilities that lie ahead. Out of the fusion of horizons between Marxism, Christianity, and a finitist ontology, there has emerged a new post-theistic way of thinking—a vision of man that did not exist before. Yet we recognize in this vision the presence of those earlier traditions whose hidden destiny (we can now say in retrospect) was to allow this newer vision to be. Should we not believe that, in the even greater vision of our global future, we shall see the triumphant presence of the dreams of all those who have gone before?

We who now live are parts of a humanity that extends into the remote past, a humanity that has interacted with nature. The things in civilization that we most prize are not of ourselves. They exist by grace of the doings and sufferings of the continuous human community in which we are a link. Ours is the responsibility of conserving, transmitting, rectifying and expanding the heritage of values we have received that those who come after us may receive it more solid and secure, more widely accessible and more generously shared than we have received it. Here are all the elements for a religious faith that shall not be confined to sect, class, or race. Such a faith has always been implicitly the common faith of mankind. It remains to make it explicit and militant.[13]

# Notes

# *Notes*

### 1   Marxist-Christian Dialogue and the Radical Perspective

1. The phrase is Roger Garaudy's, and nicely sums up the methodological assumptions which characterized the first stage of the renewed Marxist-Christian dialogue, of which his own book *From Anathema to Dialogue: A Marxist Challenge to the Christian Churches* is a good example.

2. For a volume of recent essays by Christians and Marxists venturing new interpretations of their respective traditions, see *The Christian Marxist Dialogue,* ed. Paul Oestreicher, especially the articles by the Roman Catholic theologian Johannes Metz and the Marxist philosophers Milan Machovec, Roger Garaudy, Leszek Kolakowski, and Milan Prucha.

3. Though I am using this schema for purposes of convenience in the analyses that follow, it should be noted that no satisfactory account of the issues in the one area can be given in abstraction from considerations relating to the other two. This is useful to remember if we are to avoid confusing differences in emphasis with differences in doctrine. Though a particular thinker may stress the significance of issues in one area (e.g., the Christian emphasis upon the doctrine of God, the existentialist emphasis upon individual freedom, the Marxist stress upon social determinants), this does not automatically imply conceptual incompatibilities with thinkers whose emphasis lies elsewhere.

4. The critics are divided on this point. Bottomore, for example, rejects Tucker's "religious" reading of Marx, and cites, as evidence against it, Marx's own disavowal of any divine status for the proletariat. See T. B. Bottomore, "Introduction," *Karl Marx: Early Writings,* pp. xii–xiii; and Karl Marx, "The Holy Family," in *Writings of the Young Marx on Philosophy and Society,* ed. Loyd D. Easton and Kurt H. Guddat, p. 368.

5. See James Luther Adams, "Is Marxist Thought Relevant to the Christian? A Protestant View," in *Marx and the Western World*, ed. Nicholas Lobkowicz, p. 375: "The atheism of Marx may not be an inextricable element in Marxism."

6. See Milan Machovec, "Tasks for the Dialogue," in Oestreicher, *Christian Marxist Dialogue*, p. 127: "On certain points I can admit quite openly that I do not know. I do not know, for example, how to deal with the problem of death in a Marxist way."

7. Gollwitzer's comment is a typical illustration of this criticism: Marxism, as a source of significance, "does not extend to cover acts which have nothing to do with the struggle for the future . . . for example, the world of inner experience and of so-called private relationships" (Helmut Gollwitzer, *The Christian Faith and the Marxist Criticism of Religion*, p. 117).

8. See Karl Marx, "Toward the Critique of Hegel's Philosophy of Law: Introduction," in Easton and Guddat, *Writings of the Young Marx*, (hereinafter, EG), p. 250.

9. I am not arguing that James, Dewey, or Whitehead, for example, might not also offer suitable resources for rethinking the philosophical possibilities of the Marxist-Christian dialogue. I have chosen to work with the secular existentialists because: (1) I am more familiar with them; (2) historically and philosophically, they are closer to the major figures and movements involved in this dialogue—for example, the Marxist humanists of Eastern Europe and the German theologians of hope; and (3) it seemed independently worthwhile to rescue existentialism from its association with a narrowly individualist or subjectivist perspective (Heidegger and the early Sartre) by stressing, instead, its capacity to enter into dialogue with contemporary Marxism as a philosophy that is both metaphysically and politically radical.

10. See Richard J. Bernstein's recent *Praxis and Action: Contemporary Philosophies of Human Activity* for a description of the remarkable extent to which such divergent post-Hegelian philosophies as Marxism, existentialism, pragmatism, and contemporary analytical metaphysics have come to focus their analysis of man on the central category of action or praxis.

11. See Peter Homans, *Theology after Freud*, pp. x, xv, for an analogous use of this method of approach to the dialogue between contemporary theology and secular thought—in this case, psychoanalytic psychology.

12. Thus Harvey Cox in his illuminating comments on "Marxist Humanism in Eastern Europe—Problems and Prospects," p. 38.

## 2   The Theology of Radical Secularity

1. For a collection of essays by these theologians which illustrates this new perspective, see *New Theology No. 5* and *New Theology No. 6*, ed. Martin E. Marty and Dean G. Peerman.

2. In contrast, say, to the existentialist individualism of the Bultmannian hermeneutic, the neoorthodox realism of the Niebuhrians, or the relatively nonpolitical or, at most, bourgeois-liberal expressions of earlier secular and radical theology (Altizer, Hamilton, the early work of Harvey Cox or Paul van Buren).

3. Wolfhart Pannenberg, "The God of Hope," p. 287.

4. Ernst Bloch, quoted in Jürgen Moltmann, "Hope without Faith: An Eschatological Humanism without God," in *Is God Dead?* ed. Johannes B. Metz, p. 27.

5. Pannenberg, "God of Hope," p. 287.

6. Richard Shaull, "Christian Faith as Scandal in a Technocratic World," *New Theology No. 6*, p. 130.

7. See Johannes B. Metz, "Creative Hope," *New Theology No. 5*, pp. 133–34.

8. See Johannes B. Metz, "The Church and the World," p. 74.

9. Johannes B. Metz, quoted in Michael Novak, "The Absolute Future," *New Theology No. 5*, p. 209.

10. Moltmann, "Hope without Faith," p. 38.

11. Novak, "Absolute Future," pp. 208–9.

12. Metz, "Creative Hope," p. 134.

13. Carl Braaten, "Toward a Theology of Hope," *New Theology No. 5*, p. 108.

14. Metz, "Creative Hope," p. 134.

15. Harvey Cox on Ernst Bloch in "Ernst Bloch and 'The Pull of the Future,' " *New Theology No. 5*, pp. 195, 197.

16. Braaten, "Toward a Theology of Hope," p. 97.

17. Metz, "Creative Hope," p. 138.

18. Richard Shaull, "Revolution: Heritage and Contemporary Option," in Carl Oglesby and Richard Shaull, *Containment and Change*, p. 228.

19. Ibid., p. 229.

20. For an elaboration of this methodological point, see Jürgen Moltmann, *The Theology of Hope*, pp. 285–88.

21. For an attempt by a radical theologian to do justice to both sets of needs, see Shaull, "Revolution," pp. 229–30.

22. Moltmann, *Theology of Hope*, p. 137.

23. Jürgen Moltmann, "Toward a Political Hermeneutics of the Gospel," *New Theology No. 6*, pp. 81, 83.

24. Shaull, "Revolution," p. 203.

25. See Metz, "Creative Hope," pp. 138–39.

26. Moltmann, "Toward a Political Hermeneutics," p. 78.

27. Moltmann's phrases, in Braaten, "Toward a Theology of Hope," p. 111.

28. Ernst Bloch, quoted in defense of this argument by Shaull, "Revolution," p. 214.

29. Metz, "Creative Hope," p. 139; Shaull, "Revolution," pp. 215–16.

30. Moltmann, *Theology of Hope*, p. 215.
31. Shaull, "Revolution," p. 229.
32. Ibid., p. 221.
33. See Moltmann, *Theology of Hope*, p. 216.
34. Johannes B. Metz, quoted in Ingo Hermann, "Total Humanism" (a report on the Salzburg Colloquium of Marxist and Christian thinkers), *Is God Dead?* p. 166; see also Metz, "Church and World," pp. 74–75.
35. Metz, in Hermann, "Total Humanism," p. 166; also Metz, "Church and World," p. 84: "Christian eschatology is not an omniscient ideology of the future, but a *theologia negativa* of the future. This poverty of knowledge is the very wealth of Christianity."
36. The terms for this distinction are Karl Rahner's; see the discussion of Rahner in Hermann, "Total Humanism," pp. 168–69. Michael Novak develops this distinction in Novak, "Absolute Future," pp. 208–9.
37. Novak, "Absolute Future," p. 209.
38. See Metz, in Hermann, "Total Humanism," pp. 171–72.
39. Johannes B. Metz, "God before Us instead of a Theological Argument," p. 301.

## 3  Radical Theology:
## A Secular Critique

1. Alasdair MacIntyre argues a similar thesis in "The Debate about God: Victorian Relevance and Contemporary Irrelevance," in Alasdair MacIntyre and Paul Ricoeur, *The Religious Significance of Atheism*, p. 26.
2. Jürgen Moltmann, "Toward a Political Hermeneutics of the Gospel," *New Theology No. 6*, p. 69.
3. It is somewhat startling to hear a secular theologian like van Buren say, "The theologian cannot even begin to consider the question why it should be this book which is decisive for his work, why it should be this rather than some other book, for that would be to consider as a serious question of theology whether there ought to be theology at all" (Paul van Buren, "On Doing Theology," *Talk of God*, p. 55). Either this is a harmless tautology ("By definition, theology cannot . . ."), in which case it does not constitute an answer to Moltmann's question; or it is a serious *petitio principii*. It is precisely the secular theologian, who shares the methods and world view of modern criticism, who should consider this *the* question with which to begin if he is to gain a hearing for his doing of theology at all. He may prefer to regard this as a question for the prolegomena to theology, but this does not alter the basic issue—it merely makes it explicit.
4. Moltmann, "Toward a Political Hermeneutics," p. 69.
5. As, for example, van Buren contends: theology is "that activity of men struck by the biblical story, in which they undertake to revise continually the ways in which they say how things are with their present circumstances in the light of how they read that story" ("On

Doing Theology," p. 53). The underlying assumption appears to be that apologetics makes sense of the contemporary world in terms of the biblical story, not (as a secular thinker might assume) vice versa.

6. See Johannes B. Metz, cited in Ingo Hermann, "Total Humanism," in *Is God Dead?* ed. Johannes B. Metz, p. 166; also Johannes B. Metz, "The Church and the World," pp. 74–75.

7. Jürgen Moltmann, *The Theology of Hope*, p. 292.

8. Richard Shaull's assertion in "Revolution: Heritage and Contemporary Option," in Carl Oglesby and Richard Shaull, *Containment and Change*, p. 228.

9. Moltmann, "Toward a Political Hermeneutics," pp. 77–81.

10. Karl Rahner, cited in Hermann, "Total Humanism," p. 168.

11. Harvey Cox, "Ernst Bloch and 'The Pull of the Future,' " *New Theology No. 5*, p. 196; Shaull, "Revolution," p. 213.

12. Hannah Arendt, *On Revolution*, pp. 18–19, 21. Rosemary Radford Ruether, in an excellent study of the history of messianism in Western thought, demonstrates a number of parallels in theme and typological options between religious and secular messianism, but nowhere disputes Arendt's basic claim; see Rosemary Radford Ruether, *The Radical Kingdom: The Western Experience of Messianic Hope*, pp. 2, 17, 21–22, 135, 160–61.

13. See John C. Raines, "From Passive to Active Man: Reflections on the Revolution in Consciousness of Modern Man," in *Marxism and Radical Religion: Essays toward a Revolutionary Humanism*, ed. John C. Raines and Thomas Dean, pp. 101–32.

14. Arendt, *On Revolution*, pp. 19–20.

15. Steve Weissman takes this position in "New Left Man Meets the Dead God," *New Theology No. 5*, pp. 23, 41–42.

16. See MacIntyre, "The Debate about God," pp. 26–27.

17. See Moltmann, *Theology of Hope*, pp. 81–82, for a similar point about the origins and future of modern historical consciousness itself.

18. The Marxist Gilbert Mury's comment on Rahner and Metz, in Hermann, "Total Humanism," p. 167; see Moltmann, *Theology of Hope*, pp. 58, 78.

19. A possible exception is Shaull, who interprets this dialectic of being "*in* but not *of* the established order" in a strictly temporal sense; in Richard Shaull, "Christian Faith as Scandal in a Technocratic World," *New Theology No. 6*, p. 132.

20. Rahner, cited in Hermann, "Total Humanism," pp. 168–70.

21. Metz, cited in Hermann, "Total Humanism," pp. 171–72.

22. The argument of such Marxist humanists as Marcuse is, according to Weissman, that "there is a difference between remaining in the universe of possibilities and saying 'yes' to this particular secular world" (Weissman, "New Left Man," pp. 34, 37).

23. This and the preceding quote are from Jürgen Moltmann, "Hope

without Faith: An Eschatological Humanism without God," *Is God Dead?* p. 32.

24. Rahner, in Hermann, "Total Humanism," p. 162; see Karl Rahner, "Christian Humanism," pp. 369–84.

25. Rahner, in Hermann, "Total Humanism," p. 168.

26. Moltmann, *Theology of Hope,* p. 92.

27. Shaull, "Revolution," p. 234; see Harvey Cox, "The Marxist-Christian Dialogue: What Next?" in *Marxism and Christianity,* ed. Herbert Aptheker, p. 28.

28. It could be argued that a nontheistic interpretation of secular Christianity (Braithwaite, van Buren) dissolves this particular question. To the extent that this is true, our earlier criticisms return with added force: Why does this version of the new Christianity insist on retaining specifically Christian language and practice? Can one simply eliminate the concept of God and leave the rest of the concepts undisturbed, or does a nontheistic reading of Christianity bring with it a profound sea change in all the other concepts as well? We shall return to these questions in Chapters 8 and 9. Meanwhile, for a criticism of the nontheistic or ethicist approach to secular Christianity, see MacIntyre, "The Debate about God," pp. 28, 29, 53.

29. Cox, "Marxist-Christian Dialogue," p. 28.

30. Shaull, "Revolution," p. 234.

31. Moltmann, "Hope without Faith," p. 37.

32. See Leslie Dewart's discussion of this problem (based on a set of distinctions taken from Henri de Lubac) in *The Future of Belief,* pp. 52 ff.

33. This argument of Moltmann's occurs in "Hope without Faith," pp. 30–31.

34. This argument is presented by Schubert Ogden in "The Christian Proclamation of God to Men of the So-Called 'Atheistic Age,'" *Is God Dead?* pp. 93–96.

35. Ibid., pp. 94–95. See also Schubert Ogden, *The Reality of God,* p. 145, where Ogden finds another source of ontological support for this new metaphysics of God in Heidegger's existential ontology. Heidegger suggests a conception of God's eternity as "a more primal and 'infinite' temporality," rather than an eternal "presence" of Being. See Martin Heidegger, *Being and Time,* p. 499, n. xiii.

36. See Carl Braaten, "Toward a Theology of Hope," *New Theology No. 5,* pp. 108–9; Ogden, *The Reality of God,* p. 153; Moltman, *Theology of Hope,* p. 110, n. 1: "If . . . the 'historic acts by which Jahweh founded the community were absolute,' then surely this means that . . . they overreach their temporal transience and move into the future—it does not mean absoluteness in the sense of intransience."

37. Thus Ogden, "Christian Proclamation," p. 94.

38. Ogden, *The Reality of God,* p. 157.

39. This distinction, as well as the issue it involves, is one which Ogden does not really handle. By making the shift from classical to processive

theism, he thinks he has taken care of the atheist's objections. The problem, however, concerns the logical and anthropological significance of theism itself. For the radical secularist, with this shift in categories, nothing in the essential has been changed.

40. Braaten, "Toward a Theology of Hope," p. 109.
41. Although for Marx, materialism, in its mechanistic or crudely deterministic form, is just as much a speculative ideology. Like idealism, it accentuates one side of the dialectical relation of nature and consciousness without referring it back to its prior setting in man's practical relation to nature; see Marx's *First, Second, Fifth, and Ninth Theses on Feuerbach,* EG, pp. 400–402.
42. See Moltmann, *Theology of Hope,* pp. 36, 272. This, according to Louis Dupré, is the proper, *practical* meaning of Marx's much-misunderstood call for the "abolition" of speculative metaphysics in favor of historical praxis. Marx means only to refuse "any speculation which is a priori with respect to *praxis.*" Thus, Marx's famous *Eleventh Thesis on Feuerbach*—"The philosophers have only *interpreted* the world in various ways; the point is, to *change* it"—is to be understood as a demand that philosophy answer to praxis, not that philosophy be dispensed with in favor of something else (Louis Dupré, "Comment" [on George Kline's "Some Critical Comments on Marx's Philosophy"], in *Marx and the Western World,* ed. Nicholas Lobkowicz, p. 434).
43. Johannes B. Metz, "Creative Hope," *New Theology No. 5,* p. 132.
44. Ibid., p. 133.
45. MacIntyre, "The Debate about God," p. 46.
46. See Harvey Cox, *The Feast of Fools: A Theological Essay on Festivity and Fantasy,* pp. 95–96: "The sad truth is that the church *cannot* be the meta-institution our world needs to instruct us in festivity, to open us to fantasy, to call us to tomorrow, or to enlarge our petty definitions of reality. . . . We have left behind the tired and useless task of 'renewing the church' and are now concerned with the recreation of the world." For a parallel in the radical reformation, see Ruether, *The Radical Kingdom,* p. 25.
47. See MacIntyre, "The Debate about God," p. 26.
48. Paul Ricoeur gives us a valuable discussion of this specific aspect of the contemporary situation of post-theistic, secular faith in "Religion, Atheism, and Faith," in Alasdair MacIntyre and Paul Ricoeur, *The Religious Significance of Atheism,* espec. pp. 59, 70, 84, 88.
49. Harvey Cox is more nearly correct when he says that "the only legitimate interest theology should have in the past is how it can help us create a new future" (*Feast of Fools,* pp. 127–28).

## 4 Marx's Sketch of a Radical Metaphysics

1. As the theologian Johannes Metz observes: if today we are in a post-theistic period, we are also in a post-atheistic period. Modern unbelief "is no longer an explicit negation of faith or primarily a system built in opposition to faith; contemporary unbelief offers itself

rather as a positive possibility of human existence, an integral way of being human without faith" ("Preface," *Is God Dead?* p. 2).

2. Nor does this assertion allow the subtle theologian to conclude that since atheism is not logically necessary to a Marxist metaphysics, therefore Marxism may in fact be logically compatible with theism. See James L. Adams, "Is Marx's Thought Relevant to the Christian? A Protestant View," in *Marx and the Western World*, ed. Nicholas Lobkowicz, p. 375: "The atheism of Marx may not be an inextricable element in Marxism"; or again (pp. 376–77): "Thus Marxists might be expected eventually to raise the radical question as to whether atheism is an indispensable and integral ingredient of Marxism." This apologetic strategy overlooks the fact that while Marx does not place primary emphasis upon the role of a critique of religion in the construction of a humanistic metaphysics, he nevertheless maintains, in good Hegelian fashion, that atheism, though it is only a ground-clearing operation for subsequent, more positive social criticism, still has its place in the overall dialectic. Though atheism contributes nothing of any positive substance to Marx's radical humanism, it maintains its validity as an essential preliminary: it clears the path and stands as a safeguard against the reentry of any kind of ontotheological thinking into philosophical anthropology. Cf. the not dissimilar position of Ludwig Feuerbach in his critique of modern and especially Hegelian metaphysics in *Principles of the Philosophy of the Future*.

3. Karl Marx, "Theses on Feuerbach," EG, p. 401.

4. Karl Marx, "Toward the Critique of Hegel's Philosophy of Law: Introduction," EG, p. 250.

5. Karl Marx, "On the Jewish Question," EG, p. 248.

6. Karl Marx, "On the Jewish Question," in *Karl Marx: Early Writings*, ed. T. B. Bottomore, pp. 20–21.

7. Marx, "Hegel's Philosophy of Law," EG, p. 250.

8. See Marx's similar critique of Bauer's attack on religion, "Jewish Question," EG, p. 226.

9. Marx, "Jewish Question," EG, pp. 222–23; "Hegel's Philosophy of Law," EG, p. 250.

10. For the notion that in Marx religion is "taken unseriously," see Nicholas Lobkowicz, "Marx's Attitude toward Religion," in *Marx and the Western World*, ed. Nicholas Lobkowicz, p. 308.

11. Karl Marx, *First and Second Theses on Feuerbach*, EG, pp. 400–401.

12. Marx, "Hegel's Philosophy of Law," EG, p. 251.

13. Marx, *Sixth Thesis on Feuerbach*, EG, p. 402.

14. For an especially felicitous summary of this aspect of Marx's criticism of Feuerbach, see Manfred Vogel, "Introduction," in Ludwig Feuerbach, *Principles of the Philosophy of the Future*, pp. xx, lxv, lxxix.

15. Karl Marx, "Critique of Hegel's Philosophy of the State," EG, p. 174.

16. Thus Lobkowicz, "Marx's Attitude," p. 330.

17. Marx, "Jewish Question," EG, p. 231.

18. Ibid.

19. Marx, "Hegel's Philosophy of the State," EG, p. 176; Karl Marx, "Critique of Hegelian Dialectic and Philosophy in General," EG, p. 317.

20. Marx readily acknowledges that it was Feuerbach who initiated this general line of criticism with the attack on Hegel's speculative metaphysics as simply a modern philosophical version of theology (or ontotheology) in disguise; see Marx, "Hegelian Dialectic," EG, pp. 316–17.

21. The phrase is Lobkowicz's, "Marx's Attitude," p. 329; but the use to which it is put here is more nearly in accord with Althusser's analysis of Marx's criticism of Feuerbach; see Louis Althusser, For Marx.

22. Thus Lobkowicz, "Marx's Attitude," p. 329; and Vogel, "Introduction," pp. xxv and lxiv.

23. Marx, "Hegelian Dialectic," EG, p. 329.

24. It is this consideration that in part leads Althusser to characterize Marx's philosophical anthropology as a "theoretical anti-humanism" (Althusser, For Marx).

25. Marx, "Jewish Question," EG, p. 231; "The Holy Family," EG, p. 368. It follows that Marx would also be opposed to the efforts of those theologians who give humanistic or secularizing interpretations to traditional religious ideas on the undialectical and contradictory assumption that it is possible to preserve the alleged existential or secular truth (kernel) of these ideas while abandoning their superhuman expression (husk). See Marx, "The Holy Family," p. 363.

26. Marx, "Hegel's Philosophy of Law," EG, p. 257.

27. See Richard Lichtman, "The Marxian Critique of Christianity," in Marxism and Christianity, ed. Herbert Aptheker, p. 119, for an example of this essentially mistaken reading of what Marx is trying to say.

28. Marx, quoted in Lobkowicz, "Marx's Attitude," p. 306.

29. Karl Marx, "Private Property and Communism," EG, p. 314; "Hegelian Dialectic," EG, p. 319.

30. Marx, "Hegelian Dialectic," EG, p. 331.

31. For part of this analysis, see Louis Dupré, "Marx and Religion: An Impossible Marriage," New Theology No. 6, p. 153.

32. It is only in this dialectical sense that it could be said that atheism is philosophically "unnecessary" for Marx's position. But see note 2 above.

33. Marx, "Hegelian Dialectic," EG, p. 314.

34. Feuerbach, Principles, pp. 68, 70, 72–73; and Vogel's introduction, pp. lxiv, lxxx.

35. Feuerbach was not unaware of this fact. The genuine atheist, he said, is not the man who denies the divine subject in order to relocate the attributes of religion in man. The atheist is, rather, he who denies the

divinity of those human attributes. Of course this is just Marx's point: Feuerbach's atheism and humanism are still, by the latter's own criterion, religious in nature. They are therefore expressions of a secularity that is still alienated, still not radically secular. Marx, on Feuerbach's terms, would be one of those genuine atheists who deny the applicability of the divine attributes to man either as individual or as species.

36. Althusser, *For Marx,* p. 229.

37. Marx, "Hegel's Philosophy of Law," EG, p. 257. As Engels later asserts in "The Holy Family," "it is man, actual living *man*" who "is understood as the essence, the basis of all human activity and situations" (EG, p. 385).

38. Marx, "Hegel's Philosophy of Law," EG, p. 250.

39. Marx, "Hegel's Philosophy of the State," EG, p. 170.

40. Marx, "Hegelian Dialectic," EG, pp. 324, 325.

41. Marx, *First Thesis on Feuerbach,* EG, p. 400.

42. Marx, "Private Property and Communism," EG, p. 312; "Hegelian Dialectic," EG, p. 321, where he acknowledges his debt to Hegel for this phenomenology of labor, which, however, the latter expressed in speculative or alienated form. See also Richard Lichtman, "The Marxian Critique," *Marxism: First Course,* p. 98.

43. Marx, "Private Property and Communism," EG, p. 314.

44. Ibid.

45. Ibid., p. 313.

46. Feuerbach, *Principles,* p. 37.

47. Marx, "Hegelian Dialectic," EG, p. 317.

48. Feuerbach, *Principles,* p. 24.

49. Marx, *Sixth Thesis on Feuerbach,* EG, p. 402.

50. See Lichtman's analysis of Hegel's treatment of this dialectic, *Marxism,* pp. 10, 21.

51. See John Findlay, *Hegel: A Re-examination,* p. 164. Findlay appears to believe, on the contrary, that these formulations can be indifferently exchanged with one another.

52. Hegel, quoted in Findlay, *Hegel,* pp. 60, 162, 164.

53. Findlay, *Hegel,* p. 164.

54. Ibid., pp. 164, 174.

55. Marx, "Hegel's Philosophy of the State," EG, p. 156.

56. If radical finitude is taken as ontologically fundamental, then the ex-fundamental category, "God," would simply be an inverted way of pointing to the fundamental mystery which is the givenness of finite being. The mystery of being would then be the positive mystery of finitude, not of some nonfinite, transcendent negation or ground of finite being. Here again it is Marx, not Feuerbach, who carries through to its logical conclusion the implications of Feuerbach's observation that finitude must be conceived as the (dialectical) negation of God.

See Alexandre Kojève, *Introduction to the Reading of Hegel,* who similarly argues that in Hegel we encounter the first systematic attempt to overcome the ontotheological foundations of previous metaphysics and to construct a radically atheistic or finitist ontology: "Hegel was the first to try to formulate a complete *philosophy* that is atheistic and finitist in relation to Man (at least in the great *Logik* and the earlier writings). He not only gave a correct description of *finite* human existence on the 'phenomenological' level, which allowed him to use the fundamental categories of Judaeo-Christian thought without any inconsistency. He also tried (without completely succeeding, it is true) to complete this description with a metaphysical and ontological analysis, also radically atheistic and finitist. [That is, with a doctrine of "a natural World that has no beyond—i.e., where there is no place for a God" and a doctrine in which "Being . . . must be essentially temporal—that is, finite. . . ."] But very few of his readers have understood that in the final analysis dialectic meant atheism" (p. 259, n. 41).

57. Feuerbach, *Principles,* p. 71.
58. Karl Marx, "The German Ideology," EG, p. 407.
59. Marx, "Hegelian Dialectic," EG, p. 331.
60. Ibid., pp. 331–32.
61. Ibid., p. 332.
62. See Feuerbach, *Principles* pp. 72–73, for a similar question; and Althusser, *For Marx,* pp. 188–89, though in a slightly different context.
63. Marx, "Hegel's Philosophy of Law," EG, pp. 257–58.
64. Marx, "German Ideology," EG, pp. 435–36.
65. Marx, *First Thesis on Feuerbach,* EG, pp. 400–401; see Karl Marx, "The Poverty of Philosophy," EG, p. 494.
66. On this point, see also Lichtman, *Marxism,* vol. II, p. 91; Althusser, *For Marx,* pp. 188–89; and Shlomo Avineri, *The Social and Political Thought of Karl Marx,* p. 16.
67. Feuerbach, *Principles,* pp. 72–73.
68. Ibid., p. 63.
69. Marx, "Hegel's Philosophy of Law," EG, p. 257.
70. Karl Marx, "An Exchange of Letters," EG, p. 212.
71. Dupré provides a passage from Marx's doctoral dissertation of 1841 in which Marx already links "the philosophization of the world" with "the secularization of philosophy" (Louis Dupré, *The Philosophical Foundations of Marxism,* p. 75).
72. Marx, "Hegel's Philosophy of Law," EG, pp. 263–64.
73. This universalist dimension to Marx's concept of the proletariat emerges most clearly in a passage from "Hegel's Philosophy of the Law," EG, p. 263. See Avineri, *The Social and Political Thought,* pp. 57–62, for a perceptive analysis of this phenomenon.
74. Karl Marx, "Critical Battle against French Materialism," EG, p. 392.
75. Marx, *Eighth Thesis on Feuerbach,* EG, p. 402.

76. Marx, "Private Property and Communism," EG, p. 310.

77. For a lengthier treatment of this theme in the history of ideas, see Nicholas Lobkowicz, *Theory and Practice: History of a Concept from Aristotle to Marx,* pp. 135–39.

78. Before Hegel and Marx, and again afterward, the concept of action has been interpreted in Western philosophy primarily in ideological—that is, *ethico-political* terms. It is Marx and Hegel who give it the distinctively Marxian sense of material—that is, productive *socioeconomic* activity. On this point see Lobkowicz, *Theory and Practice,* pp. 278–79.

79. Marx, "Private Property and Communism," EG, pp. 304, 310. Marx mentions in particular such traditional dichotomies in philosophical anthropology as: freedom and necessity, individual and society, essence and existence, subjectivism and objectivism, spiritualism and materialism, activity and passivity.

80. Roger Garaudy, *Karl Marx: The Evolution of His Thought,* p. 82.

81. See Avineri, *The Social and Political Thought,* p. 6, for the analysis of this paragraph. As Dupré also points out, Marx did not look to French materialism for his ontology, since he rejected its mechanical interpretation of materialism. From the French philosophers he borrowed, rather, his affirmation of man's natural being, their opposition to any supernatural view of man, and their socialist conclusions. Marx's materialism, in other words, was not directed against humanism in favor of a theory of nature as something which exists apart from man and to which man could be reduced. It is directed, rather, against an idealist mystification of man's practical capacities. See Dupré, *Philosophical Foundations,* pp. 143–44, 173 n. 2.

82. See Lobkowicz for an account of these years, *Theory and Practice,* p. 193; also Avineri, *The Social and Political Thought,* p. 124.

83. See Lobkowicz, *Theory and Practice,* p. 196. As Marx charged: "The philosopher . . . is only the organ whereby the creator of history, the Absolute Spirit, *retrospectively* becomes conscious after the movement of history has ended. The philosopher's participation in history is reduced to this retrospective consciousness, the philosopher appears post festum" ("The Holy Family," EG, p. 383).

84. See Lobkowicz, *Theory and Practice,* p. 234.

85. Avineri, *The Social and Political Thought,* p. 126.

86. *Marx's Dialectic: A Methodological Note.* There is of course an inversion in Marx's method which parallels this inversion in ontology. If, in good Aristotelian or phenomenological fashion, we view the appropriateness of a philosopher's method in terms of its adequacy to the objects under investigation, then we should expect that the finitude of man's being will be reflected in the method of philosophical analysis Marx employs. Marx in fact does reject Hegel's speculative interpretation of the dialectical method. Hegel begins, says Marx, by initially abstracting certain guiding ideas from empirical reality. But then he inverts their relationship to reality and, divorcing the development of the Idea from

its original empirical matrix, he attempts to depict the Idea, the concepts and categories of logic, as the true subject of reality, thus reducing the empirical phenomena to contingent appearances (EG, 441). The result is an ideological distortion of empirical reality and the construction of an arbitrary ideality. Marx opposes to Hegel's methodological procedure an opposite, scientific approach which attempts to derive the order of ideas from the order of reality rather than from an alleged necessity inherent in the logic of the Idea. Over against the methodological procedures of speculative Reason, Marx intends to reestablish the priority of a finite Understanding grounded in the dialectic of sensuous (empirical) praxis (EG, 370).

What, according to Marx, is the nature of a dialectical method which will avoid the distortions that result from Hegel's speculative misuse of dialectic? It is a method which begins with a different, finitist concept of reason. Rationality or intelligibility is the ever-incomplete and ongoing emergence of structures of meaning from particular existences and their interrelationships. Marx's dialectic is not a necessitarian logic of abstract and eternal ideas but an attempt to describe those shifting types and constellations of determinations which define particular finite things at any given moment as being the sorts of things they are. "Empirical actuality is thus understood as it is. It is also pronounced rational . . . through its own rationality . . . [not] because the empirical fact in its empirical existence has another [speculative—i.e., alienated] meaning than its own" (EG, 157). Universals are thus viewed by Marx not as the predetermining predicates of finite actuality but "as the actual essence of what is the actual-finite, that is, what is existing and determinate," as the finite predicates of empirical actuality which is "the *genuine subject* of the infinite" (EG, 166). "Reason," says Marx, is an ever-emergent feature of the ongoing actualization of individuals as the most concrete thing possible: "What is rational . . . is found in the reason of the actual person becoming actual, [not] in the movements of the abstract concept becoming actual" (EG, 170). It is not universal concepts but particular existences that are methodologically primary for Marx. (See Garaudy, *Karl Marx*, p. 96).

Just as Marx was more heavily indebted to Hegel than to Feuerbach in his description of the phenomenon of human finitude, here too, despite his stated reservations, it is to Hegel that he is primarily indebted for his insight into the application of dialectical analysis to finite reality. It is from Hegel rather than from Feuerbach that Marx appropriated his twofold conviction that (1) it is the metaphysician's task and within his capacity, contrary to traditional assumptions, to conceptualize and rationalize the logic of temporal, historical existence—to describe or, if need be, to construct another logic of being that can render coherent and intelligible those complex features of human, historical reality (motion, contradiction, development, totality) which had either eluded the grasp or at least not received their proper due from Western ontology (see, Garaudy, *Karl Marx*, p. 89; and Lichtman, *Marxism*, vol. I, p. 26); and that (2) a dialectical method of analysis is that other logic which provides the necessary tools for analyzing (and acting upon) the objective, rational structures or meaning of historical (for Hegel, spiritual) existence.

All of this—the reliance upon Hegel's dialectical concept of historical reality, as well as the critical reservations about Hegel's speculative distortion of that method, may be heard in Marx's methodological pronouncement to Ruge: "We develop new principles for the world out of the principles of the world" (EG, 214).

In starting his analysis from the actual, empirical world, Marx does not, in other words, mean to give up the Hegelian attempt to make sense of the world and history as a whole. Though he rejects any idealist methodological a priorism, he is equally firm in his refusal to lapse back into the narrowly piecemeal approach of positivistic methodology. A major feature of dialectical analysis is the holistic analysis of particular existences in the larger setting or ensembe of their social relationships and historical development as a whole. Though a dialectical analysis of historical reality cannot start, as Hegel believed, from a purely logical conception of development out of the original unity of a simple Idea, nevertheless it does start from a "pregiven complex, structured whole" (Althusser, *For Marx,* pp. 198–99). As Marx himself puts it: "My analytical method does not start from man but from the economically given social period" (quoted in Althusser, *For Marx,* p. 219). The universals disclosed in a dialectical analysis of particular existences and their social wholes are not reflections of a suprahistorical subject of investigation but, rather, as Marx says, of "*many units*"—that is, of "the ensemble of social relationships" as they are dialectically constituted at any given stage and place in man's historical development (EG, 169).

It follows that such a method cannot deliver the eternal truths of a speculative metaphysics of history. For a radical metaphysics, "these ideas, these categories are no more eternal than the relations which they express. They are *historical and transitory products*" (EG, 480). Rather, Marx's dialectical method is itself a critical instrument in furthering the dynamics of a changing, developing sociohistorical reality. Its categories reflect, as Hegel saw better than Feuerbach, not the fixed or predetermined attributes of an abstract species being, but the dynamic, developing capacities of man's collective productive activity.

We are now in a better position to appreciate the force of Althusser's criticism of those who see in Marx's dialectic nothing more than the rejection of Hegel's system (husk) with a retention, unchanged, of his underlying method (kernel). It is Althusser's opinion that one cannot reject the outer shell of Hegel's system and preserve some inner core of method unchanged, even though remarks by Engels suggest as much. In negating the substantial predicates of God (the inverted ontotheological content of Hegel's system), Marx is not simply standing Hegel's system right side up again. He is transforming and eliminating this ontotheological content altogether and in its place proposing a radically finitist anthropology and ontology. Hence the

method appropriate to the description of this new content must itself
be radically new, however indebted to its earlier, Hegelian
formulation. Its approach, its claims, and the results it delivers must be
*toto caelo* other than and opposed to those suggested by the notion that
Marx has retained Hegel's method while dispensing with his system. In
place of a priori (speculative, ideological) analysis, Marx proposes a
posteriori (empirical, scientific) analysis; in place of absolute
knowledge of the eternal truths of Reason, the historical and transitory
products of finite Understanding; in place of arbitrary abstraction and
paraphrasis of existing facts, or pseudo-explanations masquerading as
depth accounts of the supernatural significance of ordinary facts, a
rigorous attempt at concrete, spatially and temporally circumscribed
descriptions and explanations of specific stages in the historical
development of particular ensembles of social relationships (EG, 488).

    The critic of Marx can continue to employ this kernel-husk
metaphor, as do Marx and Engels themselves on occasion. But the
evidence, both textual and conceptual, weighs against this traditional
approach to Marx interpretation.

5   The Radical Perspective in
Contemporary Metaphysics

1. Ludwig Feuerbach, quoted by Ronald M. Green, "Ernst Bloch's
   Revision of Atheism," p. 128. Green's article is a good illustration of
   the failure of a critic to see the radical implications of what Feuerbach
   or, in our day, Ernst Bloch is up to: he sees them both as engaged in
   anthropologizing religion, attempting to preserve the kernel of
   religious experience via a critique of religion—and finds nothing
   inherently problematic about such an attempt.
2. The quotations in this paragraph are taken from Maurice
   Merleau-Ponty, "Religion," *In Praise of Philosophy,* pp. 41–47.
3. Johannes B. Metz, "Preface," in *Is God Dead?* ed. Johannes B. Metz,
   p. 2.
4. Merleau-Ponty, *In Praise,* p. 45.
5. See Rosemary Radford Ruether, *The Radical Kingdom: The Western
   Experience of Messianic Hope,* p. 162.
6. Jean-Paul Sartre, *Nausea,* p. 176.
7. This phrase is from Joseph Arntz, "Must Man Be an Atheist Because
   He Is Man?" *Is God Dead?* p. 43.
8. See Jean-Paul Sartre, *Being and Nothingness,* p. 81.
9. Maurice Merleau-Ponty, *Signs,* p. 242.
10. See Arntz, "Must Man Be An Atheist?" for a more extended
    discussion of Sartre's and Merleau-Ponty's views on the metaphysical
    ultimacy of contingency.
11. See John Wisdom, *Other Minds,* espec. chap. 7, for a similar analysis of
    the temporal logic of perceptual terms.
12. One thinks here also of William James's analysis of the future-oriented
    nature of experience in *Pragmatism,* espec. chaps. 5–7.

13. See Wolfhart Pannenberg, "Appearance as the Arrival of the Future," in *New Theology No. 5,* ed. Martin E. Marty and Dean G. Peerman, pp. 112–29, for an extended analysis of the link between the concepts of the future and contingency as illustrated by the phenomenon of perception.

14. This is certainly one of the cardinal insights of Martin Heidegger's *Being and Time;* see espec. para. 65, p. 378.

15. Again, see Heidegger, *Being and Time,* pp. 378–89.

16. For further comments on Aristotle's concept of being and time, see Pannenberg, "Appearance," pp. 125–26.

17. See Heidegger, *Being and Time,* p. 378.

18. Even the non-temporal or eternal truths of reason are, according to Merleau-Ponty and Heidegger, to be explained temporally as regards their conceptual origins and pragmatic function: such truths function "to open a whole temporal cycle in which the 'acquired' thought will remain present as a dimension, without our needing henceforth to summon it up or reproduce it. What is known as the non-temporal in thought is what, having thus carried forward the past and committed the future, is presumptively of all time and is therefore anything but transcendent in relation to time. The non-temporal is the acquired" (Maurice Merleau-Ponty, *Phenomenology of Perception,* p. 392). See also Heidegger, who speaks of infinite time as a derived mode of primordial finite temporality (*Being and Time,* p. 379). The eternal, in other words, is that which is true or valid for all times, not something which transcends time altogether. It is eminently temporal, not atemporal.

19. See Heidegger, *Being and Time,* para. 65.

20. As Eugene Fontinell observes of the seminal thinkers involved in the emergence of twentieth-century metaphysics, "It is almost always misleading to apply the traditional use of these terms to their thought" ("Reflections on Faith and Metaphysics," p. 20). For an exhaustive study of Heidegger's linguistic innovations and their philosophical import, see Erasmus Schöfer, *Die Sprache Heideggers.* A summary and commentary on Schöfer's study appears as an appendix to my doctoral dissertation, "The Logic of Language and Persons: A Methodological Introduction to the Interpretive Metaphysics of Heidegger" (New York: Columbia University, 1968), pp. 311–39.

21. To say that man's nature is something that is still coming to be is not to imply that at some future date it might conceivably reach a specific end. It is rather to say that man's way of being is permanently futural, that there are always possibilities still before it, no matter what the specific content of those possibilities might be. It is important to distinguish, in other words, between philosophical assertions about the general futural nature of man's being (what Heidegger calls ontological statements) and empirical assertions about specific future possibilities (what Heidegger calls ontic facts). This distinction is one to which we shall shortly return; see note 23 below.

22. This concept of man's being as ek-sistence, a process of self-transcendence made possible by the power of the future, may be taken as a contemporary secular version of the traditional religious and idealist concept of man's spirit. Rudolf Bultmann, for example, observes that the power of the spirit, which in the biblical writings is linked to the possibility of human freedom, "is nothing else than being open for the genuine future, letting oneself be determined by the future. So Spirit may be called the power of futurity" (*Theology of the New Testament,* vol. I, pp. 334–35).

23. Pannenberg, "Appearance," p. 128. Pannenberg goes on to add that man must (temporarily?) accept this uncertainty "since he himself does not yet live in the final future, but rather is ever again surprised by what comes upon him from the future." The phrase "does not yet live in the final future" indicates of course the distance that separates the theologian from the philosopher. What happens here is that the theologian confuses the ontological "not yet," which stands for a permanent structural feature of man's finite being, with the ontic "not yet" of a specific future state or end, the alleged final future of the biblical-eschatological hope. He confuses a general structure or way of being with a particular state or end of being. In any case, the existence or nonexistence of that future goal of being in no way alters or accounts for the futural manner in which man exists.

24. John Macquarrie, *Martin Heidegger,* pp. 30–31, 51. Macquarrie's book is an excellent brief introduction to Heidegger's philosophy and its implications for theology.

25. Jean-Paul Sartre, "Existentialism Is a Humanism," in *Existentialism versus Marxism,* ed. George Novack, p. 84.

26. Ibid., pp. 73–74, 77–78.

27. Sartre, *Being and Nothingness,* p. 617.

28. Ibid., pp. 622–23.

29. See the critical reaction to Sartre's concept of freedom by Georg Lukacs, Roger Garaudy, and Herbert Marcuse, in *Existentialism versus Marxism,* ed. Novack.

30. Merleau-Ponty observes that nothing is gained by replacing a theistic with a humanistic perspective if one then turns around and ascribes to man quasi-theological—that is, absolutized—capacities and needs; see Merleau-Ponty, *In Praise,* p. 44. Also Arntz, "Must Man Be an Atheist?" p. 42.

31. John F. Bannan, *The Philosophy of Merleau-Ponty,* p. 17. See Jean-Paul Sartre, *Situations,* pp. 159–60.

32. See Bannan, *The Philosophy of Merleau-Ponty,* pp. 267–68. Note the striking similarity between Merleau-Ponty's rejection of Sartre's philosophical ideal and the later Wittgenstein's rejection of the methodological ideal embodied in his earlier work; see Ludwig Wittgenstein, *Philosophical Investigations,* and *On Certainty.*

33. Merleau-Ponty, *In Praise,* p. 39.

34. See Martin Heidegger, *Brief über den Humanismus,* p. 71.

35. Ibid., p. 61. See also Gilbert Ryle, *The Concept of Mind*, p. 328: "Man need not be degraded to a machine by being denied to be a ghost in a machine. He might, after all, be a sort of animal, namely, a higher mammal. There has yet to be ventured the hazardous leap to the hypothesis that perhaps he is a man."

36. Heidegger, *Humanismus*, p. 96. The theist's reductive reading of this concept of our "worldly" being is of a piece, Heidegger says, with his reductive interpretation of other terms associated with it—for example, "atheism," "humanism," and so on.

37. Ibid., p. 100.

38. Ibid., pp. 100–101. For Merleau-Ponty too, the concept of man's ek-sistence as a process of transcendence is understood, at least in part, in terms of man's capacity for reaching out to a world; see Bannan, *The Philosophy of Merleau-Ponty*, p. 116.

39. Heidegger, *Humanismus*, p. 101.

40. Martin Heidegger, "The Age of the World-View," p. 281.

41. Ibid., pp. 281, 283.

42. See Heidegger, *Being and Time*, p. 78.

43. Heidegger, *Humanismus*, p. 101.

44. Maurice Merleau-Ponty, *Sense and Non-Sense*, p. 179.

45. Merleau-Ponty, "Preface," *Phenomenology of Perception*, pp. xvii, xx.

46. See the discussion by P. F. Strawson of the difficulties involved in trying to provide a logical justification for the possibility of induction, *Introduction to Logical Theory*, pp. 248–63; see also his discussion of the logically prior status of our prereflective beliefs about the world, *Individuals: An Essay in Descriptive Metaphysics*, p. 247.

47. Merleau-Ponty, *Phenomenology of Perception*, p. 398.

48. Ibid., "Preface," p. xvii.

49. See Macquarrie, *Heidegger*, pp. 58–59, for an example of the attempt to force the ontology of the secular existentialist, in this case Heidegger, into theistic terms.

50. This is the argument Schubert Ogden makes in "The Christian Proclamation of God to Men of the So-Called 'Atheistic Age,'" *Is God Dead?* pp. 90–93.

51. Merleau-Ponty, *Sense and Non-Sense*, p. 179.

52. Merleau-Ponty, "Preface," *Phenomenology of Perception*, p. xiv.

53. Ibid., p. xvii. Note that this is not to say that the notion of an idea for which one can live or die is henceforth illegitimate. The absoluteness of contingency, if we may use that phrase, does provide a general criterion for values and action: those ideas or programs of action are worth fighting for which extend the openness, the freedom and creativity, of man's being. See Rosemary Ruether's discussion of Camus' development of an ethic of revolt from out of a philosophy of radical finitude in *Radical Kingdom*, p. 135 ff.

54. Merleau-Ponty, *In Praise*, pp. 43–44.

55. Ibid., pp. 25–26.
56. Sartre, "Merleau-Ponty," *Situations,* p. 218.
57. Merleau-Ponty, *In Praise,* p. 44.
58. Merleau-Ponty, *Phenomenology of Perception,* p. 63.
59. Merleau-Ponty, *In Praise,* p. 47.
60. Ibid., p. 35.

### 6 The Metaphysics of Marxist Humanism: Being and Man

1. *Socialist Humanism,* ed. Erich Fromm.
2. Gajo Petrovic, *Marx in the Mid-Twentieth Century,* p. 22. Roger Garaudy's explanation of this shift in theoretical focus points to the underlying social changes that made it possible: "For Marx and Lenin, the fundamental problem was the construction of a new social order. For this reason, the problems of subjectivity were well down in the list of priorities, although they were not entirely ignored. But these problems are now primary, and they can be formulated as follows: will new *human* relationships automatically develop hand-in-hand with the construction of new *social* relationships?" ("Creative Freedom," in *The Christian Marxist Dialogue,* ed. Paul Oestreicher, pp. 141–42).
3. See Milan Machovec, "Tasks for Dialogue," in *The Christian Marxist Dialogue,* p. 130; and Milan Prucha, "Marxism as a Philosophy of Human Existence," ibid., pp. 247–48.
4. As Garaudy observed: "One could say that in the second half of the twentieth century, Marxism has emerged from a theological slumber of twenty-five years" ("Creative Freedom," p. 140).
5. See, for example, Prucha's comment that "the 'economic-philosophic manuscripts' provide abundant evidence of how far from the truth is the idea that Marx neglected the meta-historical existential difficulties" ("Marxism as a Philosophy," p. 249).
6. Hence Garaudy's remark, that "Marxist thought needed not so much to change as to wake up" (in "Creative Freedom," p. 140), strikes me as fundamentally untrue both because of the historical realities it overlooks and because of the conceptual distance between the Hegelian ambience of Marx's early writings and the terminology of contemporary metaphysics.
7. Petrovic, *Marx,* p. 34.
8. Ibid.
9. Ibid., p. 81.
10. Ibid., p. 56.
11. Prucha, "Marxism as a Philosophy," p. 251.
12. Bronislaw Baczko, "Marx and the Idea of the Universality of Man," in *Socialist Humanism,* ed. Fromm, p. 172.
13. Petrovic, *Marx,* p. 30.
14. Bloch's major work is *Das Prinzip Hoffnung.* Other works of Bloch

available in English include: *Man on His Own: Essays in the Philosophy of Religion; A Philosophy of the Future; Spirit of Utopia;* and "Man as Possibility."

Articles in English on Bloch include: Harvey Cox, "Ernst Bloch and 'The Pull of the Future,'" in *New Theology No. 5,* ed. Martin E. Marty and Dean G. Peerman; Jürgen Moltmann, "Hope without Faith: An Eschatological Humanism without God," in *Is God Dead?* ed. Johannes B. Metz; and Jürgen Moltmann, "Introduction," in Bloch, *Man On His Own.*

15. Bloch, "Man as Possibility," p. 281. In *A Philosophy of the Future* (p. 96), Bloch hints at the more specific social-visionary implications of these abstract ontological assertions when he tells us that "not only the specific existent, but all given existence and being itself, has utopian margins which surround actuality with real and objective possibility."

16. A quotation from Bloch's *Das Prinzip Hoffnung,* cited in his *Philosophy of the Future,* p. 111.

17. Bloch, "Man as Possibility," p. 283.

18. Moltmann, "Hope without Faith," pp. 29–30.

19. Bloch, "Man as Possibility," pp. 277–78. For Hegel, says Bloch, "The final in-and-for-itself would be only the in-itself mediated with its contrary on a higher level. In other words: the initial thesis . . . is not so much developed into a something new, as developed-out and reproduced at a higher stage. In spite of lively e-motion . . . in spite of a constantly starting process, the world for Hegel is 'ready.' Accordingly, there is no possibility that might not already be realized" (*Philosophy of the Future,* p. 55).

20. Bloch, *Philosophy of the Future,* pp. 55–56. Cf. Aristotle's definition of the "essence" of a thing as its "what-it-was-ness" *(to ti ēn einai).*

21. Cox, "Ernst Bloch," p. 194.

22. See Bloch, "Man as Possibility," p. 277. It should also be noted that this finitist interpretation of the unconditional will be used to overcome the traditional necessitarian or deterministic character of Marxist metaphysics and thus to provide the ontological basis for a radical affirmation of human freedom by these new Marxists.

23. Moltmann's phrase in "Hope without Faith," p. 31.

24. Ibid., pp. 31–32.

25. Bloch, *Man on His Own,* pp. 222–23.

26. Bloch, *Philosophy of the Future,* p. 96. See Cox, "Ernst Bloch," p. 198.

27. Bloch, *Man on His Own,* p. 161.

28. In *The Christian Marxist Dialogue,* ed. Oestricher, pp. 247–66.

29. Prucha, "Marxism as a Philosophy," pp. 253–54.

30. Ibid., pp. 254–55.

31. Ibid., p. 255.

32. Ibid.

33. Ibid., p. 257.

34. Ibid., pp. 256–57.

35. Ibid., p. 259.
36. Ibid., pp. 258–59. The deeper significance and hidden irony of Prucha's remark was apparently lost on at least two theologians who enthusiastically interpreted it as a fascinating or paradoxical call to Christians to return to their traditional concept of the transcendence of God. Thus John C. Bennett, "Christian Responsibility in a Time That Calls for Revolutionary Change," in *Marxism and Radical Religion: Essays Toward a Revolutionary Humanism*, ed. John C. Raines and Thomas Dean, p. 60; and Jürgen Moltmann, "The Revolution of Freedom: Christians and Marxists Struggle for Freedom," *Religion, Revolution, and the Future*, p. 64. It should be clear that Prucha had almost the opposite intention in mind.
37. This and the following passage are from Roger Garaudy, *From Anathema to Dialogue: A Marxist Challenge to the Christian Churches*, pp. 94–95.
38. Bloch, *Man On His Own*, pp. 154–55, 159.
39. Cox, "Ernst Bloch," p. 193; cf. pp. 192–93.
40. See Carl Braaten on Bloch, "Toward a Theology of Hope," *New Theology No. 5*, p. 97; and Cox, "Ernst Bloch," p. 193.
41. See Petrovic, *Marx*, p. 65, for a discussion of the ontological basis of Marxist anthropology and its radicality as a doctrine of man. In a similar context Prucha argues that " 'To be human' does not mean a role which we take upon ourselves as humans to enact; through the dialectic of engagement and withdrawal it offers indications as to the structure of reality" ("Marxism as a Philosophy," p. 259).
42. See Roger Garaudy, "Communists and Christians in Dialogue," pp. 208–9. Garaudy has in mind of course the passages from Marx's *Manuscripts of 1844*, especially the essay "Alienated Labor," in which Marx describes man's unique characteristics as a species being (a term Marx borrowed from Feuerbach); see Karl Marx, *Writings of the Young Marx on Philosophy and Society*, ed. Loyd D. Easton and Kurt H. Guddat, pp. 293–95. See also Marx's comments on man's first historical act, in "The German Ideology," EG, pp. 409, 419–21.
43. See Garaudy, "Communists and Christians," pp. 207–8; and Sartre's interpretation of the relation between Hegel, Kierkegaard, and Marx, in terms of this thesis-antithesis-synthesis metaphor, in Jean-Paul Sartre, *Search for a Method*, pp. 8–14. See also Marx's *First Thesis on Feuerbach*, EG, p. 400, in which he describes his philosophy as a synthesis of Hegel and Feuerbach.
44. See Garaudy, "Creative Freedom," p. 154; also Arthur Lessing, "Marxist Existentialism," p. 182, for a description of Sartre's Marxist existentialism, which here clearly parallels the concerns of Marxist humanists like Garaudy as resting in a "recognition that the qualitative existence of human beings constitutes the foundation of all human life."
45. For a good example of this genre, see Sartre's essay, "Materialism and Revolution," in *Existentialism versus Marxism*, ed. George Novack,

pp. 85–109, an article written for *Les Temps Modernes* in 1946, in which Sartre attacks his French Marxist contemporaries, drawing in part on the young Marx to make his points (see his n. 1, p. 85, and n. 2, p. 88); see also Sartre, *Search for a Method*, p. 34.

46. Again, for a good example of this tendency, see Sartre's essay, "Existentialism Is a Humanism," in *Existentialism versus Marxism,* ed. Novack, pp. 70–84. This essay appeared at about the same time as the essay attacking orthodox Marxism cited above.

47. This neo-Marxist exegesis of the early Sartre is typical of its kind and comes from Milan Prucha, "Marxism and the Existential Problem of Man," in *Socialist Humanism,* ed. Fromm, pp. 138–48, espec. pp. 140, 142–43. Other examples of this initial European Marxist response to Sartre's existential humanism may be found in *Existentialism versus Marxism,* ed. Novack: e.g., Georg Lukacs, "Existentialism or Marxism?," pp. 134–53; Roger Garaudy, "False Prophet: Jean-Paul Sartre," pp. 154–63; and Herbert Marcuse, "Sartre, Historical Materialism, and Philosophy," pp. 165–72. The neo-Marxists tend to direct similar charges against Heidegger's version of existentialism.

48. Prucha, "Marxism and the Existential Problem of Man," p. 141. The relevant discussion from Heidegger occurs in his essay, "The Age of the World View," pp. 269–84. According to Heidegger, "It is certain that as a consequence of the liberation of man the modern age has produced subjectivism and individualism. But it is just as certain that no age before this has created a comparable objectivism, and that in no previous age did the nonindividual in the form of the collective come into its own. The essential point here is the necessary interplay between subjectivism and objectivism. It is precisely this mutual conditioning which points in turn to deeper processes" (p. 278). It is interesting to note in this connection that the later Sartre tries to override the differences between existentialism and Marxism by assimilating the Marxist doctrine of the primacy of material existence over consciousness to the Sartrean principle of the priority of existence over essence. Whether or not this is a sleight of hand, as Lukacs charges, it is a tacit acknowledgment of the divorce between Sartre's earlier existentialism and classical Marxist materialism. See Sartre, *Search for a Method*, pp. 31–32. Sartre's lengthy footnote on the relationship between praxis and reflection makes it clear, in any case, how complex this issue really is.

49. Gilbert Ryle, *The Concept of Mind,* pp. 16, 18–20, 22–23 Though approaching the problem from a different tradition, Heidegger makes the same general point as Ryle: "What are we to understand *positively* when we think of the unreified *Being* of the subject, the soul, the consciousness, the spirit, the person. . . . The person is not a Thing, not a substance, not an object. . . . How is the kind of Being which belongs to a person to be ascertained ontologically in a positive way?" (*Being and Time,* pp. 72–73). See pp. 68–71, where Heidegger distinguishes between the categories of human being (existentialia) and the categories of nonhuman things as "the two basic possibilities for characters of Being." P. F. Strawson makes a similar distinction in

*Individuals: An Essay in Descriptive Metaphysics* between the two kinds
of basic fundamental particulars, material bodies and persons, each of
which is a logically primitive category. According to Strawson, it is
possible to predicate both bodily and personal predicates of the
logically primitive phenomenon of persons. This dualism within the
concept of persons is never satisfactorily resolved, however. Thus
Heidegger's critical observation applies to Strawson as well: "When,
however, we come to the question of man's Being, this is not
something that we can simply compute by adding together those kinds
of Being which body, soul, and spirit respectively possess. . . . And
even if we should attempt such an ontological procedure, some idea of
the Being of the whole must be presupposed" (*Being and Time*, p. 74).
See Heidegger's comments in *Brief über den Humanismus*, pp. 65–68,
where he argues that even the bodily predicates of persons are
different, ontologically speaking, qua bodily predicates, from the
bodily predicates of nonhuman things: "The body of man is something
essentially different from the animal organism." Does Strawson really
speak to this issue? For a contemporary philosophical effort to follow
up on this suggestion of Heidegger, see Maurice Merleau-Ponty, *The
Phenomenology of Perception*, especially "Part One: The Body." See also
Marx's intriguing comments on the human character of the body and
the senses in his essay "Private Property and Communism," EG (e.g.,
p. 309: "The *senses* of social man *differ* from those of the unsocial").

50. Thus Machovec, "Tasks for the Dialogue," pp. 126–27.

51. See Heidegger, *Being and Time*, p. 78: "The compound expression
'Being-in-the-world' indicates in the very way we have coined it, that it
stands for a *unitary* phenomenon. This primary datum must be seen as
a whole. But while Being-in-the-world cannot be broken up into
contents which may be pieced together, this does not prevent it from
having several constitutive items in its structure. Indeed the
phenomenal datum which our expression indicates is one which may,
in fact, be looked at in three ways." The concept of
being-in-the-world, rather than persons (with its traditional associated
problems) represents Heidegger's attempt to rework the sort of
ontological problematic pointed to by Marx in his *First Thesis on
Feuerbach* and posed at a later date and in a different tradition by Ryle
and Strawson.

52. See Petrovic, *Marx*, p. 62. Petrovic argues that Marx's dialectical or
natural-humanist concept of praxis overcomes the dualism of Western
anthropology by showing rather that "the question of man's
relationship to the world is wider and more fundamental than the
question of the relationship of spirit to matter (or subject to object)
and that the latter is only a distorted form of the former." As his
terminology suggests, Petrovic is here obviously indebted to
Heidegger's criticism and solution referred to in the notes above.

53. This is Heidegger's criticism of the Marxist concept of praxis in
*Humanismus*, p. 88: "The modern metaphysical essence of labor is
anticipated in Hegel's *Phenomenology of the Spirit* as the self-establishing
process of unconditional production; i.e., the objectivization of the

actual through man experienced as subjectivity. The essence of
materialism is concealed in the essence of technics, about which,
indeed, a great deal is written, but little is thought."
54. See Bloch, "Man as Possibility," p. 280; also Moltmann on Bloch,
"Hope without Faith," p. 29. For Merleau-Ponty too, praxis is "that
middle ground between subject and object" which is the original,
prereflective or lived, experiential matrix of our "meaningful contact
with things" and which therefore precedes our reflective discrimination
of subject from object. Marx's concept of praxis is perhaps an example
of what James calls a "double-barreled" term, a term logically prior to
the derivative distinctions of epistemological or metaphysical theory.
55. See Louis Dupré, "Comment, in *Marx and the Western World*, ed.
Nicholas Lobkowicz, p. 434. The reference of course is to Marx's *First
Thesis on Feuerbach*, EG, p. 400.
56. Karl Marx, "Private Property and Communism," EG, pp. 304, 310.
57. See Karl Marx, "Toward the Critique of Hegel's Philosophy of Law:
Introduction," EG, p. 250; and Karl Marx, *Sixth Thesis on Feuerbach*,
EG, p. 402; also, Prucha, "Marxism and the Existential Problem of
Man," p. 143.
58. Karl Marx, "Private Property and Communism," in *Karl Marx: Early
Writings*, ed. T. B. Bottomore, p. 165.
59. Ibid.
60. Karl Marx, "Free Human Production," EG, p. 281; see also Garaudy,
"Creative Freedom," pp. 155–56.
61. Garaudy, "Creative Freedom," p. 156.
62. Marx, *First Thesis on Feuerbach*, EG, p. 400.
63. Garaudy, "Creative Freedom," p. 156.

7   The Metaphysics of Marxist
Humanism: Man and the World

1. Roger Garaudy, "Creative Freedom," in *The Christian Marxist
Dialogue*, ed. Paul Oestreicher, p. 144.
2. See Milan Machovec, "Tasks for Dialogue," *The Christian Marxist
Dialogue*, p. 118.
3. Garaudy, "Creative Freedom," p. 146; cf. pp. 144–46.
4. Machovec, "Tasks for Dialogue," p. 130.
5. Garaudy, "Creative Freedom," pp. 146–47. As Garaudy says
elsewhere: "We thus reach the highest level of the dialogue, that of
the integration by each of us of that which the other bears in himself,
as other. I have said previously that 'the depth of a believer's faith
depends upon the strength of the atheism that he bears in himself.' I
can now add: 'The depth of an atheist's humanism depends on the
strength of the faith that he bears in himself' " (Roger Garaudy,
"Communists and Christians in Dialogue," in *New Theology No. 5*, ed.
Martin E. Marty and Dean G. Peerman, p. 221).
6. Garaudy, "Creative Freedom," p. 163.

7. Ibid., p. 139.

8. Ibid., p. 162.

9. Ibid., pp. 163, 148.

10. Ibid., p. 163.

11. Bronislaw Baczko, "Marx and the Idea of the Universality of Man," in *Socialist Humanism,* ed. Erich Fromm, p. 173.

12. Garaudy, "Creative Freedom," p. 163; see also Harvey Cox, "Ernst Bloch and 'The Pull of the Future,' " *New Theology No. 5,* p. 199.

13. See Gajo Petrovic, *Marx in the Mid-Twentieth Century,* pp. 191–92; also Richard J. Bernstein, *Praxis and Action: Contemporary Philosophies of Human Activity,* p. 71; and Jürgen Habermas, *Knowledge and Human Interests,* p. vii.

14. See Petrovic, *Marx,* pp. 182–83.

15. For a fuller discussion of the foundations of epistemology in praxis, see Bernstein, *Praxis and Action,* pp. 73–74; Leszek Kolakowski, *Toward a Marxist Humanism,* pp. 46, 66; and Jean-Paul Sartre, *Search for a Method,* n., pp. 32–33.

16. See Louis Dupré, "Comment," in *Marx and the Western World,* ed. Nicholas Lobkowicz, pp. 434–45; also, Bernstein, *Praxis and Action,* p. 43.

17. Petrovic, *Marx,* p. 197; cf. p. 63.

18. Dupré, "Comment," p. 434.

19. Petrovic, *Marx,* p. 196.

20. Ibid., p. 177; see Martin Heidegger, *Being and Time,* pp. 27–28, 32.

21. See Petrovic, *Marx,* p. 120.

22. Ibid., p. 57.

23. Ibid., p. 23.

24. See Arthur Lessing, "Marxist Existentialism," p. 161, for a discussion of this point as it applies to the later Sartre's attempt to construct a Marxist existentialism.

25. Ernst Bloch, *A Philosophy of the Future,* p. 140. Bloch argues that an attempt to construct a "commonwealth of freedom" in history must be grounded, ontologically, on "positively-possible, possibly-positive meaning in the *surrounding cosmology*" (ibid., p. 139).

26. Ernst Bloch, "Man as Possibility," p. 279.

27. Cox, "Ernst Bloch," p. 200.

28. Ernst Bloch, *Man On His Own: Essays in the Philosophy of Religion,* p. 222.

29. Bloch, *Philosophy of the Future,* pp. 96, 56.

30. Bloch, "Man as Possibility," p. 280.

31. Cox, "Ernst Bloch," p. 202. Metz has also noted this link between the process of contemporary secularization and the underlying sense of the priority of the future; see Johannes B. Metz, "Creative Hope," *New Theology No. 5,* p. 131.

32. Cox, "Ernst Bloch," pp. 202–3; see Steve Weissman's original challenge in "New Left Man Meets the Dead God," *New Theology No. 5*, pp. 32, 34.
33. Garaudy, "Creative Freedom," p. 149.
34. Ibid., pp. 150–51.
35. Machovec, "Tasks for Dialogue," p. 122; cf. p. 123.
36. Karl Marx, "The Holy Family," cited in Baczke, "Marx and the Idea of the Universality of Man," p. 174; see Karl Marx, "The Holy Family," EG, p. 385.
37. Baczke, "Marx and the Idea of the Universality of Man, p. 174.
38. Bloch, "Man as Possibility," p. 280.
39. Jürgen Moltmann, *The Theology of Hope*, pp. 107–8. As Bloch contends, "Not only thought can be experimental, but *world history itself is an experiment*—a real experiment conducted in the world and aimed towards a possible just and proper world. . . . And so of course it is not fact but only an imperilled *fieri* of true being, with no ontology other than that of not-yet-being" (Bloch, *Philosophy of the Future*, p. 112).
40. Moltmann, *Theology of Hope*, p. 269.
41. Ibid.
42. Iris Murdoch, "The Existentialist Political Myth," p. 62.
43. Ibid., p. 63.
44. Bloch, "Man as Possibility," p. 280.
45. Ibid., p. 279.
46. Ibid.
47. Bloch, *Philosophy of the Future*, pp. 89–91.
48. Ibid., p. 96.
49. See Ernst Bloch, "Man and Citizen According to Marx," in *Socialist Humanism*, ed. Fromm, p. 202; Machovec, "Tasks for Dialogue," pp. 121–22, 126–27; Carl Braaten, "Toward a Theology of Hope," *New Theology No. 5*, p. 96; and Jürgen Moltmann, "Hope without Faith: An Eschatological Humanism without God," in *Is God Dead?* ed. Johannes B. Metz, p. 27.
50. See Sartre's argument against Hegel, in Lessing, "Marxist Existentialism," p. 175.
51. Sartre, *Search for a Method*, p. 30.
52. Ibid., p. 31; cf. pp. 6–7.
53. Martin Heidegger, *Brief über den Humanismus*, p. 87. Sartre himself agrees that "Marxism . . . has been the most radical attempt to clarify the historical process in its totality" (Sartre, *Search for a Method*, p. 29).
54. Sartre, *Search for a Method*, p. 29; see Lessing, "Marxist Existentialism," p. 181.
55. Paul Lehmann, "Christian Theology in a World in Revolution," in *Openings for Marxist-Christian Dialogue*, ed. Thomas W. Ogletree, p. 116.

56. Ibid.

57. See Sartre's "Marxist" definition of the nature and task of philosophy, in Lessing, "Marxist Existentialism," p. 161; also Garaudy's rather similar criteria for evaluating competing world views: (1) which most fully recognizes man's responsibility for his own history? (2) which gives him the most effective method for realizing that responsibility? (Garaudy, "Creative Freedom," p. 163). For the original version of these two criteria, see Karl Marx, "Toward the Critique of Hegel's Philosophy of Law: Introduction," EG, pp. 257–58.

58. See Sartre's comment on Marxism, *Search for a Method*, p. 30.

59. Ibid., p. 7.

60. Ibid., p. 8. "Every philosophy," Sartre reminds us, "is practical, even the one which at first appears to be the most contemplative. Its method is a social and political weapon." This holds true not only for the dialectical method of Marxism but also for the analytic rationalism of the Cartesian bourgeoisie, the practical-empirical skepticism of the British ideologists of liberalism, and the pragmatic method of classical American philosophy.

61. See Rosemary Radford Ruether, *The Radical Kindgom: The Western Experience of Messianic Hope*, p. 282.

62. See Karl Marx, "Alienated Labor," EG, p. 295; and Karl Marx, "Private Property and Communism," EG, p. 310.

63. Sartre, *Search for a Method*, p. 34.

64. See Herbert Marcuse, "The End of Utopia," *Five Lectures*, pp. 62–82.

65. Sartre, *Search for a Method*, p. 34. Lessing notes that Sartre himself attempted to retain the theoretical assumptions of a free consciousness, despite his apparent move to a Marxist framework, because they provided (1) "the basis for a critique of material and economic life which deprives us of freedom," and offered (2) "the philosophy which ultimately Marxism aims for in overthrowing economic oppression" (Lessing, "Marxist Existentialism," p. 181). The difficulty with this attempt, as Lessing and numerous other critics of Sartre's Marxist existentialism have pointed out, is that the philosophy of freedom from which Sartre operates is not that doctrine of concrete social freedom which Marx intended but, rather, an empty, abstract, metaphysical or even quasi-theological notion of freedom applied to the individual, a kind of reversion to a pre-Marxist Cartesianism which, on Sartre's own analysis, must be ruled out. Sartre appears to give himself away when he remarks that, while Marxism is to absorb, surpass, and conserve the insights of existentialism, it is nevertheless with the un-Marxian end in view that "Marxist thought will have taken on the human dimension (that is, the existential project) as the foundation of anthropological knowledge." Thus it is existentialism, not Marxism, which for Sartre "will cease to be a particular inquiry and will become the foundation of all inquiry." See Sartre, *Search for a Method*, p. 181.

66. Karl Marx, *Das Kapital*, vol. III, p. 873, cited by Sartre, *Search for a Method*, p. 34. See also the last chapter of Robert Paul Wolff, *The*

*Poverty of Liberalism,* entitled "Community," pp. 162–95, for a splendid sketch of the nature of the Marxian social ideal on the far side of the alienated conditions of a world shaped by the dictates of material necessity.

## 8 Radical Christian Thinking: Limits and Transcendence

1. I shall not be calling what emerges on the Christian side of this three-cornered dialogue "theology," but simply "Christian thinking." I shall be contending that thinking which is both radical and Christian can no longer be considered theological if one observes even minimal etymological proprieties. What I shall be describing is a kind of thinking done by persons who, though they stand in a positive relation to the linguistic and historical tradition of Christianity, have rejected those aspects of the tradition which involve talk about God or its logical equivalents, together with those theoretical positions which follow from such talk. Such thinking belongs to a larger family of intellectual possibilities which I have elsewhere labeled "post-Christian thinking," though a more accurate term in this context would be "post-theistic thinking."

   In deciding to explore further the possibilities of a thinking which is Christian but not theological, the radical Christian accepts that part of Marxist criticism which applies to theistic thinking. However, he does not subscribe to the further inference that therefore it is no longer possible to think in a distinctively Christian way about being, man, or the world. Like the Marxist humanist, the radical Christian has accepted the challenge to rethink his own tradition along the lines suggested by the new ontology of finitude. If this should mean (as indeed it does) that the resulting position is not of a theistic sort, this does not mean that such thinking should give up its claim to being Christian anymore than the Marxist humanist, having arrived at an ontology that is not materialist in the traditional, more positivistic sense, need give up his claim to be extending in new directions the possibilities contained in the Marxist tradition.

2. Similarly, P. F. Strawson treats the category of persons as a limit concept. Along with the co-primary category of material bodies, it is a basic or fundamental category of metaphysics. See Strawson, *Individuals: An Essay in Descriptive Metaphysics,* p. 11.

3. Ludwig Wittgenstein, *Tractatus Logico-Philosophicus,* 5.633; 5.632; 5.641; 5.621; 5.63.

4. Ibid., 6.44; 6.45.

5. Martin Heidegger, *Being and Time,* pp. 102, 416, 417, 321; Martin Heidegger, *Sein und Zeit,* p. 297; Martin Heidegger, *Vom Wesen des Grundes,* p. 44.

6. Heidegger, *Being and Time,* pp. 224, 400; also, pp. 494–95, n. vi, and p. 496, n. xv, in which Heidegger acknowledges his debt to Jaspers both for the term "limit situation" and for his philosophical analyses of "the basic existential-ontological signification of 'limit situations.'" The

phenomenon of "being-toward-death" is ontologically significant for
Heidegger, given his finitist perspective, because it is that "primordial
limit situation" which is of particular help to the philosopher in
answering one of the basic questions put to a radical (i.e., finitist)
anthropology: "How is the totality of that structural whole which we
have pointed out to be defined in an existential-ontological manner?"
(p. 224). Heidegger has already said that part of the significance of the
earlier *Lebensphilosophie* is its insistence that "the relationship of life to
death . . . the bounding of our existence by death is always decisive
for our understanding and assessment of life" (a quote from Dilthey);
the task of existentialist phenomenology has been to formulate this
insight "in a more radical manner" (pp. 494–95, n. vi.)

7.  Ibid., p. 310 (italics are Heidegger's).

8.  Ibid., p. 173.

9.  Ibid., p. 321.

10.  Ibid., p. 356.

11.  See Wittgenstein, *Tractatus*, 6.431: "As in death, too, the world does
not change but ceases."

12.  See ibid., 6.43: "If good and bad willing changes the world, it can only
change the limits of the world, not the facts. . . . In brief, the world
must thereby become quite another. It must so to speak wax or wane
as a whole. The world of the happy is quite another than that of the
unhappy."

13.  Martin Heidegger, *Was ist Metaphysik?*, p. 51.

14.  See Heidegger, *Being and Time*, p. 358. See also the connections
Wittgenstein draws between the limit experiences of "wonder at the
existence of the world," "feeling absolutely safe," and "seeing the
world as a miracle" (in Ludwig Wittgenstein, "Lectures on Ethics,"
pp. 8, 11, 16).

15.  Heidegger, in his discussion of conscience and guilt, makes a similar
point: "The Self, which as such has to be the basis for itself, can never
get that basis into its power; and yet, as existing, it must take over
being-a-basis. To be its own thrown basis is that potentiality-for-being
which is the issue for care" (*Being and Time*, p. 330).

16.  Cf. Ludwig Wittgenstein, *Philosophical Investigations*, p. 174e:
"One can imagine an animal angry, frightened, unhappy, happy,
startled. But hopeful? Why not?
"A dog believes his master is at the door. But can he also believe
his master will come the day after to-morrow?"

17.  The more practical complaint, that to date man has failed to assume
complete responsibility for the creation of his future, raises a question
of an entirely different sort. Even here, however, an ontology of
radical secularity dictates that an explanation must be found within the
particular circumstances and resources, material and spiritual, of man
himself, and not by appealing to some transcendent being. The point is
that ontologically speaking, man is capable of assuming responsibility
for his own future—and if he has not yet done so, the reasons are to

be sought in man's being, not somewhere else, whether higher or lower.

## 9 Radical Christian Thinking: The Working of History

1. Again, see Ludwig Wittgenstein's observation in *Tractatus Logico-Philosophicus,* 6.43: "The world of the happy is quite another than the world of the unhappy."
2. For a discussion of the shifting line between what is utopian and what is realistic, see Herbert Marcuse, "The End of Utopia," *Five Lectures,* pp. 62–82.
3. See my article "Heidegger, Marx, and Secular Theology," espec. pp. 201–4, for an earlier formulation of this argument.
4. One who draws such a conclusion is Peter Homans in his *Theology After Freud,* p. xiv.
5. Martin Heidegger, *Brief über den Humanismus,* p. 87.
6. See Hans-Georg Gadamer, *Wahrheit und Methode: Grundzüge einer philosophischen Hermeneutik,* espec. pp. 283–90. Gadamer is one of the leading students of Heidegger. In this book, he develops in systematic fashion, as Heidegger himself did not do, the implications for hermeneutical theory of the ontological interpretation of history found in Heidegger's *Being and Time.*
7. We may thus apply to the science of history *(Historie),* or the activity of historical interpretation, Heidegger's broader observation, "As ways in which man behaves, sciences have the manner of Being which this entity—man himself—possesses" (Martin Heidegger, *Being and Time,* p. 32).
8. See Richard E. Palmer, *Hermeneutics: Interpretation Theory in Schleiermacher, Dilthey, Heidegger, and Gadamer,* pp. 137, 165–66, 215.
9. See Rudolf Bultmann, *The Presence of Eternity: History and Eschatology,* p. 133. Bultmann is here discussing R. G. Collingwood's philosophy of history.
10. Ibid.
11. See Gadamer, *Wahrheit und Methode,* Preface to 2d ed., p. xvii.
12. Ibid., p. 340.
13. Even faith, as a first-order or prereflective, lived attitude of existential trust, is, already on this lived, experiential level, essentially linguistic in nature. Thus, it inevitably tends to structure, and in turn to be already structured by, those second-order or explicitly linguistic formulations of faith which refer to it for their empirical or existential confirmation. I want to argue therefore that changes in the way we talk about or give expression to our limit experiences represent changes in those boundary situations themselves, and not simply so many variations in ways of expressing an unchanging truth about the human condition. There is, I am arguing, no such thing as linguistically innocent experience in the case of distinctively human experience (such

experience need not of course be expressly articulated). This position seems to me an essential part of a radically secular (worldly and embodied) interpretation of man's being.

14. See Emilio Betti, *Die Hermeneutik als Allgemeine Methodik des Geisteswissenschaften*, p. 35.
15. See Palmer, *Hermeneutics*, p. 234.
16. Gadamer, *Wahrheit und Methode*, p. 279; cf. Palmer, *Hermeneutics*, p. 224.
17. Gadamer, *Wahrheit und Methode*, p. 448; cf. Palmer, *Hermeneutics*, pp. 209, 244.
18. Gadamer, *Wahrheit und Methode*, pp. 339–40.
19. Harvey Cox, *The Feast of Fools: A Theological Essay on Festivity and Fantasy*, p. 133. See chaps. 8 and 9 for a comparison of radical theology, theology of hope, and what Cox calls a "theology of juxtaposition." Cox writes: "What theological method will help solve the problem that arises from our ambivalent attitude toward history? . . . It cannot try to smooth over the obvious contradictions in these dimensions of faith and experience nor attempt to reduce or reconcile them to each other. Rather it will accept and even exemplify the differences among these dimensions by juxtaposing them to each other. . . . A method of juxtaposition in theology should begin with 'radical theology' by recognizing that our present is one of discontinuity and *is* real, not simply transient" (p. 131). See Jürgen Moltmann, *Religion, Revolution, and the Future*, p. 9.
20. This is the historical-hermeneutical analogue to the ontotheological dilemma of the Marxist and the Christian when, after each has agreed to an ontology of the open future, one says that this is precisely what he means by the absence of God, while the other says that this is precisely what he means by the presence of God. See Roger Garaudy, *From Anathema to Dialogue: A Marxist Challenge to the Christian Churches*, pp. 92, 94–95; and Leslie Dewart, *The Future of Belief: Theism in a World Come of Age*, p. 58. My own discussion of this theological question, and a suggested resolution, occurs in "Heidegger, Marx, and Secular Theology," pp. 200–202.

## 10 The Future of Religion in a Secular World

1. For a fuller statement of this position, see Richard Shaull, "The End of the Road and a New Beginning," in *Marxism and Radical Religion: Essays Toward a Revolutionary Humanism*, ed. John C. Raines and Thomas Dean, pp. 27–48.
2. Ibid. See also Herbert Marcuse, "Marxism and the New Humanity: An Unfinished Revolution," in *Marxism and Radical Religion*, ed. Raines and Dean, pp. 3–10.
3. See Shaull, "End of the Road," pp. 36–37. James Luther Adams describes similar developments in the left or radical wing of the Reformation—for example, the principle of radical laicism: "It has been

claimed that by analogy this conception of the free church led to the idea of the democratic state" ("Is Marxist Thought Relevant to the Christian? A Protestant View," in *Marx and the Western World,* ed. Nicholas Lobkowicz, p. 386). Franklin H. Littell discusses these contributions at some length in "The Radical Reformation and Revolution," in *Marxism and Radical Religion,* ed. Raines and Dean, pp. 81–100.

4. The radical Christian thus finds himself in agreement with the Nietzschean-Marxian observation of Ernst Bloch that the greatest paradox of religion (specifically, of Christianity) has been its elimination of deity itself and its dialectical transformation, by way of its alleged opposite, atheism, into an assertion of an open space ahead for man. See Ernst Bloch, *Man On His Own: Essays in the Philosophy of Religion,* p. 160.

5. Even a theologian such as Shaull appears willing to make a distinction similar to the one presupposed by the Marxist humanist at this point between the biblical perspective, which still has its validity, and the biblical world view or story in which it was originally expressed. As Shaull says, "No old world-view can be restored, or even translated into contemporary idiom" ("End of the Road," p. 37). Again: "Obviously, this story as it has come down to us no longer has the power to create or sustain this perspective on life and the world. But that need not keep us from accepting such a perspective or putting it to the test" (ibid., p. 47). It is not entirely clear, however, whether in making this distinction Shaull is yet free of the kernel-husk method of separating an unchanging essence (the biblical perspective) from its accidental form of expression (the biblical world view or story). The Marxist humanist, on the other hand, as one who draws on this perspective (in contrast to the theologian, who accepts it), appears to be in somewhat less danger of committing this particular error. Paul van Buren returns for a second and rather different sort of look at the problems contained in the notion of retelling the old story in his article, "The Situation of Christian Radicals," in *Marxism and Radical Religion,* ed. Raines and Dean, pp. 133–50. Reminding his erstwhile critic (see chap. 3, notes 3, 5, and 28 of the present study) that stories are "as flexible and as open-ended as human life itself," he goes on to explain that there is therefore no necessary incompatibility between the activity of retelling a story and the gradual emergence of a story that is quite new—a story that someday may no longer be viewed so much as a religious story as it will "a human story of men" (ibid., pp. 146–50).

6. Karl Marx, *Capital,* vol. I, pp. 53–54. See John Dewey's outwardly similar but undialectical observation that "upon the social side the future of the religious function seems preeminently bound up with its emancipation from religions and a particular religion" (*A Common Faith,* p. 67). The difference of course lies in Marx's more dialectical appreciation that the social emancipation of the religious function is possible only through a prior (though simultaneous) emancipation of the social world from the structures of its own secular alienation.

7. Thus Ernst Bloch: "And the end of religion . . . is not simply no religion but—carrying Marxism further—the inheriting of religion, a meta-religious conscientious knowledge of the last problem of whither and why: *ens perfectissimum*" (*Man on His Own*, p. 163).

8. Paul van Buren, in his opening remarks to a conference on "Marxism, Religion, and the Liberal Tradition" held at Temple University in April, 1969.

9. Harvey Cox, "The Marxist-Christian Dialogue: What Next?" in *Marxism and Christianity*, ed. Herbert Aptheker, p. 28. See Jan Lochman, *Church in a Marxist Society*, p. 186: "The special contribution of the Marxists is to remind Christians of the importance of historical and social 'immanence.' The special charisma of Christians is to bear witness to the Marxists about the relevance of 'transcendence.' "

10. For a discussion of the term "pro-existence" and its significance for the dialogue of Marxist humanists and Christian radicals, see Paul Oestreicher's introduction to his edited volume, *The Christian Marxist Dialogue*, pp. 1–29.

11. St. Paul, I Corinthians 15: 24–25, 28. "When all things are subjected to him, then the Son himself will also be subjected to him who put all things under him, that God may be everything to everyone" (v. 28). See also Isaiah 49:6.

12. Rosemary Radford Ruether, "Messiah of Israel and the Cosmic Christ," p. 16 (unpub. ms.).

13. Dewey, *A Common Faith*, p. 87.

# Bibliography

# Bibliography

## Marxism, Historical and Contemporary

Althusser, Louis. *For Marx*. New York: Vintage, 1970.

Arendt, Hannah. *On Revolution*. New York: Viking, 1963.

Avineri, Shlomo. *The Social Political Thought of Karl Marx*. Cambridge: Cambridge University Press, 1970.

Bernstein, Richard J. *Praxis and Action: Contemporary Philosophies of Human Activity*. Philadelphia: University of Pennsylvania Press, 1971.

Bloch, Ernst. "Man as Possibility," *Cross Currents* 18:3 (Summer, 1968), 273–83.

_____. *Man On His Own: Essays in the Philosophy of Religion*. New York: Herder and Herder, 1970.

_____. *A Philosophy of the Future*. New York: Herder and Herder, 1970.

_____. *Das Prinzip Hoffnung*, 2 vols. Frankfurt a. M.: Suhrkamp, 1959.

_____. *Spirit of Utopia*. New York: Herder and Herder, 1970.

Cox, Harvey. "Marxist Humanism in Eastern Europe—Problems and Prospects," *The Correspondent*, No. 33 (Winter, 1965), 30–44.

Dupré, Louis. *The Philosophical Foundations of Marxism*. New York: Harcourt, Brace and World, 1966.

Feuerbach, Ludwig. *Principles of the Philosophy of the Future*, tr. and intr. by Manfred Vogel. Indianapolis: Bobbs-Merrill, 1966.

Findlay, John. *Hegel: A Re-examination*. New York: Macmillan, 1962.

Fromm, Erich, ed. *Socialist Humanism*. Garden City, New York: Doubleday and Company, Inc., 1956.

Garaudy, Roger. *Karl Marx: The Evolution of His Thought*. New York: International Publishers, 1967.

Green, Ronald M. "Ernst Bloch's Revision of Atheism," *Journal of Religion* 49:2 (April, 1969), 128–35.

Habermas, Jürgen. *Knowledge and Human Interests*. Boston: Beacon Press, 1971.

283

Kojève, Alexandre. *Introduction to the Reading of Hegel.* New York: Basic Books, 1969.

Kolakowski, Leszek. *Toward a Marxist Humanism.* New York: Grove Press, 1969.

Lichtman, Richard. *Marxism: First Course,* 2 vols. Berkeley, Calif.: Fybate Lecture Notes, 1970.

Lobkowicz, Nicholas, ed. *Marx and the Western World.* Notre Dame, Indiana: University of Notre Dame Press, 1967.

————. *Theory and Practice: History of a Concept from Aristotle to Marx.* Notre Dame, Indiana: University of Notre Dame Press, 1967.

Marcuse, Herbert. *Five Lectures.* Boston: Beacon Press, 1970.

Marx, Karl. *Capital,* vol. I. London: n.pub., 1930.

————. *Karl Marx: Early Writings,* ed. T. B. Bottomore. New York: McGraw-Hill, 1964.

————. *Writings of the Young Marx on Philosophy and Society,* eds. Loyd D. Easton and Kurt H. Guddat. Garden City, New York: Doubleday and Company, Inc., 1967.

Novack, George, ed. *Existentialism versus Marxism.* New York: Delta, 1966.

Petrovic, Gajo. *Marx in the Mid-Twentieth Century.* Garden City, New York: Doubleday and Company, Inc., 1967.

Wolff, Robert Paul. *The Poverty of Liberalism.* Boston: Beacon Press, 1968.

## Marxist-Christian Dialogue

Aptheker, Herbert, ed. *Marxism and Christianity.* New York: Humanities Press, 1968.

————. *The Urgency of Marxist-Christian Dialogue.* New York: Harper and Row, 1970.

Bennett, John C. *Christianity and Communism Today.* New York: Association Press, 1962.

Dean, Thomas. "Heidegger, Marx, and Secular Theology," *Union Seminary Quarterly Review* 22:3 (March, 1967), 191–204.

Garaudy, Roger. "Communists and Christians in Dialogue," *Union Seminary Quarterly Review* 22:3 (March, 1967), 205–12.

————. *From Anathema to Dialogue: A Marxist Challenge to the Christian Churches.* New York: Herder and Herder, 1966.

———— and Quentin Lauer. *A Christian-Communist Dialogue.* Garden City, New York: Doubleday and Company, Inc., 1968.

Girardi, Giulio. *Marxism and Christianity.* New York: Macmillan, 1968.

Gollwitzer, Helmut. *The Christian Faith and the Marxist Criticism of Religion.* New York: Charles Scribner's Sons, 1970.

Lochman, Jan. *Church in a Marxist Society.* New York: Harper and Row, 1970.

MacIntyre, Alasdair. *Marxism and Christianity*. New York: Schocken, 1968.

Oestreicher, Paul, ed. *The Christian Marxist Dialogue*. New York: Macmillan, 1969.

Ogletree, Thomas W., ed. *Openings for Marxist-Christian Dialogue*. Nashville, Tennessee: Abingdon Press, 1969.

Raines, John C., and Thomas Dean, eds. *Marxism and Radical Religion: Essays toward a Revolutionary Humanism*. Philadelphia: Temple University Press, 1970.

West, Charles C. *Communism and the Theologians*. New York: Macmillan, 1958.

## Contemporary Religious Thinkers

Bultmann, Rudolf. *The Presence of Eternity: History and Eschatology*. New York: Harper and Brothers, 1967.

_____. *Theology of the New Testament*, vol. I. New York: Charles Scribner's Sons, 1951.

Cox, Harvey. *The Feast of Fools: A Theological Essay on Festivity and Fantasy*. New York: Harper and Row, 1969.

Dewart, Leslie. *The Future of Belief: Theism in a World Come of Age*. New York: Herder and Herder, 1966.

Fontinell, Eugene. "Reflections on Faith and Metaphysics," *Cross Currents* 17:1 (Winter, 1966), 15–40.

Homans, Peter. *Theology after Freud*. Indianapolis: Bobbs-Merrill, 1970.

MacIntyre, Alasdair, and Paul Ricoeur. *The Religious Significance of Atheism*. New York: Columbia University Press, 1969.

Marty, Martin E., and Dean G. Peerman, eds. *New Theology No. 5*. New York: Macmillan, 1968.

_____. *New Theology No. 6*. New York: Macmillan, 1969.

Metz, Johannes B. "The Church and the World," in *The Word in History*, ed. T. Patrick Burke. New York: Sheed and Ward, 1966. Pp. 69–85.

_____. "God before Us instead of a Theological Argument," *Cross Currents* 18:3 (Summer, 1968), 296–306.

_____. ed., *Is God Dead? Concilium*, vol. 16. New York: Paulist Press, 1966.

Moltmann, Jürgen. *Religion, Revolution, and the Future*. New York: Charles Scribner's Sons, 1969.

_____. *The Theology of Hope*. New York: Harper and Row, 1965.

Ogden, Schubert. *The Reality of God*. New York: Harper and Row, 1966.

Pannenberg, Wolfhart. "The God of Hope," *Cross Currents* 18:3 (Summer, 1968), 284–95.

Rahner, Karl. "Christian Humanism," *Journal of Ecumenical Studies* 4:3 (Summer, 1967), 369–384.

Ruether, Rosemary Radford. *The Radical Kingdom: The Western Experience of Messianic Hope*. New York: Harper and Row, 1970.

Shaull, Richard. "Revolution: Heritage and Contemporary Option," in *Containment and Change*, by Carl Oglesby and Richard Shaull. New York: Macmillan, 1967. Pp. 177–248.

Van Buren, Paul. "On Doing Theology," in *Talk of God*, Royal Institute of Philosophy Lectures, Volume II, 1967–68. London: Macmillan, 1969. Pp. 52–71.


Contemporary Secular Thinkers

Bannan, John F. *The Philosophy of Merleau-Ponty*. New York: Harcourt, Brace and World, 1967.

Betti, Emilio. *Die Hermeneutik als Allgemeine Methodik des Geisteswissenschaften*. Tübingen: J. C. B. Mohr (Paul Siebeck), 1962.

Dewey, John. *A Common Faith*. New Haven: Yale University Press, 1934.

Gadamer, Hans-Georg. *Wahrheit und Methode: Grundzüge einer philosophischen Hermeneutik*. Tübingen: J. C. B. Mohr (Paul Siebeck), 1960.

Heidegger, Martin. "The Age of the World-View," *Measure* 2:3 (Summer, 1951), 269–84.

————. *Being and Time*. New York: Harper and Brothers, 1962. (*Sein und Zeit*. Tübingen: Max Niemeyer Verlag, 1963.)

————. *Brief über den Humanismus*. Bern: Francke, 1947.

————. *Vom Wesen des Grundes*. Frankfurt a.M.: Vittorio Klostermann, 1955.

————. *Was ist Metaphysik?* Frankfurt a.M.: Vittorio Klostermann, 1960.

James, William. *Pragmatism*. Cleveland: Meridian, 1955.

Lessing, Arthur. "Marxist Existentialism," *Philosophy Today No. 1*, ed. Jerry H. Gill. New York: Macmillan, 1968. Pp. 158–83.

Macquarrie, John. *Martin Heidegger*. Richmond: John Knox Press, 1968.

Merleau-Ponty, Maurice. *In Praise of Philosophy*. Evanston, Ill.: Northwestern University Press, 1963.

————. *Phenomenology of Perception*. New York: The Humanities Press, 1962.

————. *Sense and Non-Sense*. Evanston, Ill.: Northwestern University Press, 1964.

————. *Signs*. Evanston, Ill.: Northwestern University Press, 1964.

Murdoch, Iris. "The Existentialist Political Myth," *The Socratic* (1956), pp. 52–63.

Palmer, Richard E. *Hemeneutics: Interpretation Theory in Schleiermacher, Dilthey, Heidegger, and Gadamer*. Evanston, Ill.: Northwestern University Press, 1969.

Ryle, Gilbert. *The Concept of Mind.* New York: Barnes and Noble, 1949.

Sartre, Jean-Paul. *Being and Nothingness.* New York: Philosophical Library, 1956.

_____. "Existentialism is a Humanism," in *Existentialism versus Marxism,* ed. George Novack. New York: Delta, 1966. Pp. 70—84.

_____. *Nausea.* New York: New Directions, 1964.

_____. *Search for a Method.* New York: Knopf, 1963.

_____. *Situations.* Greenwich, Conn.: Fawcett, 1965.

Schöfer, Erasmus. *Die Sprache Heideggers.* Pfullingen: Neske, 1962.

Strawson, P. F. *Individuals: An Essay in Descriptive Metaphysics.* London: Methuen, 1959.

_____. *Introduction to Logical Theory.* London: Methuen, 1963.

Wisdom, John. *Other Minds.* Oxford: Blackwell, 1952.

Wittgenstein, Ludwig. "Lectures on Ethics," *Philosophical Review* 74 (1965), 3-16.

_____. *On Certainty.* Oxford: Blackwell, 1969.

_____. *Philosophical Investigations.* New York: Macmillan, 1953.

_____. *Tractaus Logico-Philosophicus.* London: Routledge and Kegan Paul, 1955.

# Index

# Index

Absolute future, 31–33, 39–41
Action. *See* Praxis
Adams, James Luther, 254, 277–78
Alienation: and God, 4–5, 47–49,
101; Hegel on, 76–78;
Heidegger on, 109; ideological,
109, 128, 130, 144, 148, 194,
242; Marx on, 58–67, 76–78,
175; and necessity, 144–45; and
praxis, 76–78; and religion,
58–67, 230–33, 235; and
transcendence, 76–78, 194
Althusser, Louis, 71, 266
Altizer, Thomas J. J., xi
Anthropology. *See* Man
Anxiety (*Angst*), 182–85, 195
Arendt, Hannah, 36–37
Aristotle, 69, 130; on being, 127;
on essence, 98, 103; on the
future, 98–99; on time, 98,
127–28
Atheism, 113; and existentialism,
90–92; Feuerbach on, 91,
254–56; in Hegel, 257; in Marx,
5, 57–58, 68–69, 91, 254, 256;
Merleau-Ponty on, 91–92; and
Sartre, 45, 91–92; and theism, 5,
21, 23, 45–46, 69
Avineri, Shlomo, 86

Being: Aristotle on, 98, 103, 127;
as finite, in Bloch, 126–30; as
finite, in existentialism, 95–101;
as finite, in Hegel, 257; as finite,
in Marx, 87–89; as finite, in

Marxist humanism, 126–34; as
finite, in radical Christian
thinking, 174; as futural, 20,
188; and God, 45, 188–90, 256,
277; as historical, 207–8,
216–17; mystery (contingency)
of, 173, 185, 191–95, 198, 230,
256
Being-in-the-world, 7, 12, 141–42;
and historical being, 208–9; as a
limit concept, 179–80, 183–84,
191–92; and persons, 269; two
ways of, 198–99; and the world,
107
Being-toward-death, 182–84, 275
Bergson, Henri, 115
Betti, Emilio, 214
Biblical tradition. *See* Christian
(biblical) tradition
Bloch, Ernst, 122, 131–33, 166–67,
234; on being as futural, 20; on
being as "not-yet-being,"
126–30; on biblical eschatology,
21, 27–28; on the biblical God,
20; on the biblical view of man,
24; bibliography on, 265–66; on
Christianity, 278; on
contingency, 128–30; on Hegel,
266; on the Kingdom of God,
38; on man, 23–24, 42–43, 135,
141–42; on nonbeing, 129–30;
on the past, 159–60; on
possibility, 126–27; on praxis,
141–42; on religion, 261; on
temporality, 127–28; and
theology, 129–30, 134; on the

100, 102, 257; and historical being, 216–17; as a limit phenomenon, 182–85; Marx on, 74–75; and Marx's dialectic, 258–61; and the mystery of being, 256; and self-transcendence, 43–44, 74–75, 99–100; theistic and post–theistic views of, 44; and the world, 42

Finitude, ontology of: and attributes of traditional ontology, 95, 100–101, 186–87, 194–95; and Bloch's cosmology, 156; Bloch's ontology as, 126–30; and Bloch's philosophy of man, 135; existentialism as, 90–117; and freedom, 266; and history, 203–17; as incomplete, 172–73, 177, 180; and the Marxist-Christian dialogue, 243; Marxist humanism as, 121–70; Marx's, 87–89; and Marx's anthropology, 72; as "materialistic," 49; and the meaning of life, 180, 182; Prucha on, 130–33; radical Christian thinking as, 171–226, 274; and radical secularity, 94–95; theological critique of, 172–73, 177, 180; versus theological perspective, 91–92, 131–34

Fontinell, Eugene, 52, 262

Freedom: and finitude, 191–94; and the future, 87–88, 191–94; God's, 32–33; and grace, 21–23, 33, 43, 191–94; in Hegel, 87–88; and Jesus, 222–26; in limit situations, 185, 195; Marxist humanism on, 136–40, 143–45; and necessity, 87–88, 137–40, 143–45, 147–49, 164–65, 234–35; and praxis, 87–88, 136–40, 143–45, 147–49, 164–65; radical Christian view of, 191–94, 222–26; and religion, 234–35; and self-transcendence, 43–44; and transcendence, 136–40, 143–45; Young Hegelians on, 87–88

Freud, Sigmund, 52

Fromm, Erich, 122

"Fusion of horizons," 215, 218, 220, 243. See also Hermeneutics

Future: argument from, 31–32, 49–52, 200–201; Aristotle on, 98–99; Bloch on, 127–28, 130; and ek-sistence, 263; eschatological, 24–25; and finitude, ontology of, 98–100; and freedom, 87–88, 191–94; as mode of God's being, 21–23, 32–33, 46–47, 188–90; Hegel on, 87–88; and history, argument from, 222; inner-worldly versus absolute, 31–33, 39–41; and Jesus, 24–25; as limit phenomenon, 191; and man, 102–3; Marxist humanism on, 161–65; openness of, 190; the party of the, 236–40; and past, 159–61; and praxis (action), 87–88, 199; radical Christian view of, 187, 200–201; and spirit, 263; and temporality, 98–100; and transcendence, 87–88, 187, 263; two concepts of, 189–90, 192–93, 200, 262–63; visions of the, 19; and world, 199; Young Hegelians on, 87–88

Gadamer, Hans Georg, 209, 215

Garaudy, Roger, xii, 122, 234, 247; on faith, 270; on finitist ontology, 133–34; on humanism, 146–49; on man, 136; on Marx, 85–86; on Marxism, 146–49; on Marxist humanism, 265; on necessity, two kinds of, 144–45; on religion, 232; on the world, 157–58; on world-views, criteria for, 273

*Geschichte*, 208, 210. *See also* History

God: as absolute future, 32–33; as alienating, 4–5, 47–49, 101; argument from, 44–49; attributes of, and man, 47–49, 73; attributes of, reinterpreted, 21–22, 46–47, 100–101, 173, 186–88; Bergson on, 115; and Bloch's ontology, 129–30, 155; and contingency, 256; as Creator, 96–97, 112, 185; critique of, xiii–xiv, 44–49, 96–97, 107, 116–17, 172–76, 206; death of, 179, 187; and